Doing More with Life

Doing More with Life

Connecting Christian Higher
Education to a Call to Service

edited by

Michael R. Miller

BAYLOR UNIVERSITY PRESS

Studies in Religion and Higher Education 3

Editorial Advisory Board

Book Design by Gryphon Graphics
Cover Design by Joan Osth

Unless otherwise indicated scripture quotations are from the *New Revised Standard
Version Bible*, copyright 1989, Division of Christian Education of the National
Council of the Churches of Christ in the United States of America. Used by
permission. All rights reserved.

Excerpts appear by permission from the following:
    "Liberal Learning and the Light of Faith: An Initiation into Wholeness," *The Cresset:
    A Review of Literature, the Arts, and Public Affairs* (Trinity 2004).
    "Integrating Heart, Mind, and Soul: The Vocation of the Christian Teacher," in
    *Gladly Learn, Gladly Teach: Living Out One's Calling in the Twenty-First Century Acad-
    emy* (Mercer University Press, 2005), ed. John Marson Dunaway.
    "Behind the Scenes of Hollywood," *Crisis Magazine*, 14 June 2005; and "Some Great
    Calling," *The Baylor Line*, 15 March 2005.

Library of Congress Cataloging-in-Publication Data

Doing more with life : connecting Christian higher education to a call to service /
edited by Michael R. Miller.
        p. cm. -- (Studies in religion and higher education ; #3)
    Includes bibliographical references and index.
    ISBN 978-1-932792-80-5 (pbk. : alk. paper)
    1. Vocation--Christianity. 2. Education (Christian theology) 3. Service (Theology)
4. College teachers--Religious life. 5. Education, Higher. I. Miller, Michael R.

    BV4740.D65 2007
    248.8'34--dc22

                                    2006036037

Printed in the United States of America on acid-free paper with a minimum of 30%
pcw content.

To Sara, my wife, who has blessed my life in countless ways.
You are my treasure, my vocation, my love.

Contents

Acknowledgments

I deeply appreciate the many people who brought this book, and the conference that preceded it, together. It goes without saying that such projects do not happen by themselves. To all of you I say, I am honored to be your colleague.

The 2005 Callings Conference was successful because of the hard work of a number of talented people, many more than I can properly mention in this space. Special thanks are given to Tom Butler, executive director of Mount St. Mary's Callings Program, and Roxanne Stefanik, assistant director of Callings. Both Tom and Roxanne are tremendous gifts to the Mount community, and I thank you for your leadership, friendship, and always cheerful encouragement. I am also indebted to the talented people who generously served on the 2005 Callings Conference Program Committee: Sean Adams, Mary Kate Birge, Dennis Cali, Michael Epstein, John Larrivee, Connie Monroe, Fr. William Parent, and Susann Samples. Thank you for sharing your insights and gifts. And I am very appreciative for the wonderful support the conference received from President Thomas Powell and his executive staff; thank you for your expression of confidence in the Callings Conference.

A conference depends on its speakers or presenters for its success, and we enjoyed an especially eloquent and energetic group who kept us thinking about vocation. Our speakers included: Kevin Buckley, Dennis Cali, Laurie Cassidy, Kendra Creasy Dean, Germain Grisez, Jeanne Heffernan, Thomas

Hibbs, Carol Hinds, Karen Jackson-Weaver, Charlene Kalinoski, Patti Kreke, John Larrivee, Fr. Thomas Looney, William Mattison, Bill Millard, Fr. William Mills, Gael Mooney, Susan Mountin, Timothy Muldoon, Stephen Butler Murray, Jessamyn Neuhaus, Stanley Nevins, Marc Parisi, Katie Schmidt, Philip Sutton, Deborah Wallace Ruddy, David Weber, and Tim Wolfe. Thank you for accepting our invitation and gracing us with your presence.

I happily acknowledge my debt to the wonderful people at Mount St. Mary's who truly know how to put on a great show. Such standouts include Sean Adams, assistant dean and director of campus activities, who was involved in the conference several months before I got on board; I am convinced that without Sean's leadership the conference would never have happened. All of the members of the Office of Communications, led by executive director, Duffy Ross, are also among the conference's heroes. Working with Fawn O'Hara, Kate Charuhas, Barb Ruppert, Rita Beard, Trevor James, and Lindsay Muller proved to be one of the greatest joys in planning the conference; I remain constantly amazed by your creative talent and your tireless efforts to promote the Mount and its projects.

Special thanks are also extended to J. B. Brewer, David Sheads, and Lisa Reed in the Media Center and to their capable student workers; Steven Rohlfs, rector of Mount St. Mary's Seminary, for his great support; Howard Williams and Dawn Alexander, along with all of those at dining services who kept us well fed; Barb Knott and Brian Ecker in accounting and financial affairs; George Gelles, director of conferences and special programs; Linda Junker and Deborah Guzinski of institutional research; Tom Kiniry, director of public safety and his wonderful officers; Barbara Jacobs and the rest of the information technology team; and Pam Zusi, executive director of development, who so generously supported the conference with her ideas and enthusiasm.

I am also very grateful for the hard work of Chris Bucklaew, who oversaw registration, and Christine Joyner, who graciously coordinated the mailing and the general organization of the conference and provided tremendous help with the editing of this book. I am grateful for the many student workers who completed so many administrative tasks so well and for Alison Kopreski and Amberly Battersby, who created a special slide show for the conference.

I also wish to thank my colleagues at the Mount for their support. I cannot name them all here, but I will note how grateful I am for the friendship and support of those whom I work with the most, the members of the Philosophy Department (past and present): Richard Buck, Bill Collinge, Trudy Conway, John Donovan, Molly Flynn, Brian Henning, Josh Hochschild, Sean McGrath, Thane Naberhaus, Fr. Paul Redmond, David Rehm, Jessica Wahman, and George Winnes.

At the completion of these projects I am once again overwhelmed with gratitude for my wife, Sara, who generously helped me with the conference, and who endured me while I was editing this book; I can't thank you enough for your love and support.

Preface

Questions of vocation have always been discussed at institutions of higher education in one way or the other, in large part because the work of colleges and universities naturally makes students think vocationally. That is, universities and colleges are designed to help students answer the question, What are you going to do with your life? Higher education clearly helps the student select a certain major and a likely career path, but it also naturally provides opportunities to ponder deeper vocational questions: a thrilling in-class debate leads one student to drop out of school and join the military; the near-death of a roommate challenges another to repair her relationship with her mother; a casual compliment from an admired teacher stimulates a desire in another student to one day run for public office; a chance encounter with a friend-of-a-friend-of-a-friend leads to thoughts of marriage; a required service-learning project sparks a desire to serve God's people through ordained ministry. These opportunities to reflect and wonder are repeated throughout one's years in college—in the classroom, residence, and dining hall; in the library; and at the corner bar.

The conversations with their peers, parents, teachers, and mentors that flow from these wonderful moments of awakening often center on discovering where the students' interests, talents, and plans may lead them. Often, on secular and religiously affiliated campuses alike, the conversations also focus on discovering what God may want the student to do. All these questions and conversations, and more, are examples of the natural way in which students think vocationally.

At my university, Mount St. Mary's in Emmitsburg, Maryland, questions about vocation exploded on campus after we received a $2 million grant to engage in a campus-wide theological exploration of vocation. The grant, one of eighty-eight funded by the Lilly Endowment, quickly made vocation a hot topic. Although many students, faculty, administrators, and staff initially may have asked, what does vocation have to do with me? the campus began to think more explicitly about vocation, and about God's role in our discovery and fulfillment of our vocation.

Although the particular questions asked and discussed varied tremendously, the employees on campus were very interested in learning whether their jobs were in fact their vocation. Some employees saw a direct association between their vocation and their jobs, such as those teaching theology or working in campus ministry, in large part because of the religious nature of their work. Many more on campus believed their job was their vocation (even if their job was not noticeably religious or they themselves were not especially religious) because they enjoyed it, did it well, or recognized they were helping others; since such a job was a perfect match with their interests and God-given talents, to their minds the job had to be their vocation. For example, many teachers on campus referred to their teaching as their calling, since their talents and love for the job confirmed that they were "made to teach." Still others—staff members, administrators, and professors teaching in various disciplines—resisted the notion that their jobs were somehow connected with vocation. After all, it was argued, does having a vocation to teach math change the way a math teacher teaches? Is the assistant registrar or a carpenter engaging in a spiritual act when the one is registering a student or the other is repairing a broken window? Is an administrator really cooperating with God's providential plan when she works on next year's budget?

Interestingly enough, others on campus rejected the general notion that any job, no matter how important the job may be or how much someone may enjoy it, could properly define one's vocation. Members of this group see themselves to be more than a teacher, administrator, or staff member. These folks expressed the belief that they are first and foremost known by God as being a spouse, a parent, or a member of a religious community. These central relationships, and not the particular means they use to earn money, define their vocation. Still others on campus see their vocation in even broader terms, for they primarily understand themselves as called to a certain form of discipleship and not to a job or state in life. This means that they either felt God's call to belong to a particular faith community—Catholic, Jewish, Protestant, or Buddhist—or to live a particular life defined by a certain moral code. Some on campus questioned these definitions of vocation, noting that they were too generic to actually be a vocation. After all, it was argued, since every marriage is to a certain person just as every career is in a certain job, vocation must be particular. Still others privately wondered if non-Christians could actually have a vocation.

The campus, which collectively held these different opinions about vocation, was repeatedly brought together by the events funded by the grant. The ensuing conversation about vocation was always interesting, and the campus enjoyed the spirit of investigation. And yet, I personally felt a growing sense of frustration. Although I was learning new ways to think about vocation, I became frustrated that even those of us actively engaged in this campus-wide reflection could not agree on a common definition of vocation. Such disagreement was not surprising, given the diversity of those engaged in the conversation, but I came to realize that our difference of opinions were not always just variations on a common theme, like the difference between apples and oranges, but were occasionally at odds, like the difference between apples and hammers. As an unfortunate result of these differences, participants in the discussion on campus appeared to spend more time and effort explaining and defending their particular view of vocation than learning how to discover and ultimately to live our vocation better. We simply were not getting somewhere fast enough, at least to my thinking. Clearly, there was a need for a new way of thinking about vocation. This new way should help unite the variety of opinions about vocation and still allow for the particular aspects of one's understanding to stand firm. A common language, or at least a common recognition of what vocation is and what it does, was needed.

My hope of finding this new way of thinking about vocation was the inspiration for Mount St. Mary's first annual Callings Conference and ultimately for this book. Since my goal was to help myself and others better understand what we mean when we mentioned vocation, I selected a broad theme: What does it mean to be called by God? So, thanks to the great work of many people, folks from across the country gathered at our campus in north-central Maryland on a beautiful April weekend in 2005 to share their wisdom on this question. It is my hope that the chapters in this book, all of which were initially presented at the Callings Conference, will help the reader better understand his or her sense of vocation as well.

This book is an attempt to bring some order to the wonderful diversity surrounding competing definitions of vocation. The book has three parts. After an introduction that examines common definitions of vocation and reaffirms the essential elements of what it means to be called by God, part 1 illustrates how vocations transform us into new, Christ-like persons. Part 2 then demonstrates how God calls us to serve others through our vocation. Finally, part 3 provides a further exemplification of how these two essential elements of vocation—transformation and service—work in a university setting, notably explaining how the university in general and faculty in particular help students discover and live out their callings.

It is my great hope that you enjoy this book. All of the writers informed me, in one way or the other, that writing their chapter helped them better understand not only vocation in general, but also their own vocations. I am honored to serve as the editor of this book, for I feel I learned the most of all.

Michael R. Miller
Easter 2006

Introduction

A Vision of Vocation

Michael R. Miller

The idea of vocation is often discussed in Christian society. Ordained members of the church frequently preach about vocation, and many consistently ask their congregations or parishioners to reflect God's call in their lives. Sunday school teachers and youth ministers routinely encourage young people to "answer the call" when it arrives. Likewise, Christian friends and family members regularly challenge each other to think vocationally when they discuss the joys and challenges of living a Christian life. Many parents also discuss vocation with their children, as when they point out to their children that a developing talent or interest may mark a new way of life or a future career. Such conversations have had their effect: Christians universally know that they are called by God.

In spite of all this talk about vocation and the rather common belief that everyone is called by God, Christians surprisingly find it quite difficult to explain what it means to have a vocation. They typically know that they have a vocation, and that their vocation comes from God. Most will equate their sense of vocation with a feeling of joy, an inner confidence, or a scriptural reference. But when you press them to provide definitive and particular examples of their personal vocation, many stall. If you ask any number of questions, including those that attempt to distinguish a sense of calling from a personal preference or attraction, most struggle to articulate what they claim to know. Such experiences remind me that the topic of vocation is a great mystery, for it involves God's action in our lives. Spiritual maturity is often identified when one recognizes that one does not know all the answers. Hence, one should not rush into an explanation of mystery. When we wander into God's realm, a world we cannot fully understand, we must tread lightly.

Consider the following example of someone struggling to make sense of her calling. Jenn is a young faith-filled college student who believes that God has a plan for her. In spite of her confidence that she is called by God, she agonizes over what God might want her to do. At one point in her life Jenn wondered if God wanted her to do something remarkable with her life, like become a missionary, start an international aid organization, or bring peace to a war-ravaged country. On further reflection, Jenn came to realize that God was not calling her to these noble acts. Instead, Jenn believes that God is calling her to another task, to be a filmmaker. Her logic is simple and sound, and rests in her great interest in films and all things related to Hollywood. Since God gave her these interests, she reasons, and since God would not call anyone to something she did not like, it follows that God must be calling her to work in the industry she loves. However, Jenn is an excellent science student with a caring attitude, and several teachers and her parents have urged her to consider a career in medicine. Jenn likes the idea of helping sick people, using her God-given talents for the common good, but what about her love for movies? Can't she help the common good, she wonders, by telling a really good story in film?

Prayer and conversation have led Jenn to consider the possibility that her calling may not be tied to her achieving a remarkable deed or even holding a job at all, but may be best expressed as doing the ordinary things of life, such as loving her family in an extraordinary way. And why not, she wonders. After all, her father has spent the last thirty years doing odd jobs around town, including driving a furniture delivery truck, checking in books at the library, and making potato chips in a local factory. He has been a wonderful father, husband, friend, and brother. God certainly had a plan for her father and he must be living it out, even if his jobs did not support the common good in the obvious way, working as a doctor might. But what divine plan was her father fulfilling, she wonders, when he was driving a truck, working at a counter, or operating a machine? Can living your vocation really be as simple as living a good life? Jenn's reflection is complicated by the fact that her father does not believe in God. Regardless of his lack of faith, this young college student recognizes that her father is a remarkably good man. But how can her father have a vocation if he does not believe in the one extending the call?

What is Jenn to do? She debates whether she should follow her heart and move to Hollywood or make good use of her God-given talents and enter medical school. Should she reject both options and join a missionary group,

or enroll in a graduate program in peace studies? Or maybe she should follow her father's example and not concern herself with finding any particular
job or completing any particular task. Maybe it would be best if she simply
concerned herself with becoming a better person and lived her life as it came
to her.

Clearly, understanding vocation is a difficult matter. Jenn fears her decision
is hopelessly complex, so she is certain she will not be able to decide what
God wants her to do. As a result, she is paralyzed by indecision, even though
she is confident that she is called to do something with her life. But what?

The difficulty Jenn faces in determining her vocation centers on her inability to define what it means to be called by God. Like Jenn, we need to determine if we are simply called by God to personal fulfillment, a life in which we
satisfy our natural (but often unidentified) longing to love and serve others?
Or are we called by God to particular tasks, such as a specific job, activity, or
manner of life, that make successful use of the unique talents we were given
or acquired through life? If so, must that particular task have a set outcome,
such as a remarkable improvement in someone else's life or the betterment of
the common good, perhaps? And does that same call to some particular task
change or stop when the circumstances of our lives change as well? Or is
God's call better defined as a more universal invitation to live a particular kind
of life, the life of holiness defined by our baptism? And not to forget the question of Jenn's father—does God call all people, including those who do not
believe in him? If so, to what does God call everyone?

Given the great variety of answers that might be given to such questions,
some people resist any effort to explain what it means to have a vocation. They
argue that an answer is *not needed*, since the great majority of Christians already
understand that a vocation is an invitation from God to do something with
their lives. Satisfied with this somewhat vague answer, they reject attempts to
say more. Other people resist efforts to define vocation because they think that
to do so is *impossible*, since no definition could correctly portray the variety and
fullness of God's call. And finally, some resist answering the question since an
answer is *not faithful*, since all efforts to define God's call essentially limit God's
operation and thereby deny the mysterious nature of God.

There is something to these objections, but they are not sufficient. First,
although it is helpful to understand that God is calling us, this fact alone does
not make it clear to what God is calling us, or why. Without this additional
knowledge we are less likely to find and follow the divine invitation. Second,
although it cannot be denied that God acts in ways that are often beyond
human understanding, this does not mean that we still cannot comprehend
in a meaningful way what it means to be called by God. God's transcendent
nature cannot require that we remain in the dark concerning his operation
in our lives, since it is unimaginable that God would not want us to reflect
on the nature of his call—even if our understanding does not perfectly capture the fullness of the divine operation. And finally, although it is patently

wrong to claim God's ways are not mysterious, our efforts to understand God do not limit God. God is certainly more than we can ever know in entirety, but our limitations in understanding God's call—no matter how severe they may be—do not limit God's operation in our lives any more than our inability to fully grasp the incarnation or the Trinity limit God's being and grandeur.

So, it is our right to ask the question: What does it mean to be called by God? In fact, it may be necessary for us to ask this question and to seek an answer. That is, if we are being invited by God to do something with our lives we ought to investigate what we are being called to and why—if only so we can better judge if we want to accept the invitation. It is important to realize here that the invitation offered through God's call is not for the benefit of God, who needs nothing, but for our own. If God is calling, it is likely that he is calling us to something he knows will be good for us and others. Thus, if we fail to investigate this question, we may also fail to realize our end, the very thing God knows will bring us happiness.

So, once again, what does it mean to be called by God?

The word *vocation* is derived from the Latin verb *vocare*, "to call." This little fact just invites us to ask a further pertinent question, Who is calling? The answer, in short, is God. But if God is calling, who is God calling? Everyone. It is incongruous to suggest that God just invites a few to participate in his divine plan. God does not just invite the priests, ministers, or those interested in public ministry to work with him. Nor does he simply have a plan for those who are holy, or talented, or strong. God is love, and hence he stands for all and with all; no one can be "outside of the loop." As created children of God we are made for a reason, and God has a plan for us to reach that end. That plan is linked to our vocation. We, in fact, bind ourselves to God when we strive to live the life to which we have been called. It is truly one of God's great mysteries that the infinitely wise and powerful Creator has a plan for us to follow but that he does not force us to follow it. God made us to be free. We have the power to say no, and with God's help we may have the wisdom to say yes. In its own way our choice to serve God or ourselves, to answer or reject his invitation, proves the fact that God is calling us to something.

That God calls everyone is commonly accepted. What is uncommon, however, is clear understanding of what God is calling us to. It is my thought that each of the different visions of vocation that have been given throughout the centuries feels right when considered alone, but none successfully contains all that belongs to the notion of vocation.

CALLED TO DISCIPLESHIP

One of the popular definitions of vocation is linked with belonging to a faith community or performing certain acts as a member of a particular faith.

Hence, according to this tradition, to have a vocation is to live as a Christian disciple. This vision of vocation is the oldest and one of the most common definitions, and it marks a Christian as someone set apart. The call to belong to God is very biblical, for like Abraham all those called by God are called to leave their past and sent on a journey to the land of discipleship (Gen 12:1). We are set apart through anointing (1 Sam 10:1) and baptism (Mark 15:15-16) when we are called to become disciples (Matt 4:18-22). Although all are welcome at the banquet (see Luke 14:15-24; Luke 3:29), no one by himself or herself can guarantee membership into the community (Matt 7:21; Matt 25:1-13). Scripture makes it quite clear that God alone offers the invitation to "come and follow" him (Matt 19.21; Mark 8:34). This invitation remains universal, however, for the call to membership in the Christian community is extended to both non-Christians and to believers who have fallen away from active membership in the church.

Paul clearly recognized that a vocation marks as different those who believe. When he refers to the Christians in Rome as people "who are called to belong to Jesus Christ," he is reminding them of their vocation to reject their former life and to adopt the new Christian way of living (Rom 1:6).[1] Paul repeats the same theme when he reminds the church at Thessalonica that God is "exhorting and encouraging you and insisting that you conduct yourselves as worthy of the God who calls you into his kingdom and glory" (1 Thess 2:12). He also shares with the church that those who have died in faith—who have successfully responded to Jesus' call—acknowledged themselves to be "strangers and aliens on earth" (Heb 11:13). Such passages confirm that the Christian vocation is to no longer love the things of the world (1 John 2:15; Rom 12:2), but to keep God's commandments (John 14:15; 1 John 2:3-6).

This particular call to be set apart as a Christian is supported by many, including the witness of Christian martyrs. For example, Ignatius of Antioch begs the members of the Christian community not to stand in the way of his execution. He recognizes that his death will make clear his rejection of his past, for "[t]he greatness of Christianity lies in its being hated by the world."[2] Thus, he urges his friends not to interfere so that they "do not give back to the world one who wants to be God's." Augustine of Hippo suffered in his own way when he was struggling to accept his vocation to be a Christian. Augustine's detailed and moving description of his moment of conversion demonstrates how important he believed this decision was. He knew that if he accepted God's invitation to become a Christian, there could be no turning back; he would be set apart, living for God and not the world. Writing of this decision, Augustine noted that while he was moving to a decision, "he still hesitated to die to death and to live to life."[3]

More contemporary Christians have also presented this vision of vocation as the fullest expression of God's call. In fact, Søren Kierkegaard felt it necessary to educate the Christians of his day—who Kierkegaard thought were far too comfortable in their faith—that having a vocation means one is being called by God to live the life of a disciple. Although many people were familiar with the teachings of the Christian faith, Kierkegaard believed that the majority of these cultural Christians lacked the passion needed to be an authentic Christian.[4] Thus, afraid of what the cost of faith may be, they do not properly live their vocation. Abraham, Kierkegaard's model of faith, suffered tremendously because of the burden of his call,[5] yet Abraham, when his name was called by God, "cheerfully, freely, confidently, loudly" answered: "Here I am."[6] For Kierkegaard the "knight of infinite resignation" may appear absolutely ordinary and in the world, but the one who has answered God's call ultimately stands apart from the ordinary world as "a stranger and an alien." That is, although it may be almost impossible to distinguish the "knight of faith" from the rest of the crowd, the one who follows his Christian vocation is always living in a "moment of infinity" which allows him to do the remarkable: "to concentrate the whole substance of his life and the meaning of actuality into one single desire."[7] This single desire is the hope of the Christian who has a vocation, who has answered the call. Thanks to this divine invitation, such an individual recognizes that he or she is not like others in the world, for the individual, like Christ, does not belong to the world (John 17:14). Kierkegaard argues that Christians cannot be "benchwarmers who do not take part in the dance" but must be committed men and women who live as Christ desires, thereby expressing the "sublime in the pedestrian."[8]

Other theologians also support the idea that vocation is a call to discipleship. Like Kierkegaard, Dietrich Bonhoeffer recognized the intense demands membership in the church can place on our lives. In his book *The Cost of Discipleship*, Bonhoeffer stressed that Christians must live as they are called to live—that is, to live the gospel. Reflecting on Matthew's immediate response to Jesus' call (Mark 2:14), Bonhoeffer notes that "there is no need for any preliminaries, and no other consequences but obedience to the call. Because Jesus is the Christ, he has the authority to call and to demand obedience to his word. . . . There is no road to faith or discipleship, no other road—only obedience to the call of Jesus."[9] John Henry Newman also recognizes that God's call requires Christians to act. In an essay entitled "Divine Calls." Newman notes that the saints are "working out their salvation with fear and trembling, yet ascribing the work to Him who wrought in them to will and do of His good pleasure; obeying the call, and giving thanks to Him who calls, to Him who fulfills in them their calling."[10] Thus, according to Bonhoeffer and Newman, we have and fulfill our vocation when we do what God demands.

However, in spite of this great support, some argue that this vision of vocation does not provide a complete picture. Critics note that such a view of vocation is typically articulated only when the Christian community is suffering from religious persecution or attacked by cultural forces that challenge faith. For this reason the call to membership in community through certain actions, albeit necessary, appears to many already living in a Christian culture or society to be overly general and impersonal. That is, this sense of call does not necessarily invite anyone to something beyond the faithful fulfillment of the requirements of membership, which may or may not lead to persecution. Nor does this account fully consider the particular details of the life of the one called, especially his or her unique talents or interests. Thus, it appears that if one already identifies himself or herself as a Christian, there would be no sense of God calling someone to do something more, short of martyrdom.

CALLED TO ACTION

Vocation is also often associated with God's invitation to perform certain jobs. This second vision of vocation, unlike the first, is much more concerned about where the one called spends his or her day. That is, this second view of vocation accepts that Christians are in some way called to be set apart from others, but it emphasizes that God calls each and every person to complete a particular set of acts. This sense of calling is divided into two subsets: the first links vocation to particular jobs found within the church, such as priest or minister; the second links vocation to any occupation for which we are particularly well suited by talent or interest.

Serving within the Church

The first subset of the second vision of vocation is best identified as the belief that particular individuals are called to specific ministries within the church. Although such a response can be very public, as often witnessed by the work and witness of ordained ministers and religious sisters or brothers, a response to God's invitation to give one's life to the church may also be relatively private, as when someone dedicates her life to working as a lay missionary, a Christian educator, or with an international NGO such as Lutheran World Relief or Catholic Relief Services. The essential element of this definition of vocation is that the one responding to the call works through the church, by doing church-related acts of charity or ministry, including feeding the poor, educating the unchurched, ministering to the sick or imprisoned, or even completing the relatively ordinary administrative duties required to help the church minister to others.

The belief that vocation is a call to ministry within the community also has its roots in the Bible. A large percentage of the call stories in the Bible center on an invitation to serve others in a particular way in God's name. Moses was called to lead God's people (Exod 3:4-22); Isaiah to preach (Isa 6:1-10); Paul to teach the Gentiles (Acts 9:15); and Stephen, plus six others who were also filled with the Spirit and wisdom, were called to serve the community (Acts 6:1-6). Saint Paul mentions several of the Holy Spirit's gifts (1 Cor 12:1-11); these spiritual gifts highlight just some of the different ways we can serve in Christ's name: leading, teaching, healing, giving prophecy, and discerning spirits.

Countless holy men and women have felt this call to serve others as well, and their lives reflect the diversity of the calls given to do God's good work. Thérèse of Lisieux's vocation was to the monastery, and she found both profound joy and occasional sorrow in living that life. Augustine, Luther, Wesley, and many others were called to lead and preach. Others, like Thomas Aquinas, Orthodox theologian Father Alexander Schmemann, Jacques Maritain, and Richard Niebuhr, were directed by God to teach. Mother Teresa, Albert Schweitzer, and Dorothy Day responded to God's call by serving the poor. The diversity of this call to serve is remarkable; it appears that God calls people to as many ministries as there are needs in the world. The one common feature in each of these calls is that they are completed within and through the church.

One of the problems with such a definition of vocation, however, is that vocation appears to be a rare and supernatural invitation—occasionally involving burning bushes, voices from heaven, and special spiritual insights—that is given to only a select few. And even if such remarkable occurrences are not necessary in order to be called, this sense of vocation still appears to exclude those that are not called to particular leadership or service within the church. Does this mean, according to this vision of vocation, that the Christian who works in an office or a factory, or in the home does not have a vocation? Likewise, what about those who also serve others in God's name, but who are not Christian? For example, can it be successfully argued that Gandhi was not called by God to love as he did? Can anyone honestly believe that the Dalai Lama is not likewise living out his vocation?

Serving within the World

The second subset of the vision of vocation as oriented to particular jobs eschews the link between vocation and work within the public ministry of the church; rather, it stresses that one's vocation is found in the ordinary, daily work that we do. According to this very popular notion there is no division between one's vocation and life, for all that we do in our jobs is God's work if done for God's glory. This vision of vocation respects the value of all human activities because it stresses the idea that God works through all people in the ordinary events of life. Thus, people can be called to a wide variety of occupations—doctors, teachers, factory workers, accountants, firefighters, priests, those who pick up trash—since each career becomes valuable when God calls us to it. This view of vocation is quite common today, and it receives strong support from a diverse group, including Luther, Wesley, Pope Leo XIII, and playwright Dorothy Sayers.

Martin Luther was one of the first to champion this sense of vocation. While never denying that all Christians share a common calling to live as disciples of Christ, Luther stressed that every Christian also had a unique calling to serve others in a particular profession. Therefore, convinced that our salvation does not depend on what we do but on God's grace, Luther thought it unnecessary for anyone to make special sacrifices to live a holy life, such as become ordained or enter a monastery. Thus, Luther explained, "there is really no difference between laymen and priest, prince and bishops, 'spirituals' and 'temporals,' as they call them, except that of office and work, but not of 'estate.'"[11] It was enough, he argued, for a Christian to do the work that is before him, since "all works are the same to a Christian, no matter what they are."[12] Simply put, Luther's great contributions regarding vocation and work are: 1) all people, and not just priests and religious, have a vocation; and 2) every job can be a vocation.[13]

Catholic theologians typically have not accepted all Luther's ideas concerning work, but in his watershed 1891 encyclical *Rerum Novarum*, Pope Leo XIII agreed with Luther that lay work has inherent dignity. Subsequent encyclicals including *Quadragesimo Anno* (1931), *Gaudium et Spes* (1965), *Laborem Exercens* (1981), and *Centesimus Annus* (1991) reaffirmed this belief. Together these documents demonstrate that the Catholic Church recognizes that lay men and women are doing God's work at their jobs: "Let Christians follow the example of Christ who worked as a craftsman; let them be proud of the opportunity to carry out their earthly activity in such a way as to integrate human, domestic, professional, scientific and technical enterprises with religious values, under whose supreme direction all things are ordered to the glory of God."[14] Following the church's teaching, numerous lay Catholics understand today (in ways they did not just decades ago) the dignity and value of their work. Present in the world where ordained ministers do not have regular contact, Catholic laity are called to understand their work as their apostolate, since it is a Christian leaven for society.[15]

Although contemporary theologians accept the benefit of recognizing one's job as a vocation, some are critical of this vision of vocation. For example, Miroslav Volf noted in *Work in the Spirit* that Luther's views about vocation and work cannot stand when one considers that some jobs are inherently alienating, even if not immoral.[16] Yet, since Luther argues that any moral work (excluding working as a hit-man, for example) has the standing of a vocation, it would appear that Luther must believe that even the mind-numbing, dangerous, and degrading work at a slaughterhouse must be a vocation as well. Likewise, Volf notes that Luther's vision of vocation does not equate well with modern patterns of employment, where people routinely switch jobs throughout their working life.[17] Are we to assume that God called someone to one job, only for that person to lose the job a month later after it was downsized? Other concerns also arise with this view. Namely, it does not commonly address what happens to one's vocation after one leaves work.

Does the teacher or the doctor no longer have a vocation when they retire to home at the end of the day, or from their career? Does such a vision of vocation exclude those who do not have the opportunity or ability to work, or do not get paid for their work?

CALLED TO PERSONAL FULFILLMENT

In recent decades many have articulated a new way of looking at vocation. Recognizing the insatiable and universal desire for happiness, this vision of vocation suggests that living a life vocationally is best seen as being and doing what makes you an authentic and complete human being. Influenced by the work of Erikson, Piaget, and James Fowler, this vision of vocation certainly does not rest in the shallow claim that God calls us to "look out for number one"; such a self-serving sense of vocation is ultimately self-defeating. Rather, proponents of this third vision of vocation emphasize that a vocation is a gift that must be shared with others; like all invaluable gifts (e.g., love and faith), vocation is a gift that must be given away to be enjoyed.

Those who are seeking their vocation need to go no further than to explore their gifts and desires, and to recognize where they find joy. As Parker J. Palmer writes in *Let Your Life Speak: Listening for the Voice of Vocation*, "Before you tell your life what you intend to do with it, listen for what it intends to do with you. Before you tell your life what truths and values you have decided to live up to, let your life tell you what truths you embody, what values you represent."[18] The expectation here is that when you understand yourself well, you will also come to understand why you were given your unique gifts—to serve others. As theologian Frederick Buechner notes, vocation is best defined as "[t]he place where your deep gladness and the world's deep hunger meet."[19] This holy place, this intersection between your joys and the world's needs, may be found in a particular state in life or membership in a faith community. This sacred spot may be found in your job, whether working within the structure of the church or in a secular office building. What matters here is not that you end up in a particular spot, but that you made the journey of self-discovery.

Sharon Daloz Parks, author of *Big Questions, Worthy Dreams*, says that the image of a journey is a fitting metaphor for the vocation of human development, since "[o]ur desire to soar is readily fused with a conviction of aliveness, a confidence of spirit. Journey language is a language of transcendence, crossing over, reaching and moving beyond. When we feel we are not yet *what* we ought to be, we are prone to feeling we are not *where* we ought to be."[20] This sense of longing motivates us to engage in the virtues of self-discovery: courage, surrender, sacrifice, and love. The journey metaphor is especially fitting for Jews and Christians, Parks notes, because it harkens to the Promised Land, the Kingdom of God, the promise "envisioned primarily as something not yet fulfilled" but on the horizon.[21] To seek your vocation, therefore, is an exciting and lifelong process, since your vocation may change as you develop. You may be called to one thing at twenty, another at twenty-five, and still another at forty. Rather than fear such changes, those who recognize they are on a journey should enjoy the ride.

This view affirms that everyone, Christians and non-Christians alike, receives the invitation to develop as a human being; everyone is called to become a better person; everyone is called to live a mature faith life, which is best characterized by using our talents to make the world a better place. In striving to live this life one allows oneself the chance to fulfill the deepest longing of the human heart; one will become the person one was meant to be—a whole and authentic person.

Although such a vision of vocation appeals to many today, it has its share of critics. First, if one's vocation is tied to personal enhancement, some wonder if anyone will ever complete his or her calling. That is, since everyone can always improve who they are, can anyone ever be at rest in his or her vocation? Does the journey never end? Second, in spite of assurances otherwise, some believe that the call to personal satisfaction remains fundamentally self-serving, since the view essentially allows the individual (and not the Christian community or even society at large) to define both the end and the means of his or her calling. That is, the individual is generally allowed to decide for himself or herself what counts as service to others, and which actions bring personal satisfaction. Critics of this view worry that without the proper mentoring or guidance from the church individuals will naturally avoid making the necessary but sacrificial acts required of true service to others. Finally, some critics point out that such a view of calling does not properly involve God, for little or no divine participation is required when people are "finding themselves" through the particular activities they enjoy and can do well. Although the secular language of self-knowledge and self-fulfillment may be in line with the religious sense of calling,[22] critics argue that any approach that does not recognize God as the source and end of the call should not to be identified with vocation.

A NEW DEFINITION?

Given these diverse, somewhat contradictory, and possibly inadequate definitions of calling, what is a Christian to understand about his or her vocation? Once again, what does it mean to be called by God?

Now, I hesitate to answer the very question that I have so often asked the reader to ponder. I do so not because I do not have a definition to give, but because I recognize just how difficult it is to explain properly the great mystery of vocation. If the preceding reflection on vocation has not made it clear, God's ways are mysterious. We may understand in part why God does what he does, but we will never understand fully since God is simply too great for us to comprehend.[23] Hence, I think it unreasonable to expect that the manner in which God directs our lives through our vocation would be crystal clear. There are, in fact, great advantages in presenting multiple definitions for complex things. For example, it is quite fitting that we have four gospels and not just one; the life of Jesus is so multifaceted no one author could accurately capture all that Jesus is in one account. The differences between the Gospel of John and the synoptic gospels are revealing, as are the differences that appear among the synoptics. Likewise, maybe an assortment of definitions explain vocation better than any one definition.

However, with a great admiration for the previous definitions given, I believe something more needs to be done to help us understand what we are talking about when discussing God's call in our lives. My effort here is not to replace the different visions of vocation that have so well served Christians for centuries, but to highlight central themes common to all three. If the definition given here does not capture the fullness of vocation, so be it. It remains my hope that what is presented now will serve some purpose, if only to engender more conversation on this very important topic. So, finally, what does it mean to be called by God?

I believe that to be called by God is a divine invitation to respond to the grace present in one's life. In answering that call every aspect of our life, including the most ordinary and the extraordinary, is transformed. The end result is that we are no longer simply interested in our own good, but are newly dedicated to the well-being of others. Serving them and not ourselves makes us more human, more saintly, and more Christ-like.

God abundantly gives his grace to his creatures, and every person is gifted with certain talents and interests that are part of his or her calling. The range of gifts is as broad as there are people, for there appears no limit to God's generosity. When anyone acts in relation to these gifts, whether they are particular talents or interests, that person is responding vocationally—even if he or she does not know it. Why? Because God has made us in such a way that we always choose what we perceive to be good.[24] This means that all the particular things we choose—this meal, that outfit, this job, or that activity—are chosen because we think that possessing the object or doing the activity will make us happy. Unfortunately, our choices may in fact harm us, which is not the particular choice God would want for us; however, the act of choosing itself is exactly what God wants us to do, for humans were made to choose.

Choices lead to actions and actions to habits, which in turn lead to the development of character. That is, our choices eventually make us into the persons we are. For example, if a young girl consistently explores her musical talents and interests she will become musical. Likewise, if an old man is selfish he has most certainly chosen to focus on his needs and not the needs of others throughout his life. This kind of development, for good or bad, is our response to the grace present in our lives. It is certainly God's hope that we respond well to his grace. If we do we have accepted the invitation and we are acting vocationally. It is important to note that according to this argument people can be fulfilling their vocation even if they are not aware that God is present in their lives, or that God gifted them with particular talents or interests. Christian or non-Christian, old or young, rich or poor, reflective or unaware—it makes no difference. To act vocationally, in this sense, is to choose.

Accepting one's vocation, like falling in love, transforms the individual. We become new persons when we accept our calling and live it out, for everything we are is made anew. Like the period before we find our love, the search for vocation is often lonely and laborious. But when we find our calling, we know it; nothing feels the same as it did before. Again, like falling in love, we discover our vocations in different ways. Some individuals in loving relationships discover their love for the other slowly, in fits and starts. There may be an initial flush of attraction that is soon followed by a relative cooling off in the relationship; individuals may question if they want to spend their live with the other, and they may separate for a time before coming to a decision. Others fall in love in an instant, certain that they have found their soul mate. Regardless of the manner in which one falls in love, the end result is the same: a certain knowledge that the beloved is meant for oneself. This comfortable and confident feeling pulls one through one's life, for one makes decisions in light of that love, and it sustains one when one feels alone, depressed, or tired.

This transformative aspect of a calling can come as a shock, for accepting and living a vocation always redirects our lives in particular directions. Once accepted we are not the same, and even ordinary things are radically changed for the better. It is said that near-death experiences are moments of extreme clarity. If we "live like we are dying," to echo the title of the Tim McGraw hit, we would likely recognize that tomorrow is a gift and we have to think about what we will do with it.[25] Maybe we, like the character in the song, would come to say that we now "loved deeper" and "spoke sweeter" and "gave forgiveness we'd been denying." Simple things we once ignored would now become important and activities once thought crucial could suddenly lose their value. The remarkable book *Tuesdays with Morrie* is certainly successful in jolting people into a new way of thinking.[26] It is difficult to read this little book and not resolve to do things differently, if only to sustain our dear relationships better. Hopefully we do not have to face death directly to understand what makes life worth living. An exploration, acceptance, and living out of vocation can have a similar power to transform. When we recognize our call, we know it. Suddenly, when we live out this call, all the events in our daily life are judged against this new way of seeing the world. We are not the same.

The excitement of discovering and accepting our vocation is linked to the recognition that we have a role in God's plan for the universe. Both awe inspiring and frightening, God calls us to participate in this plan. I am convinced that one of the greatest lessons of life is to learn that the universe was not made simply for us, but for all of us. This means that our needs are not central to the world. Trusting that God knows what is best—accepting that "God is God and we are not"—is a notoriously difficult lesson to learn, but once we understand our place in God's plan everything makes more sense.

This purpose, the reason we were created, has both a general and particular aspect. In the most general sense everyone is called to serve God and neighbor (Matt 22:37-40). Living the great commandment will make us into the persons God wants us to be, for we will grow in discipleship the more we live as Christ lives. Jesus' great commandment to love God and neighbor is not two requests but one, for we love God when we love our neighbor and vice versa. The particular calling we are given is simply an exemplification of our general call, and is very much united to our given graces. Thus, our talents and interests will lead us to choose one particular activity over another. As long as the job or activity we do serves the other in accordance with God's law, we can be said to be acting rightly. However, I believe that the better choice, the one that is more vocationally oriented, will likely model itself after Jesus' example. That is, often the choices that we recognize as the ones that signify our vocation are sacrificial. Like Jesus, we discover our particular purpose in life when we learn to die to self (Gal 2:20). Our sacrifice, when done in the proper spirit of trust and love, does not cost us as much as we imagine (Phil 3:7-8). For example, the parent who sacrifices sleep to care for a sick child, the co-worker who accepts a difficult task outside of her job description to bring a necessary project to completion, the volunteer at the mission who rises early to cook a needed breakfast, the neighbor who picks up trash in his neighborhood—all serve joyfully when aware of their calling. In this sense, vocation pulls us out of ourselves and our needs. It pushes us to see the other and to serve in joy.

CONCLUSION

In summary, I believe that God calls everyone to step out of their own immediate needs and to live for others. That is, every valuable definition of vocation directs us to consider the other. Discipleship demands that we live for Christ and his church. As members of the community of the faithful we are called to sacrifice our own identity and our particular concerns for the well-being of the whole. In this sense the disciple's eyes are not directed on self, but the end—life with God. Likewise, all work—either directly linked with the ministry of the church or not—finds value especially when we put our individual talents and aspirations to the service of others. Such efforts, even if demanding, will make us whole. That is, we will be living a fully human life if we share our gifts with others. As Jesus' life shows, nothing is more affirming and fruitful than living your life for the other. To be happy like Christ, who was perfectly whole, we must live like Christ—which means to die to self.

So Jenn asks: What is my vocation? Should I go to Hollywood and make movies or become a doctor? Should I follow my interests or my talents? Should I focus on completing a particular job or just living a good life? My answer to Jenn is for her to follow the option that would make her more Christ-like. That is, she needs to determine if one choice will transform her and give meaning to what she does with her life? Is one choice less about serving her immediate and personal needs and more about the happiness she will gain by helping others? Is one choice calling her to a sacrificial love that will ultimately redeem her?

If Jenn can answer these questions, then I think she knows where her vocation can be found. If not, she needs to talk to others, especially those who have already said yes to God's call, and get their advice. She should also continue to try things out, testing the waters so that she might better see God's will in the currents. And she should listen more, especially in prayer, so that she might come to know what really matters in life. Then she will know her vocation, and if we do likewise we will do more with our lives— even if we can never quite define our vocation.

Part One

VOCATION AND TRANSFORMATION

Joan of Arcadia and Fulfilling Your True Nature

Jessamyn Neuhaus

Joan Girardi, the central character on the CBS drama *Joan of Arcadia* (2003–2005), saw and conversed with God. Literally. God spoke to Joan, not in the whispering wind or the gurgling of a clear brook, but in contemporary American English. God appeared to Joan not in the stillness of the sunrise or the perfect beauty of a flower or even a burning bush, but in a wide variety of human forms—a piano tuner, a little girl, a server in the cafeteria, a telephone repairman, a sanitation worker. As the show's theme song, Joan Osborne's 1995 hit "What If God Was One of Us?" suggested, God appeared to Joan Girardi as "just a stranger on the bus." Moreover, every week Joan is called into God's service with cryptic but emphatic directives. God's call in *Joan of Arcadia* (*JoA*) is not socially acceptable: almost any church today would dismiss as mentally ill an ordination candidate who claimed God assumed human flesh and a human voice and issued a call to the ministry.

Indeed, the creators of *JoA* addressed this very presumption during the first season's finale, when Joan fell ill with Lyme disease and had to wrestle with the possibility that her divine visitations had been disease-induced hallucinations. In modern America, where the science of psychology and psychiatry so profoundly shape our understanding of human behavior, Joan and the viewers had to ask: Is she crazy? Or is she really called by God? But the

19

show quickly resolved that question at the beginning of the second season, when Joan faced the frightening consequences (a friend drinks to excess and must be hospitalized) of ignoring God's call. Although often reluctant to do God's bidding, Joan decided she must always at least attempt to follow God's directives.[1] Viewers certainly did not doubt that an embodied God appeared to Joan and called her into service.[2] In this sense, Joan experienced God's call in a way that most (sane) U.S. citizens never will nor will ever expect to: the literal appearance of divinity offering highly specific directives for individual behavior.

Leaving aside, however, the means of the call, did the representation of God's call on *JoA* break any new ground? Did the content and meaning of the call, as depicted on this TV show, offer viewers any significant reinterpretation of how human beings are called into God's service? In this chapter I will argue that certain aspects of God's call on *JoA* illustrated a growing, vital representation of the call: the idea that when God calls us, the call will fundamentally transform us and turn us from self-interest to a life of compassion and service to others. In short, the call on *JoA* demanded that Joan become more godlike, or perhaps Christ-like, in her interactions with others.[3] However, I will also demonstrate that while this message about God's call as demanding action in the world appeared on *JoA*, the tasks God gave Joan were also very much in keeping with an interpretation of God's call that emphasizes not transformative service but personal gain and accomplishment.

God's call on *JoA* was contradictory. On the one hand, it demonstrated to Joan that the most important task any of us face is finding the best way to be of service to humanity. But on the other hand, the show constantly emphasized that God's call did not require Joan to undertake any radical or overtly "religious" action and that fulfilling God's call would lead her to her own, individual fulfillment. In this sense, it neatly dovetailed with a longstanding but recently invigorated tradition among some American Christians who link God's will to personal gain, prosperity, and achievement. But, as I will conclude in the final section, despite the way the show undercut what I see as its most significant message about God's call, *Joan of Arcadia* was a pioneering effort to depict for a youthful audience twenty-first century spiritual issues and questions in general, and God's call in particular, in what is by far the most influential story-telling medium of our time.

IN THE BEGINNING: THE PREMISE (AND DEMISE) OF *JOAN OF ARCADIA*

During its first season (2003–2004), *Joan of Arcadia* won over critics and viewers, earning high ratings, three Emmy nominations, and a People's Choice award.[4]

Reviewers termed *JoA* a "surprise hit," and as the second season concluded, they continued to praise the show's quality writing and acting.[5] It also sparked considerable discussion among journalists, Christian commentators, and religious leaders. While some praised the show, others questioned its depiction of the divine. Some commentators and viewers found the ecumenical, almost secular, portrayal of God disturbing.[6] They criticized Joan's complete disinterest in Christianity: Joan did not pray and she did not attend church. She never mentioned Jesus, let alone the Bible. Joan's mother, Helen, was Catholic, but the show never depicted Helen worshiping in community or praying.

The media attention, of course, contributed to the popular buzz about the show. But during the second season, ratings for *JoA* dropped, dropped surprisingly rapidly for a show that received so much press and initially created such a devoted viewership.[7] Fans waited nervously for CBS to renew *JoA*, and both critics and viewers lamented when CBS announced its cancellation.[8] Commentators offered a variety of reasons why the show failed, ranging from the network's understandable reluctance to stand behind any show with dropping ratings to the suggestion that better shows simply lured away viewers.[9] Some pointed out that at least fans could be thankful that the aired episodes will be released on DVD sets, which include extra features as well.[10] Whatever the cause of its demise, the premise of *JoA* deserves some explanation in order to understand the cultural significance of how it depicted God's call.

JoA's creator, Barbara Hall, is Roman Catholic, but the "Ten Commandments of *Joan of Arcadia*" that she handed down to the writers dictated: "God can never identify one religion as being right." In addition, *JoA* always adhered to the other "commandments": "God cannot directly intervene," "Good and evil exist," "The job of every human being is to fulfill his or her true nature," "Everyone is allowed to say 'no' to God, including Joan," "God is not bound by time," "God is not a person and does not possess a human personality," "God talks to everyone all the time in different ways," "God's plan is what is good for us, not what is good for him," and "God's purpose for talking to Joan is to get her (us) to recognize the interconnectedness of all things."[11] In other words, God, as conceived by the creator and writers of *JoA*, does not represent any one religion or even any particular type of spiritual practice. As Amber Tamblyn, the actress who plays Joan, summarized: *JoA* was "not religious, we're philosophical."[12]

Yet, the premise of *JoA* required viewers to be open at least to the possibility of a divine omniscient force in the universe: Joan Girardi, a typical high school student with no interest in religion, begins receiving visitations from God during her sophomore year at her new school in Arcadia, a fictional Maryland town. The Girardi family are new arrivals to Arcadia, hoping for a fresh start after Kevin, the oldest son, was paralyzed in a car accident. Will, Joan's father, begins a new job as chief of police; Joan's mother, Helen, takes a position as an art teacher at the high school; and Joan's highly intelligent, geeky, younger brother Luke also begins high school in Arcadia.

When Joan, confused but willing, begins to attempt to follow God's vague and frequently baffling instructions, she starts to see that her work plays an important role in changing people's lives and bettering the world. The results are not always clear and are sometimes discomfiting, but Joan usually is left knowing, in a new way, the interconnectedness of the human condition. And so Joan, albeit reluctantly and complainingly, continues to obey God. She is not a meek, reverent servant of God: she resists, she argues, and God's enigmatic remarks continually frustrate her. In the pilot episode, Joan expresses understandable suspicions when the cute boy she noticed on the bus approaches her and identifies himself as God. She demands proof:

> Joan: Let's see a miracle.
>
> Cute Boy/God: How about that?
>
> Joan: It's a tree.
>
> Cute Boy/God: Let's see you make one.[13]

Joan seems unimpressed. However, when the boy relates a list of Joan's thoughts and actions that she had never revealed to anyone, such as her bargaining with God following Kevin's accident and that the "hideous song from *Titanic*" sometimes made her cry, she is much more unnerved.[14] Joan is eventually convinced that God is appearing to her. But the initial exchanges set the tone for Joan's encounters with God throughout the show.

At times, Joan and God almost banter. Joan is by turns sarcastic, exasperated, annoyed, pleading, and frustrated with God, while God is patient and calm, but inscrutable, unfathomable. Joan is even scornful, snapping at God, and literally and figuratively rolls her eyes at God's opaque messages. "I always thought you'd be nicer," she complains once.[15] In a typical conversation, Joan questions the existence of death and suffering:

> Joan: What kind of system is it?
>
> Little Girl/God: A perfect one. Trust me. [Long pause]
>
> Joan: [Impatiently] I'm *listening*. . . .
>
> Little Girl/God: I'm finished.[16]

Viewers and critics have sometimes wondered why Joan does not press further, why she seems so oblivious to the enormous implications of her conversations with God, why she seems so self-absorbed and moody; mature and thoughtful one minute, immature and insensitive the next. They wondered why someone in the presence of God whines and complains instead of standing in awed reverence.[17] But Hall had a ready and plausible answer: Joan is an ordinary teenager.[18] In the presence of God Joan acts just exactly as many other typical teenagers would. Joan's youth is absolutely central to *JoA*. It is not simply a plot convenience: it is essential to the show's depiction of God's call.

JUST BE YOURSELF: THE LIMITATIONS OF GOD'S CALL TO JOAN

Joan of Arcadia's target audience was young women.[19] Although the writers interweaved Joan's story with those of her family, offering adult viewers engaging story lines about Will's police work, Will and Helen's marriage, and their struggle to come to terms with Kevin's paralysis, the show focused mainly on Joan and her high school friends. As a result, young women comprised the majority of Joan's active and outspoken fan base, who praised the show's depiction of a teenage girl who neither looked nor acted like the standard TV or Hollywood blond babe. They embraced the "teen soap opera" elements of the show, speculating online about Joan's romantic relationships or dishing about the actor's haircuts, but they also appreciated the more complex story lines that raised complicated ethical and moral issues.[20] Significantly, they found the depictions of divinity and God's call compelling and thought provoking.[21]

It is not surprising that youthful audiences responded positively to the way *JoA* depicts God's call. In some ways, God's call on *JoA* is almost a metaphor for the individual work of growing up and searching for one's identity. God's tasks for Joan always begin with Joan taking a personal risk, an individual action, that challenges her to become more fully herself and, ultimately, create a positive impact on the people around her and expand her understanding of the moral complexities of the world. For example, in "Bringeth It On," God tells Joan—who is the antithesis of blond, perky, and popular—to try out for cheerleading. She does so; to the scorn and amazement of her few close friends. But Joan's God-given task became clear when she provides compassionate support for Brianna, an obviously troubled cheerleader who secretly gave birth then left her baby in a bathroom. Joan also publicly condemns the other cheerleaders who distance themselves from Brianna.[22] Joan, in this episode, becomes "the face of God" to Brianna and the other cheerleaders.[23] God calls Joan to try out for cheerleading not simply to teach Joan the somewhat banal lesson that "even popular kids have problems." Rather, God's call invites Joan to experience the necessity of true empathy toward others and the power of standing with those in need. God calls Joan toward universal compassion, a quality of divinity that is perhaps also the most important task of being human as well.

In another episode, God instructs Joan to attend a school dance with Ramsey, an obnoxious bully and loner attending Joan's high school. Again, to the amazement and confusion of her friends and concern of her parents, Joan invites Ramsey to the dance, and he seems to attempt to rise to the occasion. Unfairly harassed by the principal during the dance, Ramsey subsequently storms out. Joan follows and finds him firing off a handgun. She then stands in terrified witness as Will and other police officers surround Ramsey and convince him to surrender. Joan remains baffled about this task, until God reveals to her in the final scene that had Joan not reached out to Ramsey, Ramsey would likely have gone on a murderous rampage on school grounds.[24] Again, by simply listening and trying to be compassionate toward a fellow human, Joan answered God's call. Her efforts to serve as "the face of God" to others, to offer comfort to those in pain and need, not only increase her own awareness of the interconnectedness of humanity but also illuminate the desperate need for what we might call a ministry (a term never employed on *JoA*, however) of compassion. Obeying God's call has the potential to enormously change Joan; it offers her the opportunity to dramatically redirect her life toward service.

God calls Joan to do demanding tasks—at least, they seem demanding to Joan and perhaps to *JoA*'s youthful audience as well. Some adult viewers of *JoA* might wonder why Joan seems so daunted by divine orders such as "Ace your history test," "Dive off the high board," "Learn how to play chess," "Join the debate team," or "Audition for the school play."[25] And viewers of all ages may wonder why a supreme being would require so little of Joan. But to Joan, a typical teenager, they are difficult challenges that require not only risk taking but abiding faith in God's wisdom as well. God's tasks for Joan allow her to embark on a potentially deeply transformative experience of service, but Joan has to first trust that God's call will lead her to the right actions. Joan's struggles with these tasks are compellingly real to many young viewers, who themselves struggle with very similar tasks but without the benefit of direct divine guidance. But moreover, Joan's failures, and her continued faith, are compellingly real to anyone who has attempted to understand the mysteries of faith and vocation. Joan answers God's call. She is sulky, she talks back, she complains, but she answers the call and undertakes the arduous struggle toward fulfilling God's call to service.

However, while *JoA* suggested that God called Joan to transformative faith and service, at the same time it also suggested a more problematic interpretation of God's call. On *JoA*, God calls Joan as an individual, acting individually; God offers a plan that is "good for Joan, not for God," in the words of Hall's "commandment." As God explains to Joan in the pilot, the requests made of her "are not about religion, but about fulfilling [her] own true nature."[26] Despite the titular reference, Joan of Arcadia is no Joan of Arc, wielding a sword in the service of her religion and her king, and suffering enormously for doing so.[27] Instead, God's call allows Joan to develop her own best self with little or no real sacrifice. As suggested on *JoA*, God asks each of us to pursue self-knowledge, to be our best selves, to "be present" to the people closest to us, and in this way enact good in the world. I argued earlier that in this way God's call to Joan is transformative and meaningful. But I also believe that the depiction of God's call on *JoA* ultimately failed to truly challenge Joan or the viewers to consider the radical possibilities of working toward the common good. While I applaud the assertion of *JoA's* creators that God's call extends far beyond the confines of any one organized religion, the characterization of God's call as a call to "fulfill our true nature" troubles me. I believe it echoes one highly problematic interpretation of God's call: an interpretation that emphasizes our personal journey towards vocation, fulfillment, and prosperity rather than radical social change or working in community.

Again and again, God calls Joan to act, if not exactly in her self-interest, at least in the interest of those nearest and dearest to her. Notwithstanding the importance of loving-kindness toward our friends and family, *JoA* undercuts a compelling message about a divine call to active, universal compassion by emphasizing what appears to be God's will for Joan to simply be a good friend, sister, and girlfriend. God's call to Joan often seems to be limited to her own group of friends and family. For instance, when God suggests that Joan stop "underachieving" at school, she enrolls in an advanced chemistry course and meets Adam Rove, whose father, a night janitor at the police station, tells Joan about an impounded car with hand controls—exactly what Joan's brother Kevin needs. In another episode, God advised Joan to "recreate," and so she and her brother throw a party in the absence of her parents and the police arrive to tell them to quiet down. Everyone later realizes that by being called to the Girardi home, the police avoid a deadly explosion at the crack house they had originally staked out that night. In another example, when Joan questions her role in life—wondering what her special talent, her "thing," is—God tells her to join the yearbook staff. After failing as a photographer then accidentally throwing away the poetry submissions, Joan discovers an anonymously written poem. She believed it should be included, but yearbook policy demands stated authorship. Joan distributes the poem on her own, thereby significantly affirming the creativity and talent of her friend Grace, who secretly wrote and submitted the poem. And when God instructs Joan that her boyfriend needs a "gift," Joan realizes that Adam needs encouragement to pursue his art career in the face of economic odds.[28]

We can assume that God's directives involving Joan's friends and family were at least partially an effort on the part of the show's creators and writers to establish regular viewers invested in ongoing story lines. *JoA*, like all television shows, was a product, created to sell more products, and its directors and writers were ever mindful of the need to appeal to as broad an audience as possible. To that end, there is nothing in how *JoA* depicts God's call that would cause viewers to question their own religious practices. Unlike God's call as understood by Mormons or Jehovah's Witnesses, for example, God's call to Joan never requires her to convert others to a particular faith. In fact, the writers on *JoA* even allow God to poke fun at Christian doctrine. In one early episode, when Joan is still reluctant to believe God is really appearing to her, God begins to speak to Joan in the form of a newscaster on television but her father, oblivious, turns off the TV. Later, God appears again as a sanitation worker driving a garbage truck outside Joan's school:

> Joan: Oh, and by the way, the other night, it was my father that turned you off, not me.
>
> Garbage Man/God: Oh, okay. He shall burn for eternity in Hell.
>
> Joan: What?! No, he's a nice guy and he didn't mean it. . . .
>
> Garbage Man/God: I'm just kidding. Where do you people get this stuff?[29]

There was no hell waiting for Joan if she refused God's call or if she failed to fulfill the call. Remember that one of the "commandments" of the show was "Everyone is allowed to say 'no' to God, including Joan." Although she feared the possible consequences of refusing God's call, those consequences did not include divine retribution—a concept that would clearly have alienated many viewers. God's call on *JoA* emphasized free will; it depended on Joan's willingness to pursue her best self. It did not ask her to believe any doctrine or creed or follow any "religious" path.

By depicting God's call as essentially an individual message for Joan, unaffiliated with any broader set of religious or spiritual beliefs, aimed at allowing Joan to "fulfill her own true nature" rather than working in concert with a spiritual community, God's call did not require Joan to address larger issues of social justice. Joan, while completing God's tasks, came into contact with issues such as poverty, homelessness, and discrimination, but God asks only that she be aware, be present, and try to understand these issues on an individual level rather than in a social or systemic way. At the end of one such episode, Joan expresses confusion about the role God means her to play in bettering the world. God's request that Joan learn how to jump rope at the public park leads Joan to befriend a young homeless African American girl named Casper. Using her family's utility bill as evidence of residency, Joan enrolls Casper at the high school. When school authorities discover the lie, Casper disappears and a concerned Joan confronts God, who appears as another jump-roping young woman at the park:

> Joan: I wanted to help her. Get her a place. Get her dad a job.
>
> Double Dutch Girl/God: You can't fix everything, Joan.
>
> Joan: She's my friend. I want to know what's happened to her.
>
> Double Dutch Girl/God: I know you do. But sometimes it's enough to plant the seed, walk away, and let the flower grow on its own.[30]

Again, Joan serves as "the face of God" to Casper, and the "face of God" is one of compassion—but not necessarily of justice.

Joan perhaps played an important part in shaping the direction of Casper's life. But unlike in "Bringeth It On," when Joan directly confronted the people responsible (the other cheerleaders) for the suffering of Brianna, here God only asks that Joan plant the seed and walk away. Casper remained, as far as the viewers know, homeless and poverty-stricken, without a stable family, and unable to attend school. Yet God reassured Joan that her work was done, that her task need not inconvenience her further. God did not suggest that perhaps this was only the beginning of a lifelong fight against inequity. Nor could God do so, given the dictates of the show. A more sustained struggle against the injustice of the world would obviously require Joan to work in community, possibly religious community, with others—the problems shaping Casper's life could not be resolved by one individual act of compassion. And, as always, God's call begins and ends not with "fulfill the demands of service to humanity" but rather "fulfill your true nature." This depiction of God's call is in sharp contrast to that of Christians such as Catholic liberation theologians who argue that God calls us, through the life of Jesus, to enact social justice here on earth; to stand with the most oppressed, the poorest of the poor; and to fight for economic equality.[31] It is not Joan's failure to fix Casper's life that illustrates the problematic limitations of God's call on *JoA*. Rather, it is the emphasis on Joan's solitary journey and ultimate goal of "fulfilling her nature." In the end, Joan's task is not to better the world but to better *herself* and, perhaps, in the process benefit others.

It is this depiction of God's call as fundamentally concerned with our individual, personal fulfillment that I wish to criticize. *JoA* echoes a much broader trend in discussions about God's call in this regard. Michael Miller describes, in the introduction to this book, recent and compelling work by theologians who define vocation as a journey toward one's truest self and who endorse the idea that such a journey, when we use our talents to serve others, is our best contribution to the greater good. Yet, as he points out, this description of God's call contains some troubling gaps. I believe it leaves far too much room for an interpretation that allows us to justify our own desires—for happiness, for comfort, for assurances that our individual likes and dislikes are paramount in God's plan—as God's call to us.

Theologian Germain Grisez and author Russell Shaw write in a recent work on Christian vocation: "[God] calls each of us by name, and if we listen to his call and try honestly to respond, he will guide each of us personally to what is best for us and everyone else."[32] In other words, "vocation," or the call into God's service, is neither a demand for social justice (with all its attendant difficulties) nor a rigid command to lead others to a particular version of religious truth. Rather, God calls us to "embrace our God-given potential" as individuals or "accept the treasure of true self [we] already possess."[33] Many such Christian writers and thinkers urge readers to reconsider "vocation" in this way. These authors argue that this is not a selfish view of vocation, but rather one that demands service to others. Some clearly state this essential point, asserting that vocation must direct us toward service to others, that our "true self" (in the case of Joan, "our own true nature") may only develop when we devote ourselves to a higher purpose than self-gain.[34] As Christian scholar Os Guinness writes: "God normally calls us along the line of our giftedness, but the purpose of giftedness is stewardship and service, not selfishness."[35]

However, other theologians and authors seem to suggest that finding our vocation simply means doing what we like best, with God's blessing. One extreme example of how some Christian authors and leaders interpret God's call as a guarantor of personal fulfillment may be found in recent books linking Christian belief and practice to material success and the accumulation of wealth. This is not exactly a new theological development. The Puritans, for instance, believed that those who enjoyed abundant material goods and success therefore must also enjoy divine grace. Numerous published sermons and life-guidance manuals authored by Protestant clergy in the late 1800s asserted that faithful Christians, by dint of hard work and spiritual righteousness, would enjoy financial success. Recently published books, with titles such as *Becoming a Millionaire God's Way* and *The Gospel of Good Success: A Road Map to Spiritual, Emotional, and Financial Wholeness*, indicate the reemergence of the late nineteenth-century "gospel of success."[36] Similarly, Bruce Wilkinson's best-selling *Prayer of Jabez* (2000) demonstrates a rapidly growing market for books that connect Christian practice to personal achievement.[37]

While many authors do not go so far as to promise material gain to their Christian readers, they do argue that Christians must understand that the opportunity to hear and respond to God's call exists in every kind of "secular" profession and that one is "called" to succeed. Vocation, assert these authors, exists in any work that demands the best of us and, therefore, provides our best service to the world.[38] By fulfilling our own destiny, we best serve the world. Or as self-help author and therapist Marsha Sinetar argues, employing one's own gift in the service of others helps us to become "self-actualized,"[39] fulfilling the biblical mandate in 1 Peter 4:10: "Like good stewards of the manifold grace of God, serve one another with whatever gift each of you has received." It is too easy take Sinetar's statement, and others like it, as license to follow a path of individual fulfillment based on developing whatever we decide are our God-given gifts while not taking the next, necessary step—discovering how these gifts might best contribute to the greater good.

JoA very much exemplified this understanding of God's call: Joan's gift, her best ability, was acting as a catalyst for positive change among her friends, family, and community. She followed God's suggestions, attempting to decipher God's instructions, looking for the greater purpose. But as the story lines and the "commandments" made clear, Joan's primary job was doing the hard work of growing up and discovering her best self. Joan's "secular" activities—taking piano lessons, working in a bookstore, joining the chess team, working on a fellow student's campaign for student body president—led her to a deeper understanding of her own place in the world.[40] In the process, she caused a "ripple effect" by making present "the face of God" in the midst of her community. But I agree with *Time* magazine's art critic James Poniewozik, who points out the limitations of this representation of God's call on *JoA*: "God asks for hard work but not self-sacrifice. If you realize your potential, you enlarge the pie of world happiness. It's supply-side spirituality."[41] Yes, Joan's accomplished tasks of service benefit her community. But Joan always also benefits from her tasks: she gains self-knowledge, greater understanding. In obeying God's call and following her vocation, she accomplishes important work toward the project of growing up and becoming her most "authentic self."

However, Poniewozik goes on to praise *JoA* for both Tamblyn's acting and the show's insistence on the small but essential work ordinary people may accomplish:

> If God, however, is simply asking Joan to do what all teens have to do—develop an identity—Arcadia works because Tamblyn reminds us so well how tough that job is. Joan may talk to God, but she has to do the work her own, mortal self, from accepting life's unfairness to finding her niche at school. . . . Unlike most prime-time teens, Joan is neither a babe nor a brain, neither a Goody Two-Shoes nor a sarcastic rebel. She's the most extraordinarily average teen to crop up on a TV show in years.[42]

Poniewozik suggests here what I would like to discuss in more detail in the next section: although God's call on *Joan of Arcadia* sometimes suggests self-help spirituality, with an emphasis on an individual journey of self-growth rather than communities of faith working together toward the greater good, this did not render the show pointless or unduly problematic. In fact, the depiction of God's call, however limited, is key to the show's unique contributions to the cultural history of television.

A JOAN FOR THE NEW MEDIUM/MILLENNIUM

Joan of Arcadia is an old, old story: God appears to a young girl, speaks to the young girl, and delivers a call into God's service. Theophany, the appearance of God in a physical form or other type of manifestation, occurs throughout Jewish and Christian scripture.[43] But the story of a young girl's communication with God has particular resonance and fascination for Americans. In films, songs, war bond posters, suffragette propaganda, and even advertisements, Joan of Arc made regular appearances in U.S. popular culture throughout the twentieth century.[44] Is *Joan of Arcadia* simply the latest manifestation of American secular enthrallment with an old religious story? While it's true that the story of Joan of Arc definitely influenced *JoA* creator Barbara Hall, *Joan of Arcadia* is not simply another retelling.[45] Although the elements of the story are familiar, *JoA* marks a new venture for television: the representation of God's call to humanity and its attendant spiritual and moral questions for a mainstream, youthful audience.

I do not say "new venture" lightly. Virtually every single pop culture text contains recycled elements and bears traces of important cultural precedents. The creator and writers of *JoA* are not by any means the first to consider, via the visual mediums of film and television, how an individual human being might see and converse with God. Films aimed at mainstream audiences such as *It's a Wonderful Life* (1946), *The Bishop's Wife* (1947; remade as *The Preacher's Wife* in 1996), and *Michael* (1996) to name a few, portrayed angels from heaven interacting and interceding in human lives. Angels, of course, starred in the sentimental but hugely popular television series *Touched by an Angel* (1994–2003) and *Highway to Heaven* (1984–1989). And a variety of celebrities played the role of God in contemporary film comedies, most recently Alanis Morissette in *Dogma* (1999), and Morgan Freeman in *Bruce Almighty* (2003).

Although network television rarely portrays religious practice in any form, maudlin serial family dramas, such as *Little House on the Prairie* (1974–1984), *The Waltons* (1972–1981), and *7th Heaven* (1996 to the present), portray Christian families who regularly refer to their faith.[46] A few network TV shows address issues of spirituality without cloying sentimentality. The extraordinarily popular and influential animated series *The Simpsons* (1989 to the present), for instance, remains one of the few series that regularly depicts a family attending church, but it also offers pointed critiques of organized Christianity.[47] The short-lived *Nothing Sacred* (1997–1998) told the story of a Catholic priest wrestling with questions of faith. NBC aired an apocalyptic miniseries, *Revelations*, in the spring of 2005, and that fall the network premiered *The Book of Daniel*, a dark comedy depicting an Episcopal priest struggling with a drug addiction and a crisis of faith.[48]

One could also make the argument that *JoA* belongs less to the tradition of funny or saccharine representations of God and angels on the big and small screen than to the family of teen soaps such as *Beverly Hills 90210* (1990–2000), *Gilmore Girls* (2000 to the present), and *The O.C.* (2003 to the present). It is true that Joan's everyday struggles with school, friendships, and dating seem to resonant as much with viewers as do her struggles with God.[49] *Joan of Arcadia* may also be the newest addition to a growing "action chick" genre, in which women, especially young women, contend with the supernatural or possess superpowers: *Xena: Warrior Princess* (1995–2001), for instance, or the witches on *Charmed* (1998 to the present), or the psychics on *Tru Calling* (2003–2005), *Medium* (2005 to the present), and *Ghost Whisperer* (2005 to the present).[50] *JoA*, in some ways, has more in common with *Buffy the Vampire Slayer* (*BtVS*; 1997–2003) than *The Waltons*.[51] Like Buffy, Joan is at first a reluctant recipient of a special gift that allows her to better the world, and like *BtVS*, *JoA* is set mostly within a high school with numerous references to popular youth culture. Joan's closest TV parallel, however, appeared on the extremely short-lived (only four episodes aired) *Wonderfalls* (2004). *Wonderfalls* told the story of Jaye, a cynical young woman working a dead-end job at a souvenir shop at Niagara Falls who received messages from inanimate objects (although these encounters never explicitly name God as the source for these directives) that lead her to intervene for the better in other people's lives.[52]

The premise of *Joan of Arcadia*, as told to a TV audience, then, is not entirely unique. Nor is the aforementioned debate among Christians about *JoA's* depiction of God a new one. Christian leaders, theologians, and commentators in the United States began grappling with the implications of mass media during the 1920s. While condemning numerous aspects of the new "modern" culture of the post-World War I era, evangelists also quickly seized on the use of radio to spread the Word of God; and religious broadcasting played a significant role in the development of commercial radio in the interwar years.[53] In the 1950s evangelists also embraced TV's potential as a proselytizing tool, and televangelism continues to be one of the clearest ways that religion traverses popular culture.[54] In recent years evangelists have turned to video, film, and the Internet to spread the gospel.[55] But at the same time, many Christians perceived the spread of popular culture in general and of television in particular as a disturbing threat to organized religion.[56] Such criticism proliferated during the 1980s and continues to today, as the United States finds itself in the grip of what many term "a culture war": a running series of debates and disagreements between politically and religiously conservative Americans, on one hand, and politically and religiously liberal Americans, on the other, that foreground sociocultural or "moral" issues such as abortion and gay marriage, as well as the content of pop culture texts such as music videos and television shows.

The "culture wars" entrenched the opposing sides of Christian conversations about popular culture. Conservative commentators argue that pop culture, particularly television, endangers the Christian faith in the United States. They assert that TV threatens to replace the functions of church and Christian community.[57] But others counter that popular culture may be reclaimed for Christians via reworked forms of culture, such as contemporary Christian rock music.[58] Films that do directly depict religious themes create their own controversies. In 2004, millions of Americans flocked to see Mel Gibson's film *The Passion of the Christ*, igniting a new series of debates about the representation of Jesus in film and in pop culture that surpassed even the furor over *The Last Temptation of Christ* in 1988.[59] Meanwhile, liberal Christian authors urge readers to be more open to the possibility of reading and consuming mainstream popular culture in the context of Christian practice.[60] Christian writers and critics search secular films as diverse as *The Wizard of Oz, The Big Chill, Field of Dreams, Groundhog Day, Edward Scissorhands, Eyes Wide Open*, and *The Piano* for spiritual messages.[61] Scholars of pop culture, literature, and religion examine the religious meanings that may be read in *The Matrix* and the *Star Trek* series, as well as secular television shows, while Christian authors search directly for God and spirituality on the Internet, in advertising, fashion, and popular art.[62]

Christian critics need not search for religious subtexts or hidden spiritual meanings in *Joan of Arcadia*—God was central to the show's premise. Of course, predictably, some theologically and politically conservative viewers and commentators condemned *JoA* for its failure to conform to Christian scripture and doctrine, particularly in its depiction of the divine. And, also predictably, liberal Christian authors and viewers tended to enjoy Joan's contentious conversations with God and were not particularly troubled by the theological implications of the ecumenical God presented in *JoA*. But these arguments, influenced as they were by "the culture wars," failed to fully acknowledge the remarkably innovative presence of *JoA* on network television. They fell into a long-standing debate about popular culture and religion without noting the unique qualities of Joan's prime-time conversations with God and, specifically, the show's focus on God's call.

JoA did offer audiences and scholars in the fields of religious studies and popular culture an important new kind of pop culture text. As director of the Center for the Study of Popular Television at Syracuse University Robert Thompson points out, God did not miraculously intervene on *JoA*: Kevin remained paralyzed, Joan's friend Judith died after she was stabbed during a drug deal, and so on. Douglas LeBlanc, founding editor of GetReligion.org, argues that it was this aspect of *JoA* that allowed it to successfully "move spiritual TV shows beyond tear-jerking resolutions and angels who deliver lengthy speeches."[63] God, on *JoA*, scorned the supernatural, explaining to Joan on numerous occasions that there are "rules" (natural laws) that all humans must obey,[64] stating: "I put a lot of thought into the universe. I came up with the rules. It sets a bad example if I break them."[65] There were no easy answers on *JoA*. Faith was complicated and confusing, as God explained to Joan in another episode: "I understand you're confused. But there are no dilemmas without confusion, there's no free will without dilemmas and there's no humanity without free will."[66] God even poked fun at Joan's request for a quick fix to a problem:

> Joan: Yeah, well, you can raise people from the dead, so just wave your hand and fix this stupid thing.
>
> Piano Tuner/God: If you want special effects, rent *Lord of the Rings*.[67]

There were no special effects on *Joan of Arcadia*. God was simply present— present in the normal, workaday world, a world with "rules." And Joan must obey those rules.[68] As Little Girl/God explained one day on the playground, coming over to retrieve a ball from a game she and her friends are playing: "You're an instrument of God, bound by the limits of time and space. [pause] Can I have my ball?"[69]

Moreover, Joan's life and Joan herself, with the exception of God's frequent visitations, was absolutely normal. Tamblyn *looks* normal, a rarity among television actresses: critics frequently mention her frown lines and her curvy figure.[70] Although a pretty young woman, Tamblyn does not have the air-brushed perfection all too common on television. And the character of Joan led a normal life: she and her family grappled with the everyday, mundane problems facing *JoA*'s viewers. Joan was struggling to bring up her grades as she prepared to apply to colleges; the family had to adjust to Helen's full-time job; Will worked too much and relied too much on Helen for the emotional well-being of the family; unresolved tensions and sadness around Kevin's accident shaped family interactions. As writer Ashley Merryman asserts in her review of *JoA*, it is the ordinariness of Joan, and of people like Joan of Arc and Jesus, that make their stories so compelling: "The power of the story is that an ordinary little girl can change the world."[71] *JoA* took God, and Joan, seriously, but not at the expense of realism. And this was groundbreaking in terms of how television depicts God and God's call. In *JoA*, God is ordinary; literally just "a stranger on the bus." To suggest to prime-time viewers of a network television show that an unknowable but visible God, who sees and is seen and is among us always, in all kinds of forms, participating in our everyday life but not interfering with humanity's free will, and who nonetheless calls us into service, was a significant new way of televising ideas about God.

JoA took youth culture seriously as well. *JoA* spoke in the sarcastic, cynical, pop-culture-referential language of American teenagers in the twenty-first century. True, it echoed teen prime-time serials and dramatized routine aspects of growing up that adult viewers might find trite. But the premise of the show demanded that viewers take Joan's struggle to obey God's call to service to her community, into stewardship, seriously. She was ordinary, her struggles to grow up were ordinary, and *JoA* asked all viewers—teenagers and adults—to acknowledge the important ways ordinary life and an ordinary girl are in fact amazing. Moreover, despite Joan's complete lack of religious affiliation, this show also asked us to take Joan's spirituality seriously. It asked us to look closely at Joan's soul, her conscience, her efforts to participate fully in the universe. Perhaps most importantly, it asked us to watch Joan's struggles to fulfill God's call. What a welcome change from shows that depict teenagers as caricatures and constantly display the sexualized bodies of young women.[72] Joan did not fight crimes or vampires; she did not wear revealing clothing or toss back long blond hair during her conversations with God. She simply was present, listening, and trying to understand. Joan was a new kind of televised teenager: an ordinary girl with eyes and ears to see and hear God's call.

This TV story speaks seriously of spiritual quests and the call of God. God did not appear randomly to Joan, nor did God appear to simply offer comfort or guidance to Joan. God appeared and revealed a call to service. The premise of the show utterly depended on God's call: every week Joan attempted to fulfill God's call, God's specific directives. I believe there were important limitations to God's call on *JoA*. By foregrounding the way God's call to Joan asked her to "fulfill her own true nature," *JoA* depicted calling as a strictly individual journey, a "supply-side" style of spiritual work whereby Joan's efforts to improve the world often seemed to be merely a side effect of her quest toward personal growth and awareness. Although some episodes suggested that God's directives to Joan offered her the opportunity for deeply transformative moments of service and compassion to those in need, in many other episodes God's call appeared to be limited to issues surrounding Joan's own family and friends, as well as her struggles toward adulthood.

Although it is not necessarily limited to blatant self-interest, the representation of God's call as an invitation to "fulfill our own nature" too readily lends itself to an overly simplistic and self-serving interpretation of vocation. I believe it did not challenge Joan, and it did not challenge viewers, truly to grapple with the implications of how God might call us into service to others. However, as a pop culture text, it did challenge the boundaries between mainstream popular culture, specifically youth culture, and nondenominational theistic religion in a new and important way. *Joan of Arcadia* was the first mainstream network TV show to depict an otherwise normal young woman struggling to fulfill God's call to service and stewardship. As such, it has earned a place in our current discussions of what it means to be called by God.

Vocation as Proclamation of Love

Thomas Looney

In *The Story of a Soul* Thérèse of Lisieux proclaims the fruit of her lifelong struggle to grasp the fullness and significance of her vocation: "In the heart of the Church, who is my Mother, I will be love."[1] Thérèse's proclamation of the deepest meaning of her life, forged in the crucible of surrender to the truth of her existence before God, indicates both the structure and substance of every Christian vocation. Christian vocation from the side of the believer is a proclamation of the deepest word a person can utter about himself or herself in response to an encounter with Jesus, the Word of God in the midst of the church. Christian vocation is a word of love, spoken in response to the Word of love, in the midst of a communion of love, the church.

In this essay, I construct a foundational theology of Christian vocation as proclamation. This constructive project unfolds in three principal stages. First, I ground the human capacity to express a word about oneself in the doctrine of the *imago Dei*. In short, since God reveals the depth of his life through his Word, human beings created in God's image share in the capacity to utter a word that expresses the deepest truth of one's own life. Thus, Christian vocation is the deepest actualization of the human capacity to communicate the depths of one's being and person. Second, I ground the human capacity to speak an efficacious word about oneself in the concept of the

35

imago Christi. Conformed to Christ in baptism, the believer's identity is united to the identity of the Word, whose self-expression is always creative, redemptive, and sanctifying. Thus, Christian vocation is a creative, redemptive, and sanctifying word that both expresses and deepens our relationship to Christ. And third, I ground the uniqueness of the Christian vocation in the image of the church as the body of Christ. As a member of Christ's body, the identity of the believers is inseparable from the identity of the whole church. Thus, a Christian vocation is always an actualization of the life of the church, a proclamation of a particular manner of loving. In the midst of the church the Christian vocation is expressive of the *imago ecclesiae*.

IMAGO DEI

At the heart of the Christian understanding of the human person is the doctrine of the *imago Dei*. The present examination of this doctrine proceeds along two distinct, yet interrelated paths: first, a descending theological anthropology, and second, an ascending theological anthropology.[2] The first approach begins with an examination of the Christian understanding of God, and proceeds by way of analogy to speak of the various ways in which human nature corresponds to and is dissimilar from the divine nature. This approach asks the question, Who is this God in whose image we are made? The second approach begins with an examination of the experience of human persons as seekers of meaning and proceeds by way of induction to speak of God as the ground of that searching spirit. This approach asks the question, Who are we as human persons? The convergence of these two perspectives demonstrates that the human search for meaning or vocation is necessarily rooted in a desire to speak a word about oneself in relation to ultimate reality.

A Descending Theological Anthropology

The Christian understanding of the Triune God affirms that relation and self-communication constitute the nature of God. The church affirms the coeternal and coequal existence of three persons in one God: the Son is eternally begotten of the Father, and the Spirit proceeds eternally from the Father and the Son. Richard of St. Victor's development of John's assertion that God is love into the Trinitarian analogy of Lover, Beloved, and Love captures the essential truth that God is a relationship whose very being is the sharing of love.[3] Thomas Merton's later claim that "[i]nfinite sharing is the law of God's inner life" also gives voice to this truth of the church's faith.[4] The nature of God is a relationship of self-communication, a communication of love that is both spoken and received in fullness. In the relationship of love that is God, the Unbegotten One speaks a Word about himself that is of his own substance, yet distinct in relation to himself. In the eternal speaking of the Word, God communicates the fullness of his being, sharing himself in complete fullness with another. The eternal speaking of the Word is simultaneously accompanied by the eternal procession of the Spirit from the Father and the Son, for the perfection of God's self-communication requires that the gift be fully given and fully received.[5] The procession of the Spirit is the excess of the Word spoken and received, a communion of love.

If God is a relationship of persons involved in an eternal self-communication that is love itself, it follows by way of analogy that in some way relationship and self-communication form the foundational principles of the *imago Dei* in humankind. To be human is to exist in relationship, not in radical autonomy and isolation. Relationship marks human existence not in an exterior mode, as if relationship is simply an option that human persons can choose to engage in or not. Relationship marks us in an interior mode; that is, to be human is to be in relationship. Relationship is not a choice; it is the very fabric of human existence, not an addition to the nature of the human. To be human is to be in relationship with God, other human beings, oneself, and the whole of creation. To claim that relationship is at the core of human being is an ontological, not a psychological, statement. It is interesting to note that in the document "Letter to the Bishops of the Catholic Church on the Collaboration of Men and Women in the Church and in the World," the claim is made that the male-female relationship is in a fundamental way constitutive of the *imago Dei*: "From the very beginning therefore humanity is described as articulated in the male-female relationship. This is the humanity, sexually differentiated, which is explicitly declared 'the image of God.'"[6]

As beings whose nature it is to be in relationship, the human person, made in God's image, is also characterized by the capacity to communicate a word about himself or herself. It is the very nature of God to speak a word about himself, a word that shares the nature of the divine being. And so by analogy it is the very nature of the human person to speak a word about himself or herself, a word that seeks to express the fullness of who we are. In stating this, I am making, once again, an ontological claim and not merely a psychological one. To exist as a human person is to be in communication about the very nature of one's own being, even if one cannot give voice to it in a thematic way. At heart, the human person's self-communication is a word of dependence, a word of creaturely status, a word that proclaims that life itself is a gift, and simultaneously a word that proclaims that the gift received is also the gift given in the communication of self.

In the preceding brief reflections on *imago Dei* as relationship and self-communication, I have emphasized the similarities between the divine and human. It is also imperative to examine the dissimilarities. First, in terms of dissimilarity, the relationship that characterizes the life of the Triune God is fullness of being itself. The relationship of Father, Son, and Spirit in the eternal dance of mutual self-emptying love is characterized by fullness;

there is no necessity in God, no complement to God's existence. God is pure relationship. The relationship that marks human beings made in the image and likeness of God, on the other hand, is a participation in being, a dance that has a beginning in the moment of one's conception; it is a dance begun by the music of another's love. Thus, it is first and always a response to one's complement and origin; it is a dance marked from the human side by necessity and by the contingency of being. God must initiate, lead, and sustain the dance. Thus, all the steps taken in the dance, all the words spoken are a response to love's offer of the gift of existence itself. Thus, the human word is spoken not as an expression of the fullness of being, as is God's word about himself, but as a responsive word to being itself. It is fundamentally a word of obedience, a word that expresses the human desire to know oneself in relation to being itself. It is a word that cannot express the fullness of human existence in a single utterance, in a single word, but a responsive word that finds itself in ongoing formulation and various attempts at an accurate and sustainable utterance.

The relationship that is God is eternal; the relationship that is humankind is temporal. God exists in fullness of relationship from all eternity, and human existence is marked by relationship from a specific point in time—a relationship that grows to fullness through the course of history. The temporal beginning of the human as relationship marks human existence as a project, whereas the eternal nature of relation in God marks divine existence as complete. The human project is only complete in its final word about itself, a word spoken in relation to the Eternal Word; it is the word of obedience or disobedience, a word of communion or self-excommunication. Vocation as proclamation is a lifelong task, for the final word about ourselves is uttered only in death.

A second significant dissimilarity between the divine and the human in terms of relationship and self-communication is, of course, that the fullness of the Word that God speaks about himself is spoken in the Son, who shares God's very being. While faith declares that God has spoken his Word, the speaking of God's Word *ad extra* is a totally free act that does not alter God who speaks it. When the human person seeks to speak a word about herself, that word is, of necessity, spoken to another; it is spoken ultimately to the One who creates us to be in relationship with him, but also to creation itself, the existence that mediates to us the presence of the Creator. It is a word whose speaking is done out of necessity; it is a word that must be spoken, that reaches out to being itself, and that knows itself only in its speaking. This word is spoken in such a way that in the speaking one comes to know the veracity of the word, the truth of one's own existence. It is not a word of "I–Thou," but a word of "We–Thou." Since to be human is to have no existence apart from the relationships within which we find ourselves embedded, the human person cannot speak a word about "herself" that is not simultaneously a word about another. Every word we speak is spoken in relationship and about relationship that includes us but is not exhausted by us. As human persons we speak a word about ourselves, and in so doing we affirm or deny our relation to the ground of all being and life. It is in speaking a word of relation that we affirm the deepest truth of our being; yet we are free to reject relationship as the ground of our being and so utter a word of excommunication, a final word that results in complete isolation of self from being itself. Made in the image of God, who is love, we speak a word of love and so enter into communion with love itself, or we speak a word of indifference and so enter into a state of excommunication from love.

An Ascending Theological Anthropology

In terms of an ascending theological anthropology two fundamental approaches may be drawn on to demonstrate the concept that the human person experiences himself or herself as a searching spirit seeking to articulate in the midst of one's historicity a proclamation of one's own meaning and existence. To this end, I will briefly point to the work of Karl Rahner and contemporary phenomenology.

In his first major work, *Hearers of the Word*, Rahner constructs his vision of the human as that being who is capable of dialogue with the infinite; the human person is by nature capable of hearing the word spoken by infinite being and proclaiming a response to that word.[7] The human experience of self as a searching spirit confronted with the finitude of its own existence constitutes for Rahner the dynamic of the human relationship with the transcendent. The human person is by nature open to the possibility of encounter with being itself. The ground of this possibility is present as ontological offer; to be human is to be characterized by this obediential potency. To be human is to seek to respond to the ground of one's own being grasped at first indirectly and later brought to explicit consciousness through the exercise of that same searching spirit. In the human response to the ground of its own being, a word about self in relation to that ground is spoken.

From a contemporary phenomenological perspective the human person experiences himself or herself in the world as a being with a capacity to make choices, to reason, to be responsible, to grow and develop, to be social, and to be spiritual.[8] When a comprehensive description of human experience is enumerated, at the heart of that experience is a longing for a satisfaction of fullness that lies beyond the self, but that does not leave the self behind. The experience of freedom whereby we constitute ourselves in relation to the world around us is viewed as constitutive of meaning and purpose. While the directionality of our lives is determined by the complex of choices that we make, we do not construct choice itself; the necessity and capacity to choose lie in the depths of the human. An important aspect of the choice of life's direction is the experience of a spiritual dimension at the heart of existence; the choices that we make are not simply concrete particulars, but singular manifestations of a basic stance toward reality itself. We make choices against the backdrop of a horizon that frames our choices, not by the limitation of our own vision but by the ever-broadening expanse of the horizon itself. In our choosing we find the paradox of the interfacing of self-determination (i.e., we choose who we become) and of our being determined by an existence greater than ourselves. Our choices are not isolated and vacuous decisions, but decisions rendered in relation and intercommunion with a reality that is both within and beyond us. In the choices we make, we speak a word about ourselves in relation to the horizon of possibility, the horizon of existence itself.

The perspectives of Rahner and contemporary phenomenology converge in the experience of the searching subject, seeking to grasp the truth of one's own being in relation to the surrounding world. The inner dynamism of that search marks the human person as a being in relationship that seeks to speak a word concerning his or her own life.

Insights garnered from the perspectives of a descending theological anthropology and an ascending theological anthropology converge in significant ways to demonstrate that the human is a being who exists both in and for relationship. The human experience of relationship establishes the ground of being as dialogical. To be human is to exist in a mode of receptivity and response to a word that has already been spoken.

IMAGO CHRISTI

The previous section described the common experience of all human persons from the perspectives of a descending and an ascending theological anthropology. To be human is to be constituted as a relational being and to speak a word about oneself in relation to the very ground of being itself. In the present section I will examine the implications of the church's theology of baptism for the development of a theology of vocation as proclamation. In its baptismal theology the church teaches that baptism affects both conformity to Christ and insertion into Christ's body, the church. In baptism the *imago Dei* receives a christological deepening, the *imago Christi*, as well as an ecclesiological deepening, the *imago ecclesiae*. Even though these aspects are inseparable, I will first examine the Christological dimensions of the baptismal configuration and treat the ecclesiological dimensions of the baptismal configuration in the final section.

The church's faith proclaims that in the celebration of baptism, the believer, immersed into the communion of God's life, becomes a new creation. In the words of Paul, "It is no longer I who live, but Christ who lives in me" (Gal 2:20). Sacramental immersion into the passion and death of Christ not only cleanses from sin; it also confers the gift of adoption and bestows a likeness to Christ. The gift of the baptized person's configuration to Christ is expressed in the theology of the sacramental character that is said to bestow on the believer the capacity to offer Christian worship.[9] In baptism Christians are granted a share in the one priesthood of Christ, who offers acceptable sacrifice to the Father.

The claim that baptism bestows the gift of a likeness to Christ, a share in his relationship to the Father, is an ontological claim that is made at the level of being. The task of theology is to discern the implications of that ontological claim in the life of the baptized. Since all human persons already share by virtue of the *imago Dei* in the capacity to speak a word about themselves in relation to being itself, and since the Word made flesh is the self-communication of the fullness of the love of God, it stands to reason that in conformity to Christ there is in the baptized a deepened capacity to speak a word about oneself in relation to the Father. At issue, of course, is the nature of the word that is to be spoken.

At the heart of the New Testament's reflection on baptism is a theology of redemption.[10] Christians are baptized into the passion and death of Christ because in his passion and death the gift of salvation is accomplished. Christ's obedience unto death constitutes an essential aspect of the word that Christ spoke about himself, a word of self-emptying love. The celebration of baptism is an affirmation that the deepest word the church has heard from the Father is the Word of self-emptying love encountered in the life and mission of his only begotten Son. Baptism also celebrates the church's desire that each member live his or her life as son or daughter of God; pouring himself or herself forth in self-emptying love.

In baptism the deepened identity and conformity to Christ that is bestowed on the believer is expressed in the liturgy by the titles: priest, prophet, and king. The baptized person receives this new identity and accepts it as a word about the foundational and deepest meaning of his or her life. The presentation of a candidate for baptism is a proclamation of a choice made by both the church and an individual believer, not a choice regarding merely external realities such as membership in an organization, but a choice concerning a person's fundamental mode of being in the world. It is a choice rooted in the human capacity to speak a word about oneself in relation to being itself, a word that one has come to believe can only be spoken in fullness in conjunction with the Word itself. In the waters of baptism, the believer comes to receive at the hands of the community of believers the gift of adoption by which he or she is conformed to Christ. By the grace of the Holy Spirit, the *imago Dei* is more deeply conformed to Christ, and so is constituted the *imago Christi*. Having embraced this deepened identity, the believer seeks to speak a word about himself or herself that expresses the inner depth of their conformity to Christ who is priest, prophet, and king.

In the Johannine literature, Jesus, the Word made flesh, who receives the anointing of the Spirit, is presented as speaking a word about himself, a word of radical identification with God and with God's mission on behalf of humankind. Jesus proclaims: "I am the bread of life" (John 6:35), "I am the way, and the truth, and the life" (John 14:6); "I am the light of the world" (John 9:5); and "I am the good shepherd" (John 10:11). In proclaiming "I am," Jesus affirms a radical identification of both his person and his mission with the Father. In using the term "I am," Jesus proclaims an identity with the Father on the level of being. In the predicate nominatives that he uses to complete this affirmation of his deepest identity, he expresses his identification with the mission of the Father.

In the waters of baptism, the baptized is conformed to the person of Christ; she or he is established by imprint of the sacramental character as priest, prophet, and king. It is no longer the believer who lives, but Christ who lives in the believer. Thus, the "I" of which the baptized speaks is not an "I" of radical isolation over and against all that is other. Rather, the "I" is a "we"—a relationship with Christ that expresses the deepening of the image of God in which all persons are made. It also expresses a share in the mission of Christ.

Through baptism the believer is conformed not only to Christ's person, but also to participation in Christ's mission. The church's Trinitarian faith proclaims that in the mission of God *ad extra* each person of the Trinity shares in the work that is principally designated as the mission of one.[11] Thus, the faith of the church proclaims that God the Father creates through the Word, and that God the Holy Spirit sanctifies by bearing witness to the presence of the Christ. Thus, the Word shares in the work of creation, redemption, and sanctification. God the Father creates all things through his Word in the power of the Spirit. God the Holy Spirit sanctifies the world by communicating the Word spoken in Christ, in a mystery of self-abasement. The redemptive work of the Word is the work of the Father and the Spirit as well, for the Son redeems the world as the self-communication of the Father's saving love in the power of the Spirit.

If the Word creates, redeems, and sanctifies, it follows that those conformed to Christ's person and mission come to share in the creative, redemptive, and sanctifying mission of Christ. Thus, the proclamation of a human word by one who has been conformed to Christ has the capacity to be a creative, redemptive, and sanctifying utterance. Our human experience certainly suggests to us such a capacity. Through vowed commitment new relationships are created. Through love expressed, the wounds of self-loathing or recrimination are redeemed. And through steadfast loyalty to our word we are born aloft by a spirit whose origin, we sense, is not of our own making.

Yet, if our word spoken in Christ is to share in the creative, redemptive, and sanctifying capacity of Christ's own word and presence, then like Jesus we must be about the task of obedience to the Father's will. As Christ opened his heart in prayer to the Father, and so came to grasp in fullness the manner in which the word of his life was to be spoken in creative, redemptive, and sanctifying love, so the Christian is invited to a life of obedient listening in prayer in order to hear the word of self-emptying love that the Father desires us to embody in the world.

Through the waters of baptism the believer is conformed to the person and the mission of Christ. The word that the believer is capacitated to speak is a proclamation of the deepest truth of one's being and mission as a person who stands in the world *in persona Christi*. However, the analogical language of similarity in speaking of the graced human capacity of conformity to Christ needs to be balanced by attention to the manner in which our conformity to Christ lacks fullness. In Jesus' proclamation of his person and mission, a radical identity of life and mission is proclaimed. Jesus' word concerning himself, expressed in the "I am" statements in John's gospel, also reflects a perfect image of the Father's glory present in his person. Jesus' mission of kenotic love, expressed in fullness in his death on the cross, reflects a perfect image of the Father's self-emptying love in sending forth the Son. Our baptismal conformity to Christ in his person and mission, on the other hand, is for us a proclamation of who we are called and desire to be. In baptism, we have been sealed with an identity that unfolds in us as the project of our lives, our vocation. The dialogue of sacramental fidelity spoken in word in the baptismal moment is for us the task of a lifetime. Our frailty as believers suggests that although our faith tells us that God has taken hold of us in Christ, the process of our surrender has not yet come to fullness. We know only too well our own capacity for the duplicitous word as well as our frailty in living up to the word we have spoken about ourselves, even with the best of intentions.

Thus, the gift of conformity to Christ is for the believer, as is the gift of the *imago Dei* for all persons, a historical project to be lived out in the course of the particular choices of our lives. The baptized Christian, conformed to Christ in terms of both Christ's person and mission, seeks to live his or her life in total openness to all that the Father asks. The hearing of the Father's word and our attempts to speak a word concerning our lives in fidelity to what we have heard lie at the heart of the Christian understanding of vocation. Like Christ we are called to be in some analogous manner the presence of God in the world. Thus, the Christian vocation, whatever its particularities, is always an act of self-emptying love by which the Christian by grace seeks to proclaim the deepest truth of his or her life, a truth proclaimed in baptism. As priest, prophet, and king, the believer is called to respond in generous love to all that the Father desires, announcing Christ's creative, redemptive, and sanctifying presence.

IMAGO ECCLESIAE

Through the waters of baptism a twofold gift embraces the life of the believer: conformity to Christ and insertion into the mystery of Christ's body, the church. Membership in the body of Christ can be viewed from the perspective of a descending ecclesiology as well as from the perspective of an ascending ecclesiology.

A Descending Ecclesiology

Biblical and patristic tradition affirms the divine origin of the church in a variety of ways. The Gospels attest to Christ's desire to found a church in the radicalization of the demands of the Torah, the transignification of the elements of the Passover supper, and the postresurrection commission to baptize. The Epistles proclaim the church to be the work of the Holy Spirit, who effects a radical union between Christ, the head of the body, and its members (Eph 4:1-16; 1 Cor 12:12-31). Epiphanius of Salamis and Isidore of Seville view the church as having its origin in the blood and water that flowed from the side of the crucified Christ.[12] J. M. R. Tillard suggests that at the heart of the church's self-understanding is the patristic insight that the church "is the chosen people since the beginning of time—*jam ab Abel justo*—that God was preparing for himself for the eschatological era."[13] The preexistence of the church, the attribution of its existence to the will of Christ and the outpouring of the Holy Spirit, and its emergence from the wounded side of the crucified Christ underscore the divine nature and origin of the church. The church is a communion of salvation precisely because it comes to the believer as prevenient gift; it is not the product of human association, but a manifestation of God's passionate desire to communicate the gift of salvation to all.

As a communion of salvation, the church is the privileged means by which God chooses to save all humankind. In the waters of baptism the believer is embraced and taken up into an ontological reality that precedes his or her being. Thus, the believer does not give identity to the church, but receives his or her identity from the church. The vocation of believers is a call to give expression in the world to the mystery of the life of the church into which they have been inserted. Within the midst of this community of salvation, each believer shares fully in the life of Christ in a complex of mutually interdependent relationships, for it is the same Spirit that animates each and every part of the one organic body that is the church. The church is not a coming together of autonomous believers first conformed to Christ in personal relationship; it exists only as an organic whole. Thus, each and every believer is an image of the church, for no member of the church ever stands in isolation from it. Thus, the fundamental vocation of every Christian is to be a sacrament of the church, a visible sign of the deepest reality of their personhood—a personhood that defies isolation and autonomy, but is, in fact, constituted as relationship in Christ.

The analogy drawn between the incarnation and the church suggests that as the person and mission of Christ are inseparable realities, so too are the nature and mission of the church. The epistles describe the church as a community of believers exercising a variety of ministries and living a variety of lifestyles as an expression of the fullness of its life and mission. The existence of the church is an existence for others. Thus, insertion into the life of the church suggests that the believer embrace the ministry and lifestyle that the church proposes for his or her life. It is a ministry and lifestyle that reflects the truth of a person's existence as a member of the church, and that reinforces membership in the church as an existence that is intrinsically directed toward others as a word of salvation.

The church's tradition proposes two fundamental modes of existence in the body of Christ, marriage and celibacy. Thus, it may be instructive for us to examine briefly the church's faith concerning marriage and celibacy as it is proposed in the liturgy of marriage and religious profession. In both liturgical celebrations the church emphasizes the human person's capacity to speak a word in the midst of the community of the church that establishes a profound bond of relationship. The tradition of the church in the West teaches that mutual consent establishes marriage. It is the mutual proclamation of the gift of self that establishes the bond of marriage, a covenant relationship whose indissolubility makes tangible the unconditional nature of Christ's relationship with his bridegroom the church. The church's affirmation of the sacramental nature of marriage is an amazing affirmation that human words share in the creative, redemptive, and salvific power of the Word. For in the pledged relationship of marriage the church proclaims that a covenant relationship is created between the couple, a covenant that expresses their common share in the redemptive work of Christ and that will be for themselves and for those whose lives they touch an expression of the sanctifying presence of the Spirit.

In its liturgy of religious profession, the church affirms that it is the pledged word of a baptized believer spoken in the midst of the community of faith that establishes a believer in the church as a sign of the coming kingdom in which there is neither marriage nor giving in marriage. Although the church has opted not to speak of religious consecration as a sacrament, the theological history of the church in affirming the value of consecrated life including celibate commitment deems this act of commitment as a constitutive element of the church's self-expression. In the pledged relationship of celibate love, the believer speaks a word that defines his or her being in relation to the church; it is a word that communicates the truth that God alone is sufficient, while at the same time asserting that the God who is enough is served in the present order by the gift of self in service to the body of Christ and to all who are called to membership in it.

From the perspective of a descending ecclesiology, the church as a divine preexistent reality embraces the lives of those immersed into its life. The ontological structure of the church's life embodies God's call to marriage or celibacy as the fundamental lifestyles that embody the nature of the church as the sign in the world of its nature as the bride of the Lamb. In celibacy the church affirms its life is centered on Christ alone, and in marriage it simultaneously proclaims the embodiment of Christ in its very life. Since the church's life precedes both an individual's baptism as well as the individual's vocational choice, celibacy and marriage are present always as offers within the midst of the community of the church. Thus, the believer's particular call is always received in the midst of the community of the church and takes on the character of a proclamation of one's lifestyle within the body. It is a lifestyle choice that deepens both the *imago Dei* and the *imago Christi* received at conception and baptism, respectively, as these realities unfold in the historical events of the life of the believer.

In speaking of the church from the perspective of its divine origin, certain clear dissimilarities emerge between the experience of the church as a whole and the living out of the vocation of its particular members. Whereas the church itself as the body of Christ can never waver from the truth of its divine life, individual believers may through sin forsake the truth of their commitment of love in the midst of the body. The pledged love of marriage and consecrated life are not always lived in fidelity. The word spoken that proclaims the gift of one's life in the midst of the body is sometimes rescinded. Vows are not always lived in complete fidelity, and at times the lived sign of the vowed lives of married and celibate believers is obscured by the public renunciation of the pledged commitment. The utter fidelity of the word that the church speaks concerning itself in its conformity to Christ is not always mirrored in the pledged love of its members.

An Ascending Ecclesiology

In addition to a descending ecclesiology, the perspective of an ascending ecclesiology also underscores a vision of vocation as an ecclesial reality. An ascending ecclesiology suggests that the community of the church emerged out of the mission of Jesus, who did not intend to found a church, but rather to reform the community of Israel. In the experience of the gift of new life in Christ poured forth at Pentecost, the disciples were empowered to continue the proclamation of the Kingdom of God. As the disciples set about the proclamation of the good news that God had visited and redeemed the world in Jesus Christ, they established various structures and lifestyles that embodied the message of Jesus. In this perspective the choices made by the community of believers emerge out of the complex of historical circumstances in which the community finds itself. Yet, here too the structures and lifestyles of the community and its members are a mechanism by which the community expresses the deepest truth of its own life in relation to Christ. This perspective suggests a greater fluidity than a descending ecclesiology, due not only to the fluidity of historical circumstance, but also to the unpredictable movement of the Spirit, which "blows where it chooses" (John 3:8).

As the community alive in the power of the Spirit, the church is called to the ongoing discernment of God's presence and action in the world. As a member of the church, each believer is called to the discernment of his or her particular mode of service within the body of Christ. Contemporary ecclesiology affirms the importance of responding to the signs of the times, which bear indications of the manner to which the Spirit is inviting us to be conformed to Christ, in self-emptying, loving service to others. Although a contemporary ecclesiology might emphasize the prophetic or charismatic nature of the mission of the church and of the individual believer, its understanding remains that a particular vocation is a response to the movement of the Holy Spirit. The call comes to one from without, even though it is experienced in the depths of one's being through a prayerful discernment of the signs of the times. The presence of the Spirit moves us to utter a word about ourselves.

CONCLUSION

Christian faith professes that the God who calls us to salvation is a Triune God, the God whose very being is a relationship of love. The call to salvation is mediated to human persons, not as an addition to their nature, but in their very existence as creatures made in the image and likeness of God. The call to salvation is mediated to believers, not as an addition to their baptismal character but in their very existence as creatures whose nature is conformed to Christ and inserted into his body. Thus, the call to love that is the presence of love itself comes not only from without, mediated through history, but also from within, mediated through one's own personhood. To be human is to be called to love in the midst of the human community; to be Christian is to be called to love in the midst of the human community with the very love of Christ. The call to love, of course, is not a call to an abstraction, but a call to a concrete way of being and acting in the world that seeks the good of the other. Thus, in order to proclaim a word about oneself, one must discern the particular manner of loving to which one is called. This discernment, by its very nature, while it is intensely personal, is not private and so needs to be undertaken in the midst of one's relationship to the community in which one finds oneself immersed.

The attempts of Thérèse of Lisieux to discern her vocation, as well as her ultimate claim concerning her deepest desires, model this process. "I will be love," for God is love and the human person is *imago Dei*. I will be love "in the heart of the church," for conformed to Christ in baptism the human person is *imago Christi*. I will be love in the heart of the church, "who is my mother," for in the font of baptism we receive and make our own the gift of life in Christ's body, *imago ecclesiae*.

Habits, Compartmentalization, and Vocation

William C. Mattison III and Marc Parisi

One of the consistent themes of this volume is that a vocation is not simply a task that we aim to complete. A vocation is more than what we do; it concerns who we are. It entails a transformation, whereby our actions not only have an impact on the world around us but also reflect who we are and further shape our very selves.

This essay explores the dynamics of how our purposeful action reflects and further ingrains the transformation of the self that characterizes a vocation. It was prompted by the story of a young adult discerning what it means to live a vocation. While completing an undergraduate degree at Mount St. Mary's University, Marc Parisi enrolled for an optional fourth credit hour of service learning while taking a course in moral theology. His project was to direct a Christmas play for local elementary school children and critically reflect on the experience in light of class material. This youth ministry position was a way for him to combine a love of theater with another of his passions, working with kids. As the term progressed, it was clear Marc was becoming a role model for his children.

What was particularly interesting was how the role of youth minister was affecting Marc's life back on campus as a college student. Wearing this "hat" of youth minister was becoming increasingly important to Marc. In fact, as the role became more and more a part of who he was, it was difficult for him to "take off" his youth minister hat. It was shaping who he was in ways that seemed to persist even when he was "off the job." How was his work with the children related to his life back on campus? How were these seemingly disconnected roles in fact connected? These questions turned out to be a focus for discussion with his faculty adviser (and the other author of this essay), Dr. William Mattison.

Marc relayed a story to help explain how this experience as a youth minister was changing who he was. Marc's own youth minister was an important role model in his life and someone he has become closer to as he has grown older. One of Marc's first memories of his youth minister was from his freshman year of high school. At the time he thought it had very little to do with youth ministry and vocation, though now he sees its relevance to his own life. He remembered talking to his youth minister one night about a movie they had both just seen. They were out with a group of friends, not at all on any formal youth ministry outing, just to see a movie. While discussing the movie, his youth minister made the comment, "It would be a great movie to show on retreat!"

Marc remembered thinking to himself, "What? What does a retreat have to do with this movie? We're not sitting in your office; we're at a movie theater! Check the office at the door—we're talking about a movie!"

His youth minister must have sensed his confusion because she simply told him, "Marc, I'm not just a youth minister when I'm at the parish. It's who I am. I can't just hang my 'Youth Minister' hat on the back of my door at the office, flip the light off, and close the door behind me. It doesn't work like that."

For whatever reason, the hats metaphor remained in Marc's head as he grew out of high school and into college. Ever since the conversation with his youth minister in high school, the idea that it is difficult to take off certain hats has stuck with him. Indeed, as Marc began working with kids in his college years as a youth minister himself, he also found it difficult to remove the youth minister hat.

Although Marc found himself becoming more and more invested in his youth ministry theater project with the kids, working on it did not erase the other roles in his life. He was still being a student, a son, a brother, a friend— the list goes on. That semester he wore many "hats," and in each of these roles the way he acted depended on the different requirements of the particular role. Yet even while playing all these different roles, he was still only one person. The roles were not hermetically sealed from one another. There was never, as they say in the theater world, an "intermission" between one role and another, affording him an opportunity to change character or swap one hat for another.

The more Marc reflected on this reality, the more he decided he would not want to be constantly changing who he was. His work as a youth minister was not just something he did on the side; it had become an integral part of his life.[1] Marc wore his "youth minister hat" constantly, even while playing other roles in his life. While working with the kids on the theater project, his role seemed to transcend the walls of the school where he worked; he was finding it difficult to shake the title of "Mr. Marc!" He was reminded of this in the university cafeteria one day after class with some student friends. The mother of one of the kids he mentored was working there and saw Marc. She cried, "Hey, *Mr. Marc*, what can I get for you?" Marc was jarred from his college student life and reminded of his life outside the university working with kids as a youth minister. The point here is that youth minister "Mr. Marc" lives with distinct responsibilities and expectations, and they were rubbing off on plain old college student "Marc."

All agree that we tend to act differently depending on which role we find ourselves in, which hat we are wearing. For example, we act differently when with our friends than with our parents. This is understandable, and at times even necessary. There are character traits that are brought out by our friends that do not show up when we are with our parents, and vice versa. We display some character traits in some roles and not in others. Yet there are some things about us that we cannot compartmentalize so easily. This is because we possess certain character traits that are central to who we are. It is less desirable, perhaps even less possible, to compartmentalize the traits and roles in our lives that are most important to us. To keep the terminology parallel, it is difficult to take off certain hats. The types of persons we are—that is, the character traits we possess while playing the "most important" roles—seem to seep into other lesser roles we play. This happens in much the same way that Marc's high school youth minister's job affected the way she enjoyed a movie.

What has any of this to do with vocation? Some character traits are common to any true vocation, such as the virtues of justice, courage, and moderation, while other traits may be particular to one's specific vocation. When we speak of certain roles in our lives being more central to who we are, we are speaking about our vocations. A distinguishing feature of vocation is that it is not simply something one does on the side. It is a role that is deeply important to us. It is not simply "doing something," but rather being transformed into a type of person. As such, it is not surprising that who we are in that role will permeate other areas of our lives. This essay explores these dynamics for the purpose of helping us discern vocation in our lives by attempting to explain how it is that the way we live shapes our very selves. Through appeal to virtue theory, particularly as delineated by Thomas Aquinas, the goal here is to understand better why the actions that we consistently do transform the persons we are. This is the focus of the first section of the essay.

What this has to do with vocation is explored in the second section. If some facet of one's life—be it one's job, a ministry to which one is committed, or one's role as parent, spouse, etc.—may be described as "vocation" for that person, then we should expect that the transformation effected by living out that role will continue to characterize a person even when he or she is not exercising that specific role. One characteristic of living out a vocation is possessing a certain harmony or integrity, such that the character traits that we develop while in our prime vocational role, which mark who we are, are a part of us in whatever we do. Indeed, they "seep in" to other areas of our lives. Simply put, living a harmonized life is a central feature of a vocation.

Of course, this does not always happen. Our lives are "compartmentalized" when seemingly central parts of us are not woven throughout the different roles of our lives. Furthermore, just because certain traits appear consistently does not necessarily mean they are who we are called to become. The third section of this essay examines several ways and reasons why our lives might not evidence the sort of integrity that should characterize a person living out his or her vocation. In many of these situations, our lives are "compartmentalized" and fragmented, rather than exhibiting the harmony emblematic of living out a vocation.

The fourth and final section returns once again to examine the relevance of this research for discerning and living out one's vocation. How can this inquiry enable us to understand our vocation better? After all, the first and third sections reveal that though our actions shape our very selves, we may live in ways that prevent the sort of harmony that should mark one's vocation. Or we may live in a consistent manner that actually deforms us, rather than building us up into people who are flourishing by living our true vocations. However, by attending to the dynamics described here, we can identify the character traits we are developing that seem to penetrate other areas of our lives, and reflect on whether these are characteristic of the persons God is calling us to be. Furthermore, by attending to the compartmentalization and fragmentation in our lives, we can better understand what still requires conversion in our lives in order that we might live as persons of integrity, in a manner more fully consistent with who we are called to be.

PLAYING ROLES AND FORMING PERSONS: PUTTING ON HATS

We are involved in a host of different relationships and activities that make particular demands on us and that shape us into persons who can play many roles. Given these particularities, it is no surprise that we "wear different hats," or act differently based upon the role at hand. In the often dizzying array of activities we are involved in, it can be difficult to discern which of our activities and roles constitute our vocation. However, though we wear many hats, our lives are not completely fragmented. Some hats just are more difficult to remove than others. Why is this the case, and how does understanding this fact help us discern our vocation?

In a very real way, our actions, and in particular our consistent actions, make us who we are. Thomas Aquinas offers a thorough virtue theory to explain how our actions make us who we are.[2] Human persons, endowed with the powers of reason and will, act freely with purposes, or goals, in mind.[3] These goals are called intentions. With our reason we understand some things to be good (or bad), and with our wills we pursue (or avoid) them. Intentions are the purposes behind our actions. It is not enough to ask what someone does. One has to know *why* the person does it. What goal is the person seeking in this action? The things that we hold important—important enough that they guide our actions—are revealed by our intentions.[4]

Yet intentionality does not just reveal who we are; intentionality shapes who we are, or our identity. Intentional action tends toward repetition because it entails a judgment of what we consider true and good and worth pursuing. It shapes our character and identity by revealing and further ingraining what we believe to be true. This phenomenon of being shaped by repeated actions has been called the "intransitive" feature of human action.[5] By repeated intentional acts, we actually mold ourselves with certain character traits. We not only act in consistent ways, but become certain types of persons.

Thomas Aquinas, following Aristotle, labeled enduring character traits "habits."[6] They generally do not appear instantly, but rather develop over time from repeated intentional actions. Once one has a habit, the person is then inclined to act in such a manner in the future. For instance, from repeated intentional acts of generosity one develops the habit of being a generous person. Such a person can be relied on to act generously. Note that a habit does not determine one's action. One can act "out of character," so to speak, such as when a normally generous person refuses to share. When this happens we say "she's not really like that," or "that's not like him." Eventually, of course, if someone continues to act "out of character," we no longer say they are acting out of character. They have lost the old habit of generosity and developed a new one of, say, stinginess. Good habits are traditionally called virtues, and bad habits are called vices. Once one has a habit, that habit is part of one's self. It shapes how one sees the situations one encounters, and inclines one to consistent actions in those situations.

Consider Marc's work with children this past semester. Twice a week he led practice sessions for the Christmas play. He spent countless hours beyond these sessions in preparation for practices and the event itself. All the while, his intention was to help develop in the young persons entrusted to him newfound abilities as performers, a sense of responsibility and work ethic, and resulting self-confidence. He was not only performing the actions of a youth minister and role model, but Marc was doing so with the intention of serving the children's best interests, and just plain having fun. Marc's actions made *him* a certain type of person. He formed *himself* in the process of interacting with the children. Acting regularly with the intention to serve those children made him the sort of person who sees himself, his current project, and potential new situations through the lens of his commitment to serve as a role model and youth minister.

What is most important for the purpose of this essay is that habits are a part of who we are, and they incline us to a certain type of action in the future. This effect on future actions is not a mechanistic one; rather, how we actually see new situations we enter is reshaped.[7] For instance, in his early work with children, Marc might have viewed the noise, confusion, and overall craziness that always accompany working with children as a nuisance. He could have intended to avoid such situations so as not to be disturbed. Had he done this repeatedly, Marc would have developed a habit. Not only would he reliably avoid such situations, but when he entered a situation where there existed an opportunity to serve the needs of children, he would actually "see" the situation not as a chance to serve, but as an annoying situation to be escaped. Instead, we know that due to repeated, intentional acts of serving his kids' needs, Marc has made himself the sort of person who sees those needs and responds generously.

In this way, the realities of intention and habit help explain why some roles we play spill over into other areas of our lives. Now when Marc encounters his little cousins at a family event, we can expect him to be a role model there too, because his actions with the kids in his play reveal certain beliefs that Marc has. He believes in the dignity of children. He believes adults have a special responsibility toward nurturing their growth. Finally, he believes he has certain gifts for doing this work. He believes such work is important enough that it warrants putting one's other good desires aside at times (such as the desire to just sit and relax with other adults). Because of Marc's intentions while working with his youth group, and the habits his intentional actions have imprinted on his character, we can ascertain certain things he believes to be true, and trust him to act on these same beliefs in other similar situations.

The claim that habits—in Marc's case, virtues—are generalized to other areas of our lives is an important one for this essay on vocation and "wearing different hats" because habits we develop in one area of our life become part of us, such that we take them with us to other areas of life. If Marc is the type of person who is inclined to help children, presumably that work with the kids in his play shapes how he interacts with children outside of the play, say, with children in his family. It may be further generalized or hypothesized that if "college student" Marc were to encounter a family friend whose child is struggling, he would be similarly inclined to be of service. Thus our habits—be they virtues or vices—seep into other areas of our life since they incline us toward consistent types of intentional action in similar situations. The commonalities between situations elicit the exercise of the habits Marc has developed through his other experiences.

HEEDING THE CALL: WEARING HATS WELL

The relevance of this discussion for the topic of vocation should now be more clear. The reason why we might find it difficult to remove certain hats in our lives is that our actions in those arenas have transformed us into certain sorts of persons. In light of Thomas Aquinas's virtue theory, we can now see why this happens. Our intentional actions transform, or habituate, us such that the habits developed influence more and more areas of our lives. We engage in activities such as youth ministry for certain reasons, and those reasons rest on certain beliefs. If our beliefs are truly important to us, and a role is based on those beliefs, then that role will harmoniously relate to other important roles in our life, largely because the transformative process of habituation has ingrained those beliefs into who we are. Thus our most central habits are reflected in the many different things we do, and these hats just are more difficult to remove. Looking at our habits, at the sorts of character traits we have developed through our activities, is the way to discover what sorts of persons we are, and are becoming. Since one's vocation is exactly a matter of becoming transformed into a certain sort of person, this data is critical in discerning our vocation.

Before turning to the following section, it would help to take stock of the argument so far. A vocation entails a transformation and concerns not only what we do but the persons we are. People who live out a vocation, like Marc's youth minister, seem to exhibit a harmony, an integrity, in their lives. They find that who they become in living out their vocations seeps into other areas of their lives. The first section of this paper attends to ways this transformation happens through an examination of virtue theory. This next section argues that, given an understanding of vocation as a transformation of one's person, ascertaining which hats are difficult to remove will be a great help in identifying and discerning what we are called to.

Of course, there is one important issue raised by this analysis. What if the person one has become or is becoming is not who one is called to become? Unless we assume that all people are indeed living out their vocations, we cannot simply equate the habits and roles that characterize who we are with our vocation. This issue can be addressed through two questions. First, what if there is no such integrity to one's life? What if there is rather "disintegration," or compartmentalization, such that our lives are fragmented? Second, and more disturbingly, what if one's life is indeed integrated by a consistent character but that character is not who we are called to be? The claim here is that both of these situations signify a failure in living out one's vocation. Just because a trait is showing up across the board in many areas of one's life does *not* necessarily mean it is part of our vocation. The habit might not be a positive one. But since living a vocation ought to harmonize the roles in one's life, observing how habits show up across areas of our lives is an important clue in discerning whether we are living out a vocation.

MISSING THE CALL: ILL-FITTING HATS AND
COMPARTMENTALIZATION

Our lives are often not perfectly harmonious and integrated. We at times do take off even important hats, seemingly in order to do things that would conflict with wearing that hat. We are not simply talking about how different activities require different things of us. Rather, sometimes we conveniently set aside character traits that are important to us because they actually conflict (and not just differ) with those in another role. This is what we mean by compartmentalization. Understanding how and why this compartmentalization happens can also help us on the path toward identifying our vocations. If we can identify occasions when we compartmentalize, and ascertain the reasons why we do so, this data can be as helpful in our discernment as identifying those hats that are difficult to take off. In what follows we try to explain different ways and reasons why people compartmentalize roles in their lives.

There are a variety of reasons how and why compartmentalization occurs. Many of these reasons have to do with the above discussion of Thomas Aquinas's virtue theory, with its emphasis on intention and the formation of character traits called habits. Consider one way, of four proposed in this paper, that such compartmentalization might happen. Recall that Marc's activity with regard to his youth group was intentional, in that he deliberately pursued certain goals because of his beliefs in the dignity of children, his own capacity to serve their needs, and so on. Imagine another undergraduate working with Marc who does similar external actions but for very different motivations. In fact, this happens all the time with undergraduates doing service work. This first imaginary co-worker of Marc's participates in youth ministry because he wants to look good in front of others, perhaps those people who might one day be reading his résumé.

In this case, the person is still acting intentionally. He has a goal in mind, and pursuing that goal as worthy reveals certain beliefs on his part. However, in this case his intentions are different from the purpose of youth ministry. He is doing the service work with self-promotional intentions. Doing this still shapes his character, but it shapes him into the sort of person who does good actions for the sake of being seen by others. We would call such a habit a vice, rather than a virtue. We are reminded here of Christ's critical words in Matthew 6 to those who pray, fast, and give alms "so that they may be praised by others."

This type of person does develop habits that will incline him to future acts. And presumably those habits will seep into other areas of his life, shaping how he acts in other similar situations. But the habit obtained is being the sort of person who performs praiseworthy actions for selfish motives. He will do such acts again in the future, but will most likely do so for the sake of gaining recognition. To the casual observer such a person seems to compartmentalize his service work from other activities in life that are more obviously self-centered. However, on closer reflection this person has a consistency to his life. The fragmentation is not within who he is becoming, but rather between his consistent self-promotion and the purpose that any person would publicly state for meaningful activities such as service work, a career, or being a good spouse or parent. The consistency in this person's life is difficult to reconcile with vocation in any common sense of that word. By attending to the intentionality of one's activities, the person can discern more truthfully who he or she is becoming, and whether or not that can accurately be called one's vocation.

There are other, more insidious ways that our lives are compartmentalized. Not all people engage in activities in such a two-faced way as in the case of Marc's first hypothetical co-worker. Yet even people who do not engage in activities for purely selfish motives can engage in service work in a manner that seems compartmentalized from other areas of their lives. Consider a second imaginary undergraduate working with Marc. She is not there simply to look good or pad her résumé. Rather, she does "good" activities such as service work out of a sense of obligation, perceived (rightly or wrongly) as imposed by her parents, religion, or the community. Perhaps the obligation is imposed by a sense of guilt. When she performs good actions such as service work, she, too, intransitively shapes who she is. But she becomes the sort of person who acts out of a sense of obligation, and who does good things to appease her conscience so as to be able to go on in peace with other areas of her life where she can do what she really wishes.

We are not claiming that doing good actions out of a sense of obligation is never praiseworthy. At times our sense of obligation helps us to do things that we ourselves at our better moments would want to do. What distinguishes the sort of compartmentalization we describe in this second case is the complete lack of interiorization of the goods/purposes of the activity at hand. She is not simply experiencing a sense of obligation to do something she knows is right to do even though she does not "feel like it." Rather, this person intentionally does the youth ministry work because it is the sort of good activity that people should do. But she has not at all interiorized what people would publicly state the real purpose of the activity is (e.g., helping children). She is simply "going through the motions" because service work of this kind is what people are "supposed to do." The true purpose of the activity is missed.

If this is the case, it is not at all surprising that what she does in other areas of her life conflicts with her service work. This constitutes a type of compartmentalization. She intentionally performs actions that others perceive as good simply out of a sense of duty, rather than because she believes in the sorts of things that drive Marc's work in youth ministry. This will indeed form a habit in her. But she is becoming the type of person who does good acts out of duty. Unsurprisingly, when the duty has been satisfied, she will act in ways that conflict with the stated purpose of the activity at hand.

Consider a third, and less disingenuous, reason why people may act in a compartmentalized manner, or fail to keep on their worthy hats when they perform other related activities. Sometimes we engage in activities whose goals and meaning we do grasp as worthwhile and have interiorized. But due to our weakness, we also engage in activities that defy those same goals. Imagine a third undergraduate working with Marc who is genuinely devoted to the well-being of the children, and committed to serving in their best interest. As part of his role he advises the children about the dangers of excessive drinking of alcohol. Yet sometimes this young man takes his role-model hat off and acts in a manner contrary to his own advice to the youth. Or at other times, despite being genuinely committed to the youth, he finds himself making fun of some kids in the youth group with his friends back at college for their amusement. In this case his desire for friends, recreation, and escape, soon leads him to do things that conflict with a hat he wears proudly at other times. In both cases he realizes and afterward regrets how his acts defied something he himself holds important. But that recognition is not enough to prevent him from occasionally succumbing to these temptations.

Such failure is an example of what Thomas Aquinas calls "incontinence."[8] This third undergraduate's desires lead him away from his own better judgment. This results in a sort of disintegration in him that may also be called compartmentalization. He knows he is defying his integrity, and may even desire not to do so, but he at times repeats such actions anyway out of weakness of will, or incontinence.

A fourth and final source of compartmentalization in our lives can be due to a simple lack of formation/development. Sometimes we just fail to "see" connections between different but important areas of our lives. In these cases it is not so much that we intentionally act in ways contrary to important roles in our lives. Rather, those connections are simply unclear to us. A good example of this is seen in Marc's opening story with his youth minister. Given her advanced development in understanding her vocation, she was attuned to how areas of life not obviously related to youth ministry were indeed related. Marc was not aware of this connection, though not due to any active rejection of the goals of youth ministry. In fact, today he would likely see such a connection. But at the time of his movie conversation with his youth minister, watching movies was one part of his life that was unrelated to how he was involved in youth ministry. This example is very innocent. But consider how mature people might fail to see how their activities in certain areas of their lives conflict with what they believe to be an important role for them. An undergraduate might fail to see how his faith is contradicted by certain ways of living. A newlywed may fail to see how certain activities with her friends are harming her ability to be a good spouse. These examples reveal how habit formation takes time, and thus there may be times when the traits needed for some roles in our lives have not yet permeated other areas of our lives. Depending on what traits are still being further habituated, this could indicate a (generally innocent) lack of maturity/development in that calling.

Each of these four examples suggests a different sort of compartmentalization that we may find in our lives. We can examine our lives for occasions of compartmentalization in order to scrutinize the motives behind our actions. Are we doing certain things for ulterior motives? Are we playing certain roles out of a sense of duty? Sometimes our motives may be pure, but compartmentalization persists nonetheless. Are there areas in my life where I need to stand stronger, and not conveniently leave aside a role that is important to me when it is difficult to maintain the character traits it demands? Am I not seeing how an important role in my life is interconnected with other areas of my life? Questions such as these can help us identify hats we are wearing that we would just as soon not wear. Or we might see how certain of our hats need to be kept on through other areas of our lives. This awareness of types of compartmentalization in our lives can be most helpful in coming to better understand our callings.

WEARING DIFFERENT HATS: COMPARTMENTALIZATION AND VOCATION

It is time once again to place the arguments of the previous section more explicitly in the context of vocation. As should now be clear, when trying to discern one's vocation, it is not enough simply to identify the hats we find difficult to remove. Though integrity and harmony do indeed characterize the life of someone living out his or her vocation, the previous section underscores that understanding how persons are transformed by their intentional activities is not adequate to ensure they are being transformed well into the persons they are actually called to be. One can become the sort of person he or she is not called to be, thus having harmony but playing the wrong tune. Or people can be fragmented and compartmentalized such that there is need for more harmony.

This raises some obvious questions. How are people to know what their vocations are? How are they to know if they are responding to that calling or not? A vocation entails a transformation of the person one is rather than simply the actions one performs. Obviously the answer to all people's calls cannot be provided in this essay. But what this essay does is explain the dynamics of *how* people are transformed through habit formation in order to give the reader a better idea of what to look for in one's life. Therefore, in addition to explaining why habits develop as they do, the main contribution of this paper is the claim that attention to what hats are difficult to remove is critical in discerning and deepening one's vocation.

This analysis of how our intentional actions shape our very selves, such that we develop habits that then seep into other areas of our lives, has purposely been left at a rather formal level. One reason for this is rendering this discussion applicable for people of different faith commitments, or even without a faith commitment. In other words, the dynamics described thus far can apply to various people whose vocations are drastically different. In these different cases, the beliefs that are internalized will vary, and thus the transformation will look different. Yet, the process of how habituation, and compartmentalization occur remains the same.

Given the Christian perspective of both this essay and its authors, it is worth emphasizing in closing the richness of that faith tradition with regard to vocation. In each of the gospels, the kingdom of God is announced with a call to repent, to experience a change of heart, a transformation. In each of the synoptic gospels that transformation is "summed up" in the famous dual love commandment: love God with all your heart, mind, and strength, and love your neighbor as yourself (Matt 22:37; Mark 12:28-34; Luke 10:25-28). Obviously each of these general calls to conversion needs to be further specified in the lives of different believers. This process of specification, this discovery of the way one is to respond in conversion and follow Christ, is the process of discerning a vocation. Marc heard this call in his work with youth. Given that his ministry flowed from a change of heart, and that it was his way of living out love of God and neighbor, we should be unsurprised that it was difficult for him to take that hat off. Indeed, we should be grateful. It reflects a genuine and pervasive change of heart, and a desire to consistently love God and others in all he does.

The negative aspects of compartmentalization, discussed earlier, are essentially different forms of sin and human limitation. The person with ulterior motives pridefully warps the good of the activity at hand into a self-serving opportunity. The person acting out of duty is blind to the true needs that drive work like youth ministry. The person suffering a weakness of will longs to live more authentically and consistently, but is bound by more selfish desires. The person who simply does not yet see the connections between different areas of life does not seem to sin, but does reveal the ignorance that marks the broken human condition.

Each of these weaknesses may be healed, so to speak, by the grace of God. One vehicle for that grace is a better understanding of how our lives are compartmentalized, leading to revelation that with God's further help we can be healed of the disintegration of our lives that is a result of sin. This grace, through the church, is of course what makes possible the transformative change of heart, the conversion, described above whereby one attains harmony and integrity of character.

In this essay we have attempted to draw attention to those times in our lives when we see character traits from one role seeping into other roles. There is a reason this happens, and it has to do with how character is shaped by developing habits. Our vocations ought to bring about a certain harmony, such that the habits we develop in one area of life do not conflict with what is required in other areas. But even those occasions when this conflict occurs can be invaluable in discerning vocation. When it comes to some hats—for Marc, his youth ministry hat—it may seem that we never quite take them off. Hopefully, on further reflection we can recognize and be grateful that this is where we live out calling in our lives.

Transforming Artistic Vocation into a Calling

Gael Mooney

In his *Testament*, written shortly before his death, Francis of Assisi begins the story of his conversion by saying, "When I was in sin, it seemed too bitter for me to see lepers. And the Lord himself led me among them and I showed mercy to them. And when I left them, what had seemed bitter to me was turned into sweetness of soul and body. And afterward, I delayed a little and left the world."[1] In this story a person regarded to be an outcast and the very symbol of impurity during the Middle Ages was transformed before bodily eyes (those of Francis) into an object of beauty. This encounter is mysterious because we realize that it is not likely had we been present at the time that we would have "seen" what Francis described; hence, the leper's "sweetness" would have remained hidden from our view. Francis, however, crossed over from the earthly to the divine to glimpse "the simple, marvelous, transcendent truth of the symbols,"[2] and we recognize this to be a sign of the saint's holiness.

I begin this essay reflecting on the nature of the artistic calling with the story of Francis's encounter with the leper because I believe the same process of self-transformation and illumination is at play when the artist turns his or her gaze toward the beauty of the physical world with the aim of uncovering its hidden and divine source. In his 1999 "Letter to Artists," Pope John Paul

II celebrates the artist's "special relationship to beauty" when he notes that "in a very true sense beauty is the vocation bestowed on him by the Creator" and that "work that reflect[s] in some way the infinite beauty of God" serves to "raise people's minds to him."[3]

In reflecting on this theme, I will follow the definition of vocation set forth by Paul when he prays for "a spirit of wisdom and revelation as you come to know [God], so that, with the eyes of your heart enlightened, you may know what is the hope to which he has called you" (Eph 1:17-19). The same "spirit of revelation" underlies the artist's search for epiphanies of Beauty and the call to transcendence, and it is what permits us to see the world through God's eyes so as to make works of art that "raise people's minds to him."[4]

In addressing this theme, I will be reflecting on my experiences over the past several years painting on the premises of a Gothic cathedral in France—the Saint-Denis Basilica. The basilica was inspired by Pseudo-Dionysius, the sixth-century monk and theologian whose influential writings concerning the nature of theological aesthetics and divine illumination also contain valuable insights for our present inquiry reflecting on the nature of the artistic vocation. My experience observing and painting the Gothic light of the basilica has been an education in its own right: by providing firsthand exposure to a mystery that goes beyond words, this experience has demonstrated beauty's power to illuminate our minds so as to transform the way we see the world.

My essay is divided into three sections, entitled, respectively, "Seeing the Light," "Learning from Light," and "Becoming Light." Light and Beauty according to Pseudo-Dionysius are seen as reflections of God and it is in this sense that I am using the terms.[5] Hence, the three sections of this chapter correspond to the three different stages that comprise the artist's search for epiphanies of Beauty.[6] However, given that these stages are mutually related, there is no strict division between them; rather, they are intended to emphasize that the search for epiphanies of Beauty entails a progression from the earthly to the divine realms similar to that associated with any spiritual journey.

I can think of no more appropriate model for the artist's vocation and search for new epiphanies of Beauty than Francis. For by conforming his life with "unflagging desire" to Christ's teachings and way of life—the norm and archetype for Beauty—Francis transformed his life into a "resplendent mirror of all holiness" so as to "guide into the light those sitting in darkness"[7] and make apparent the way for all who follow.

SEEING THE LIGHT

The first thing about this story that strikes me, as an artist who derives inspiration from nature and the process of working from direct observation, is the impact that the saint's conversion had on his senses, for Francis of Assisi *sees* the leper transformed from bitterness to "sweetness of soul and body." Hence, the saint's inner conversion is manifested outwardly, causing him to see the leper anew, as if encountering him for the first time. This story demonstrates that the search for epiphanies of Beauty begins with an encounter with what is already there beneath reality's surface.[8]

This story thus affirms Pseudo-Dionysius's belief that "any thinking person realizes that the appearances of beauty are signs of an invisible loveliness."[9] The foregoing statement is important for our consideration of the artistic calling because by professing his belief that all creation is a reflection of God, Pseudo-Dionysius affirms the human capacity for divine revelation and underscores God's relation to the material world as Source of all creation.

Pseudo-Dionysius further suggests that God modeled the world in such a way because he recognized that "it is quite impossible that we humans should, in any immaterial way, rise up to imitate and to contemplate the heavenly hierarchies without the aid of those material means capable of guiding us as our nature requires."[10] By reflecting God's wisdom and providence, the created realm hence provides the very means by which we are able to see God's reflection in the world around us so as to discern his purpose and plan for each of us.

Beauty (when seen as a reflection of God himself) therefore becomes synonymous with the call to holiness with the result that the aesthetic and spiritual merge on the level of human experience. This merging is the basis of theological aesthetics and is what transforms the artistic vocation into a call to transcendence. Indeed, calling and beauty in Greek are synonymous: the Greek word for beauty, *kallos*, means "to call," and *kalon* is an adjective whose equivalent meaning according to one author is "the called."[11] This is why, as Pope John Paul II says in his 1999 "Letter to Artists," art "in so far as it seeks the beautiful" serves as "a kind of bridge to religious experience."[12]

So by helping us discern God's plan and purposes, contemplating the beauty of creation serves to unite the artist's intent with the divine intent of the Creator, as Pope John Paul II suggests: "With loving regard, the divine Artist passes on to the human artist a spark of his own surpassing wisdom, calling on him to share in his creative power."[13] Pseudo-Dionysius instructs us that all of creation was made in order to manifest God's plan and to enable us to grow closer to God. This is why, as Pope John Paul II recognizes in his 1999 letter, art provides "a unique disclosure of [the artist's] own being" and "a new dimension and an exceptional mode of expression for . . . spiritual growth."[14]

Bonaventure further elaborates on this theme using rich imagery, calling creatures "vestiges, that is the very footprints of God: they are roads leading to God, ladders on which we can climb to God; they are signs divinely given so that we can see God—shadows, echoes, pictures, statues, representations of God; creation is a book in which we can read God, a mirror in which the divine light shines in various colors."[15] In a passage that reads like a manifesto for artists in search of epiphanies of Beauty, Bonaventure continues this reflection on material creation:

> Whoever, therefore, is not enlightened by such splendour of created things is blind; whoever is not awakened by such outcries is deaf; whoever does not praise God because of all these effects is dumb; whoever does not discover the First Principle from such clear signs is a fool. Therefore, open your eyes, alert the ears of your spirit, open your lips and apply your heart so that in all creatures you may see, hear, praise, love and worship, glorify and honour your God lest the whole world rise against you.[16]

Hence, the things of creation are vestiges by which we can come to know God. Teresa of Avila referred to this notion saying that creatures contain "beneficial secrets" such that "in each little thing created by God there is more than what is understood, even if it is a little ant."[17] Contemplating our natural surroundings therefore provides one of the chief means by which artists may acquire the wisdom and spiritual insights needed in discerning their calling and in helping others to open their eyes to God's presence in the world around us through works of art that celebrate these gifts.

Pope John Paul II noted that artists, by virtue of their innate gifts, are particularly attuned to such vestiges in creation, when he says:

> None can sense more deeply than you artists, ingenious creators of beauty that you are, something of the pathos with which God at the dawn of creation looked upon the work of his hands. A glimmer of that feeling has shone so often in your eyes when—like the artists of every age—captivated by the hidden power of sounds and words, colours and shapes, you have admired the work of your inspiration, sensing in it some echo of the mystery of creation with which God, the sole creator of all things, has wished in some way to associate you.[18]

God in his providence and wisdom allows each of us to discern such hidden truths according to our capacity to receive them. Bonaventure refers to this idea when he says that creatures are "like stained glass windows: Just as you see that ray of light entering through a window is colored in different ways according to the different parts, so the divine ray shines forth in each and every creature in different ways and in different properties."[19] Our ability to see such spiritual realities depends largely on our openness and receptivity to a sacred reality that, by definition, exceeds our own limits. Hence, in the next section, I would like to consider the question: How can we make further progress in approaching a divine mystery?

LEARNING FROM LIGHT

Francis of Assisi used to say: "What a man is in God's eyes, that he is and nothing more." Prior to his conversion, Francis had "no experience in interpreting divine mysteries nor did he know how to pass through visible images to grasp the invisible truth beyond." He was therefore "still ignorant of God's plan."[20] Embracing the leper would change everything, allowing him for the first time to see himself and the world around him in a new light so as to discern God's presence and purposes.

How is it that we, too, might learn to discern such hidden truths? This is the challenge that artists face when they attempt to discern their calling. In fact, the situation for us in many respects is no different than that which Francis relates to us in this story. This is because, as Pseudo-Dionysius instructs us, "the most sacred things are not easily handled by the profane but are revealed instead to the real lovers of holiness." He then continues: "Only these latter know how to pack away the workings of childish imagination regarding the sacred symbols. They alone have the *simplicity of mind* and the *receptive contemplative power* to cross over to the simple, marvelous, transcendent truth of the symbols."[21] Simplicity of mind requires at the outset that we acknowledge God as the source of creation and all existence. This is crucial in order for artists to acquire an understanding of "their own being, of what they are and of how they are what they are."[22] This is what is required by each of us in order to make works of art that reflect our true authentic selves and that acknowledge our relationship to God as the unique source of our being and of all existence.

Such awareness is a form of humility and gratitude, by which we humbly acknowledge our indebtedness to God and praise him for the manifold gifts of his creation, including our own innate artistic talents. Practicing such virtues invariably changes the way we see the world, as Pope John Paul recognized when he wrote:

> Artists, the more conscious they are of their "gift", are led all the more to see themselves and the whole of creation with eyes able to contemplate and give thanks, and to raise to God a hymn of praise. This is the only way for them to come to a full understanding of themselves, their vocation and their mission.[23]

This to me is one of the most important aspects of Pope John Paul II's 1999 "Letter to Artists," for seeing "with eyes able to contemplate" is the means by which we are able to acquire precisely the kinds of spiritual insights that are needed in order to recognize Beauty's contours in the world of appearance so as to discern our calling. As will be discussed more fully later on, such insights are what enable us to "see" the height, depth, and breadth of reality, including its inherent wholeness and its goodness.

Paul similarly underscores the importance of practicing the spiritual virtues in discerning our vocation when he says: "I therefore . . . beg you to lead a life worthy of the calling to which you have been called, with all humility and gentleness, with patience, bearing with one another in love, making every effort to maintain the unity of the Spirit in the bond of peace" (Eph 4:1-3). Paul humbly acknowledged that it was through the gift of God's grace that he was able to discern his own vocation, such that "the very least of all the saints" obtained the wisdom and insights to "make everyone see what is that plan of the mystery hidden for ages in God who created all things" (Eph 3:7-9).

Artists themselves have acknowledged the fundamental relationship between art and virtue by seeking to find ways to embody such ideas in their own work. For example, Van Gogh admired the work of the Egyptians who by "faith [and] working by instinct, express all these intangible things— kindness, infinite patience, wisdom, serenity . . . by a few knowing curves and by the marvelous proportions" so as to impart to their work "style and quality."[24]

Work that embodies such spiritual values permits us to engage in a form of seeing that goes beyond surface appearances. Such seeing is the very definition of contemplation for its Latin root, *templum*, means to look "inside of things to discover divine meanings and purposes."[25] As Simone Weil has observed, such seeing requires a kind of attention or receptivity that "consists of suspending our thought, leaving it detached, empty, and ready to be penetrated by the object" who is God himself. Attention of this kind that is directed toward God is "the very substance of prayer," for it "presupposes faith and love."[26]

Artists who work with an awareness of God as the source of our existence are able to experience more fully the awe and wonder of creation, which has inspired so many works of art. Such feelings prompted Francis to compose hymns of praise, such as his celebrated "Canticle of the Creatures," in which he extols the virtues of all creation, particularly with regard to "Sir Brother Sun," who he called "radiant and beautiful and with great splendor."[27] As Bonaventure observes: "When [Francis] considered the primordial source of all things, he was filled with even more abundant piety, calling creatures, no matter how small, by the name of brother and sister, because he knew they had the same source as himself."[28]

Referring to a poem by Gerard Manley Hopkins, Garcia-Rivera shows us how approaching our work and daily lives with faith induces a "third" type of knowing that finds its home in the "in-between of heaven and earth," so that rather than beginning with the trunk and then proceeding to the branches, we "begin with the branches in order to reveal the trunk." The result is that suddenly we find ourselves "high above the ground defying the [laws of] gravity" where we are able to glimpse a "vision of the whole."[29]

The Gothic architecture of the Saint-Denis Basilica where I paint was built for the explicit purpose of making visible this idea. In building his cathedral, Abbot Suger wished to make manifest that philosophy of Pseudo-Dionyius referred to earlier by which all material creation is seen as a reflection of God. As noted by Otto von Simson, the height and soaring verticality of the Gothic "seems to reverse the movement of gravity" while, at the same time, the transparent light from the stained glass windows undermines the materiality of the stone columns.[30] Together these features induce a sense of weightlessness that makes one feel suspended between two worlds, the earthly and the heavenly.

Abbot Suger also saw such qualities present in the gems that adorned the high altar, and he spoke about them in moving terms that I believe capture the essence of what his cathedral was intended to convey:

> When—out of my delight in the beauty of the house of God—the loveliness of the many-colored stones has called me away from external cares, and worthy meditation has induced me to reflect, transferring that which is material to that which is immaterial, on the diversity of the sacred virtues: *then it seems to me that I see myself dwelling, as it were, in some strange region of the universe which neither exists entirely in the slime of the earth nor entirely in the purity of Heaven; and that by the grace of God, I can be transported from this inferior to that higher world in an anagogical manner.*[31]

The foregoing quotation by Suger conveys the essence of Pseudo-Dionysius' "anagogical approach to beauty," in which he envisions divine illumination as an ascent from the lower earthly realms to the higher celestial or spiritual realms. This ascent requires that you

> leave behind you everything perceived and understood, everything perceptible and understandable, all that is not and all that is, and, with your understanding laid aside, to strive upward as much as you can toward union with him who is beyond all being and knowledge. By an undivided and absolute abandonment of yourself and everything, shedding all and freed from all, you will be lifted to the ray of the divine shadow which is above everything that is.[32]

The foregoing is a paradoxical notion for artists who rely on their senses and imagination in making works of art, particularly in light of the previously quoted passage (included in the section "Seeing the Light") in which Pseudo-Dionysius advises that the spiritual ascent begins with the recognition of material creation seen as "signs of an invisible loveliness." However, as will be further explained below, the goal is not to suppress the expressive or creative instinct but rather to reconfigure it vis-à-vis our relationship with God.

Letting go of the things of the world is a means by which we acknowledge our human limits as finite beings in approaching a God who is transcendent and wholly other. This idea is symbolized in the mystical tradition by the cloud of darkness where Moses finally meets God. For darkness symbolizes unknowing—the apophatic or negative way—and hence, our limits as finite creatures in approaching God who is absolutely "other." This is why Pope John Paul II says that as artists approach the source of beauty they will experience this "unbridgeable gap" and glimpse the "abyss of light which has its wellspring in God."[33]

Significantly, it was by undergoing a process of purification that Moses was able to experience the extraordinary series of epiphanies on Mount Sinai. It was only after he freed himself from his passions and departed from the crowds that he heard "the many-voiced trumpets" and saw "the many lights, pure with rays streaming abundantly."[34] Hence, it is only by letting go of worldly attachments that we are able to acquire the spiritual insights Paul speaks about in his letter to the Ephesians (1:17-19) that will enable us to discern God's presence in the world around us and the purposes for which we are called.

In a particularly evocative passage, Pseudo-Dionysius refers to this process, comparing those engaged in such an effort to sculptors who as they "set out to carve a statue . . . remove every obstacle to the pure view of the hidden image, and simply by this act of clearing aside, they show up the beauty which is hidden."[35] I find this advice helpful in my work as a painter since it allows me to suspend thoughts and judgments that tend to get in the way of the immediate experience and to embark on an open-ended discovery—recognizing that I cannot know where it may lead. I find such advice particularly helpful in attempting to capture the ephemeral colors of the Gothic light of the basilica that, as a symbol of divine illumination, represent an ineffable mystery that exceeds my own limits.

Art that reflects such eternal values can open our eyes to another level of existence provided that we are receptive to such an experience. In some cases, appreciating the various levels of meaning a given work symbolizes may require that the viewer similarly engage in a process of self-transformation in order to acquire the spiritual insights necessary for discerning a work's deeper significance. That great works of art embody such levels of meaning has been acknowledged by artists. For example, when Matisse donated the *Three Bathers* by Cézanne to the Petit Palais Museum in Paris, he acknowledged this deeper level by saying that despite having owned the painting for thirty-seven years—which he admitted had sustained him at critical moments in his career—he said, "I know this painting rather well, but I hope not completely."[36]

Works of art are signs and symbols that reflect the artist's innermost thoughts and feelings. By acknowledging God as the source of our existence, the search for epiphanies of Beauty strengthens the artist's ability to make works of art that function as signs, since the works of art are taken out of the realm of the purely subjective and grounded in an objective and absolute reality. In the following section I wish to show how the search for epiphanies engages the artist in a continual process of growth and transformation into the likeness of God.

BECOMING LIGHT

Having seen the vestiges of Beauty's mysterious contours in creation, Francis of Assisi desired nothing more than to follow those footprints, to go down that road, and climb up that ladder so as to "embrace him who is utterly desirable." By following Christ's teachings with "unprecedented devotion," he transformed his way of life so as to become a "hierarchic man" who "would be lifted up on the wings of contemplation and there would be exalted with a Seraphic vision." His life thus became a sign and beacon that "guided into the light those sitting in darkness" [37] and illuminated the path for all those seeking Beauty's end.

"Becoming Light" in the foregoing context signifies several different but related aspects of the artist's search for epiphanies of Beauty. First, "becoming" signifies the eternal aspect of the artist's search for epiphanies of Beauty. Francis acknowledged in so many words following his encounter with the leper that he was embarking on a limitless path toward God when he says, "And afterwards, I delayed a little and left the world." [38]

Gregory of Nyssa explores the foregoing theme in his treatise on *The Life of Moses*, whereby he equates Moses' journey on the Sinai with a succession of steps and a never ending journey that constantly left him "straining ahead for what is still to come." This idea is vividly conveyed by the new horizons continually opening out when Moses reached the height of each new summit. [55] Gregory concludes from Moses's example that perfection lies not in achievement, but simply in progress. [39]

These are compelling words of advice for artists whose aims are, by definition, elusive and open-ended. I find Gregory's advice useful in approaching my own work since it helps me to adopt the attitude of openness and receptivity discussed earlier in the section "Learning from Light." Further, by recognizing that it is God who is leading us, not vice versa, we are more apt to adopt the attitude of patience and attention that is necessary to discern God's presence in the world around us.

"Light" in the context of the artistic vocation and search for epiphanies embodies several different but interrelated concepts. To begin with, light is a symbol for Christ—the norm and archetype for Beauty, who is himself the object of all of our inner strivings and desire to embrace Beauty as the ulti-mate goal of the artistic journey. Light, according to the Neoplatonic thought of Pseudo-Dionysius, is also the visible form of the Good, which "illuminates the mind" and "gathers together whatever may be scattered," returning them to their divine source.[40]

Considered in the context of the artist's search for epiphanies of Beauty, light takes on added significance, as a symbol of the self-detachment/self-transparency on which our ability to approach transcendent and ultimate Being ultimately depends. Teresa of Avila's *The Interior Castle* is based on this idea. The castle is a symbol for creatures made in God's own image with Christ at the center and "the difference, therefore, between it and God is the same as between the Creator and his creature." The transparent walls of the castle symbolize the self-surrender needed to approach God. Hence, progressing toward the center where God resides ultimately depends entirely on the renunciation of the autonomous, ego-driven self. It is this self-renunciation that ultimately "removes the scales from our eyes," making possible a spiritual marriage or union.[41]

With open eyes beholding the light of the resurrection, the more than seventy reclining tomb sculptures housed in the Saint-Denis Basilica interior—in French called *gisants*—serve as a metaphor for this idea. When the light from the stained glass windows is reflected on the stone *gisants*, the sculptures glow with an interior light, making them appear to have descended from on high. During such moments the *gisants* appear to me like mirrors that reflect back a world reconfigured according to heavenly norms, which permits us to "see" not merely our outer appearance but our inner truth and reality as well, so as to see ourselves as we appear "transparently" in God's eyes.

In *The Interior Castle* and elsewhere throughout the Christian mystical tradition, the aim of self-transparency is a spiritual marriage with God. Hence, self-transparency ultimately becomes a form of rapture, as Gregory of Nyssa suggests when he says:

> Such an experience seems to me to belong to the soul which loves what is beautiful. Hope always draws the soul from the beauty which is seen to what is beyond, always kindles the desire for the hidden through what is constantly perceived. Therefore, the ardent lover of beauty, although receiving what is always visible as an image of what he desires, yet longs to be filled with the very stamp of the archetype.[42]

The soul that loves what is beautiful longs to become Beauty so as "to be filled with the very stamp of the archetype." "Aroused by all things to the love of God," Francis "rose to their life-giving principle and cause." For "in beautiful things he saw Beauty itself and through his vestiges imprinted on creation he followed his Beloved everywhere, making from all things a ladder by which he could climb up and embrace him who is utterly desirable." In this way he transformed his life into "a resplendent mirror of holiness."[43]

By drawing us out of ourselves so as to embrace the One who is entirely transcendent and wholly other, the search for epiphanies of Beauty invokes this same process of becoming Beauty, becoming Light. For it is in the experience of "otherness that the in-breaking of God's glory becomes possible."[44] This is the hope to which the artist in search of epiphanies of Beauty clings, in patient expectation that by endeavoring to free the mind, senses, and imagination from such earthly constraints, in our lives and our work we, too, may become "all eyes, all light, all countenance."[45]

Part Two

VOCATION AND SERVICE TO OTHERS

Developing a Vocation of Work for Today

John Larrivee

INTRODUCTION: POSITION IS NOT ENOUGH

A number of years ago when hiking with a friend in the Rockies, we were awakened in the middle of the night by the sound of a grizzly bear approaching the campsite. Like a squadron of pilots responding to a midnight alarm, we scrambled out of the tent. Our only refuge was a tree nearby. Since I was the better climber, I hoisted my friend up to the lowest branch, bent down to pick up our knives and rope in case we were up there a while, then turned to climb up the tree myself. To my consternation, I could not: my friend was in the way. He had stopped on the second branch. He had achieved his position, which was safe, but hadn't thought about what to do once there—like climb higher! After a few gentle words from me, he got the point and ascended higher so I could follow. No more than thirty seconds later, the bear lumbered into the clearing. It pawed around the tent below us for another hour and a half while we remained up in the tree.

My friend's view of his position on the branch is a lot like the way we often think of our vocation in work: we search out the position we want, but stop when we get there without thinking about what to do once there. This is a "called to position" view of vocation. Whether we go into particular professions out of personal interest in the field, or better, in response to God's call, we still often treat our work as an end in itself, rather than a means to some greater end. This is not surprising, since a common but incomplete understanding of vocation focuses on reaching and doing certain jobs (our position) and not on how we should be completing them.

Two factors make it especially difficult to escape the "called to a position" mentality today: jobs change and people change jobs. First, a position-based idea of vocation is inadequate since for most people their position will change frequently during their lives. As a result, it becomes hard for people to contemplate what their vocation is when what they erroneously think of as their vocation has changed many times, too rapidly to provide the needed tether to God, or the lens for properly viewing work. Second, as with my camping friend, focusing on the position alone gives little guidance for what to do in any position. Our sense of being called to a particular job cannot end when we accept the position, for why would we be called to a job if we are not expected to do something once we get there? After all, what boss hires workers merely to fill slots?

We need a concept of vocation that people can carry with them to any job, throughout any change, that also guides them in what to do there. The intellectual standpoint needed to get through this is the recognition that having a vocation does not just mean working in some position, but actually means approaching one's work in a certain way. For lack of an alternative, I will call this view of vocation the "approach to work mind-set." This way of thinking about vocation includes the concept of being called to a position but also provides needed direction about what to do and how we are to work in any position.

Critiquing the "called to a position" mentality was one of the strength's of Dorothy Sayers's approach to vocation in her essay "Why Work?" She argues that our vocation in work is to do good work in our jobs as if we were working for God himself, and that this must be a means of growing toward God because we are working out his will. This concept of vocation applies to any job we might have because it is based on a way of working and viewing work, not on attaining or holding a position. However, Sayers's account doesn't go far enough, because while it properly emphasizes that work is sacred, the only advice it offers is to "work hard in whatever position you hold." But what do we do if the work itself requires reform?

In this, John Paul II's encyclical *Laborem Exercens* offers an answer: our vocation is to transform ourselves and the world. He arrives at this answer by building a spiritual theology of work, based on the fundamental Christian principles of creation, incarnation, and the suffering and redemption of Christ, which helps us see the meaning our work has in God's sight. This serves as a framework through which we can understand the higher purpose of our work—the transformation of self and the world. This perspective on vocation and work frees workers from the "called to a position" trap since it guides all to reflect on why they do what they do.

I will argue in this chapter that this call to transform the world involves several variations. First, we must be willing to use our job-related skills in service to others. This may be in one's job (a lawyer specializing in working for poor immigrants) or outside it (a mason working for the church as a mason on the weekends). However, those variations transform the world outside of work, and in some ways in jobs of direct service, but it still leaves a big hole: the transformation of work itself. Not only can most people not take such jobs, but such an approach would leave the world of work untouched by the light of Christ. Our vocation as cocreators to bring about the kingdom of God implies that we will work to change the places where we work and even the fields in which we work. I close with several examples of people who have brought such a transformation to their fields.

INADEQUACY OF POSITION-BASED CONCEPTS OF VOCATION IN AN ERA OF RAPID CHANGE

The nature of the world of work today can make it difficult to think vocationally about work. First, the array of employment options facing people is enormous. For example, the Bureau of Labor Statistics (BLS) classifies workers into more than 700 different occupations, across a similar number of industries.[1] The resulting number of firm/occupation combinations is immense. Long gone are the days in which 90 percent of the population would have specialized in some agriculture-related occupation.

The enormous job variety results from a key component of the modern labor market: change. The labor force is changing constantly in types of jobs, industries, working conditions, training, needed skills, etc. As one BLS report states, "When it comes to the things we produce and the work we perform, in fact, the one constant is change. The predominant industries and occupations of the present—and the future—are different from those of 100 years, 60 years, and even 10 years ago." The report provides some glimpses of these changes. In 1900 40 percent of U.S. workers were in agriculture versus less than 2 percent today. In the 1940s 40 percent of U.S. workers were in manufacturing versus only 11–12 percent today. In 1994 there were 1.4 million computer specialists. By 2000 this had more than doubled to 2.9 million.[2]

Moreover, not only has work changed; people have changed too. Workers are far more mobile than ever before, and move between jobs and even professions at an unprecedented rate: the average person has worked for nine different companies by the time he or she is thirty-four.[3] I myself had exceeded this number before I even hit thirty.

The explosion in potential work roles in society and the pace at which change is occurring make clearer every day the need for each and every layperson to be involved in transforming the world. The larger the number of niches, and the faster they change, the less ordained ministers can do alone to address the needs of the world. Only people in those positions can know what needs to be done and do it.

Of course, the laity must understand the need for their work in transforming their world in the first place so they can do it. The problem is that while the changes that are occurring increase the need for each person to think vocationally, they also highlight the danger of position-based vocational thinking, of identifying our work, especially our current employment, with our vocation. It will be hard both to believe we have a vocation to a position, a call from an unchanging God, and to have an idea of how to serve God when our position is changing so rapidly. Without a clear and portable concept of vocation that we can hold to wherever we are, we will find ourselves tossed around in the labor market. Instead of being able to take positions in which we can transform the world, or doing this within our own employment, we will feel increasingly lost in work. Thus, without the right mind-set for work, what I have called the "approach to work mind-set," the frequent changes will make it increasingly difficult to know how to serve God in our work, and we will instead find our work increasingly separating us from him.

Thus, the expanding gulf between the need for each of us to take charge within our own position and what we understand as our call of what to do both presents us with a spiritual danger for ourselves (increasing disconnect between a major area of our life and our relationship with the Lord) and leaves the world less and less leavened by the Spirit of Christ, which can only be brought to it by all of us, as people of faith. The task, then, is to construct a theology of vocation that is general enough to apply across the wide variety of occupations and tumultuous change workers face today. The key in this is not to limit vocation to a call to a position. Instead, vocation must be thought of as a call to *how* to work and *what* to do wherever we are.

SAYERS'S APPROACH: VOCATION AS A CALL TO HOW TO WORK AND VIEW WORK

Dorothy Sayers presents a theology of work and vocation in her essay "Why Work?" that withstands the changes present in a modern economy, for she emphasizes that God does not call us to a position but to a mentality about work. The essay had an interesting origin in World War II as wartime conditions forced people to see their work in vocational terms: that they had a role, and that doing a good job in that role was crucial to the country's survival. She argued that people should have the same mind-set out of wartime, and would if they could see "serving the work" as a means of glorifying God. The difficulty was to help people think vocationally about what they did. She argued that work

> should be looked upon not as a necessary drudgery to be undergone for the purpose of making money, but as a way of life in which the nature of man should find its proper exercise and delight and so fulfill itself to the glory of God. That it should, in fact, be thought of as a creative activity undertaken for the love of the work itself; and that man, made in God's image, should make things as God makes them, for the sake of doing well a thing that is well worth doing.[4]

Sayers's ideas of fulfilling one's calling by "serving the work" is not new. Paul encourages Christians to work as if God were their master (Col 3:23-24), and glorifying God in one's work is basic to many religious orders. However, Sayers observed that the laity typically did not live out these ideals themselves because they lacked a clear theology of vocation to help them understand how to do so.

Moreover, in an economy with rapid changes in position, in which popular notions of vocation are heavily influenced by preference for positions or careers, her argument captures a key idea in thinking about vocation: seeing vocation as a mind-set regarding how one is called to act regardless of the position one finds oneself in. Saying that we are called to work hard is like saying that we are called to, or responsible for, quality: it is position neutral. Such a view of vocation tells us that we don't have to worry about finding the specific position to which we are called (though some may be clear about that). According to Sayers, we are all called to do good work, no matter where we may find ourselves employed and even if the position disappears in a year. In this way Sayers's notion of vocation and work includes being called to a position, but doesn't limit vocation to that.

In spite of Sayers's worthwhile contribution in informing us *how* we are to work, her notion of vocation does not provide much direction concerning *what* we are to do.[5] Even serving God in serving the work cannot be an end in itself because this doesn't provide us with enough direction. As an extreme example, the mafia boss and the pornographer may wrongly claim they are properly fulfilling their vocation because they are producing "high quality" work. Thus, to overcome this possibility, a theology of work also needs to reflect on the direction or goals of the particular work.

JOHN PAUL II'S SPIRITUALITY OF WORK: VOCATION AS A CALL TO TRANSFORMATION

This is precisely the combination provided by John Paul II in his reflections on a theology of work that he provides in the encyclical *Laborem Exercens*. In it, he focuses more on the "approach to work mind-set" of vocation than on the "called to a position" sense, urging us, as cocreators with God, to work for the transformation of the world as Christ himself did.

The pope developed his theology of work within his personalist framework.[6] Work acquires value because it is done by persons who have the capacity to act in light of divine principles, given in revelation by God, who is the only possible source of value. Through "inner effort," by conducting our work in accord with the "many points which concern human work" in revelation, we can give to our work the "meaning which it has in the eyes of God." As he writes in *Laborem Exercens*:

> [A]n inner effort on the part of the human spirit, guided by faith, hope and charity, is needed in order that through these points the *work* of the individual human being *may be given the meaning which it has in the eyes of God* and by means of which work enters into the salvation process on a par with the other ordinary yet particularly important components of its texture.
>
> The church considers it her duty to speak out on work from the viewpoint of its human value and of the moral order to which it belongs, and she sees this as one of her important tasks within the service that she renders to the evangelical message as a whole. At the same time she sees it as her particular duty to *form a spirituality of work* which will help all people to come closer, through work, to God, the creator and redeemer, to participate in his salvific plan for man and the world and to deepen their friendship with Christ in their lives by accepting, through faith, a living participation in his threefold mission as priest, prophet and king, as the Second Vatican Council so eloquently teaches.[7]

Here is an answer to fill the gap left open by Sayers: a theology of work that would enable people to give meaning and direction to their effort. For this, the pope employs three principal elements of Christianity: Creation, Incarnation, and the suffering and Resurrection of Christ in the redemption of the world. These serve as a foundation for thinking about vocation in work.

WORK AS A SHARING IN THE ACTIVITY OF THE CREATOR[8]

The first principle discussed by John Paul II is the idea that we play an active role in God's creation. Made in the image and likeness of God, we are called to be creative as God is and work as he did, sharing in his creative effort, and working to transform both the world and ourselves. As the pope writes, "[M]an ought to imitate God, his creator, in working, because man alone has the unique characteristic of likeness to God. Man ought to imitate God both in working and also in resting."[9] As he did throughout his pontificate, John Paul II builds his argument on the teachings of Vatican II, here quoting from *Gaudium et Spes*:

For man, created to God's image, received a mandate to subject to himself the earth and all that it contains, and to govern the world with justice and holiness; a mandate to relate himself and the totality of things to him who was to be acknowledged as the Lord and Creator of all. Thus, by the subjection of all things to man, the name of God would be wonderful in all the earth. . . .

. . . For, while providing the substance of life for themselves and their families, men and women are performing their activities in a way which appropriately benefits society. They can justly consider that by their labor they are unfolding the Creator's work, consulting the advantages of their brothers and sisters, and contributing by their personal industry to the realization in history of the divine plan.[10]

Therefore, one implication of the dignity of being made in the image of God is responsibility to work. But this is not merely a command or a duty. Instead, it is an invitation to work with God and share in his creative work:

The word of God's revelation is profoundly marked by the fundamental truth that *man*, created in the image of God, *shares by his work in the activity of the Creator* and that, within the limits of his own human capabilities, man in a sense continues to develop that activity and perfects it as he advances further and further in the discovery of the resources and values contained in the whole of creation.[11]

Toward what ends? The same as God's: that "the name of God would be wonderful in all the earth," and for the benefit of all people, to bring about the full "realization . . . of the divine plan."

This working toward a transformation of the world is itself part of our own spiritual growth and transformation. In fact, it is the primary way in which we grow in holiness and draw closer to God and do his will because only we can do it. Each of us is best situated to transform our own position, thus the transformation of the world requires the actions of each person where they are.[12] As the pope writes, work "cannot consist in the mere exercise of human strength in external action; it must leave room for man to prepare himself, by becoming more and more what in the will of God he ought to be."[13]

These reflections should be of great comfort since they both provide direction to and assure meaning of our work. As he adds, "the knowledge that by means of work man shares in the work of creation constitutes the most profound motive for undertaking it."[14] These reflections also assist in understanding vocation more fully by helping interpret the work part of our vocation in light of our relationship to God, our families, and the world. This sense is perhaps best captured in the quote he uses from *Lumen Gentium:*

The faithful, therefore, must learn the deepest meaning and the value of all creation, and its orientation to the praise of God. Even by their secular activity they must assist one another to live holier lives. In this way

> the world will be permeated by the spirit of Christ and more effectively
> achieve its purpose in justice, charity and peace. . . . Therefore, by their
> competence in secular fields and by their personal activity, elevated from
> within by the grace of Christ, let them work vigorously so that by
> human labor, technical skill and civil culture, created goods may be per-
> fected according to the design of the Creator and the light of his word.[15]

As with Sayers's approach, this call to transforming work makes vocation
more about an attitude and way of working than holding a position. Moreover, this takes the idea of vocation that Sayers sought—serving God in serving the work—but goes further, demanding not only quality work, but work
done to transform the world. While any work can be given value by the spirit
in which it is done, we still must seek out work of value to do.

CHRIST, THE MAN OF WORK

The themes elaborated above, sharing in the creative work of God for the
transformation of ourselves and the world, find concrete expression in God
incarnate, Christ the worker whom we could observe directly. Christ was a
man who worked. The witness of Christ's life and work provides a number
of insights.[16]

As God incarnate, he too worked. Thus, work can be noble. As John Paul
II noted, "The eloquence of the life of Christ is unequivocal: He belongs to
the 'working world,' he has appreciation and respect for human work. It can
indeed be said that he looks with love upon human work and the different
forms that it takes."[17] Moreover, as Jesus worked, both as a carpenter and in
his ministry, he gave us a model to follow. As Sayers noted, "No crooked
table-legs or ill-fitting drawers, I dare swear, came out of the carpenter's shop
at Nazareth."[18] However, perhaps an even more important lesson for us in
this is that Christ lived vocationally, knowing and participating in the activity God had set before him. When found in the temple as a boy he said he
had to be about his father's business (Luke 2:49).[19] His frequent mentions of
going up to his death in Jerusalem make clear his understanding of his vocation of redeeming the world and his determination. He knew and worked
toward his goal. So too must we. So, too, must we work toward our goal of
transforming the world.

And yet, as the data on work today make clear, the ways in which this is
accomplished vary tremendously. Thus, the work of transforming the world,
which falls to all of us, must be accomplished in the many places in which we
find ourselves. Priests cannot be in every occupation, every job, every loca-
tion. The clergy, necessary as they are, cannot be the only ones required to
transform the world. Not only can they not do it, this would deny each of us
the opportunity to work with the Lord in transforming our own little spot in
the world. Lawyers are best for transforming the legal profession; accountants

are best for reforming accounting. Each of us works toward transforming the world best when transforming the position in which we find ourselves.

HUMAN WORK IN THE LIGHT OF THE CROSS
AND THE RESURRECTION OF CHRIST

While the pope's reflection on Creation and Incarnation (and not the more neutral aspect of "quality" alone) inspire us to transform the world, such opportunities may be limited by time, job type, or circumstances. Some of us may accept the call to transform our work and the world; but we may be uncertain how to proceed, or be faced with tremendous challenges to do so. Others of us, particularly with little control over our occupation and/or contact with others, may find work hard, and have little occasions for renewal, at least for some time. Finally, all of us face periods in which our work is difficult and seemingly contributes little to the coming of the kingdom of God. What will bring meaning to such toil? In this, Christians can always find refuge in the great proof of God's identification with us: the crucifixion. Christ, too, suffered, and yet this accomplished good. *Laborem Exercens* reads:

> In a sense, the final word of the Gospel on this matter as on others is found in the paschal mystery of Jesus Christ. It is here that we must seek an answer to these problems so important for the spirituality of human work. . . .
>
> Sweat and toil, which work necessarily involves in the present condition of the human race, present the Christian and everyone who is called to follow Christ with the possibility of sharing lovingly in the work that Christ came to do (John 17:4). This work of salvation came about through suffering and death on a cross. By enduring the toil of work in union with Christ crucified for us, man in a way collaborates with the Son of God for the redemption of humanity. He shows himself a true disciple of Christ by carrying the cross in his turn every day (Luke 9:23) in the activity that he is called upon to perform. . . .
>
> The Christian finds in human work a small part of the cross of Christ and accepts it in the same spirit of redemption in which Christ accepted his cross for us. In work, thanks to the light that penetrates us from the resurrection of Christ, we always find a *glimmer* of new life, of the *new good*, as if it were an announcement of "the new heavens and the new earth" (Isa. 65:17; Rev. 21:1).[20]

These ideas provide great comfort to those who recognize the call to transform the world in which they work, but have limited opportunity to do so, either because they have little control over how they work or because they believe they work in a "value-neutral" job. John Paul II makes it clear that the efforts made by these people, even if it appears they failed to accomplish the end of work, are not without meaning.

As humans, designed with a natural inclination to want to be useful, to do work of value, the suffering and Resurrection of Christ provide proof that our effort can always be meaningful in God's eyes, not from its market value, but from its contribution to the transformation of the world, and the spirit in which we do it. We Christians ought to rejoice that we have the ability to bring meaning and value to our work by the spirit in which it is offered to God. This Christian perspective on work provides a profound response to Marx's (simply material) labor theory of value, which depends only on the physical effort of the laborer involved.[21]

PUTTING IT ALL TOGETHER: USING OUR SKILLS TO SERVE GOD AND OTHERS

What would be of value? How do we work for transformation? We must acknowledge that many of us will be limited at times in what transformation we can do. Nonetheless, as the pope's discussion of work in light of the crucifixion and resurrection of Christ makes clear, all work can be of value, even that which appears to be toil. We can be assured in this even when we cannot do what we know needs to be done, or when we do not know what direction to take or what to do to connect our work with the building of the Kingdom of God. Similarly, at least for some periods of life, our callings in other parts of our life vocation may take precedence over our calling in work, leaving us with little ability to work toward that transformation. This was the case with Paul and his ministry, and certainly is often the case for many parents and children with aging parents. Even in these circumstances, however, we must never let our temporary inability cause us to forget the need to be ever vigilant in looking for ways in which we may transform the world.

What are we to do if we have greater opportunity? Our vocation in work as transforming the world as God would have it involves everything from ordained ministry, to lay service work, to volunteering, to transforming the environment in which we work and even our fields. Surely some are called to engage in inherently transformative work, using professional skills for others, either directly in ministries of service in religious life or in professional careers (e.g., accountant for a diocese, chef at a soup kitchen, attorney for low-income families). But most of us are called to other occupations. Thus, we need ways in which even explicitly nonreligious or nonservice work may be made into a means of transformation.[22]

One way our vocation in work involves an obligation to use the skills we develop in our work is in service to others. For example, a corporate lawyer may provide free legal work for a program for inner-city youth, and a carpenter may volunteer to repair the church hall. If we have been given such gifts, we must use them for others.

Nonetheless, that does not go far enough either. What of the total transformation of the work world itself? One part of this is changing where we work. Many of us are employed at places in which the conduct at work is inconsistent with what God would want, and our vocation is to change that. This might be as simple as helping everyone there be more polite or caring, or as broad as changing a company policy.

And yet we can go further to transform even our own professions. Just as we ourselves need transformation to become more faithful to God's vision for us, so our professions need that as well. In some cases, the gifts of the profession need refinement so that they can be used in service to the world. In other cases, the field itself needs reformation. As the passage from *Gaudium et Spes* quoted by John Paul II above makes clear, we must subject the "earth and all that it contains" to "relate . . . the totality of things" to God so that "the name of God would be wonderful in all the earth."[23]

How great a transformation is required of us? As Christ taught in Luke 12:48, "from the one to whom much has been entrusted, even more will be demanded," so the extent of transformation will depend upon the gifts we have in amount and in type, and in light of the other calls we have in our life at the time. For many, the clearest transformation will be within our own workplaces, where we work, rather than in our professions, and in this a CEO may have greater freedom or ability than a janitor. Nonetheless, the call applies to all our work: to always be alert for such opportunities, and to constantly do what we can to achieve it. Taken together, viewing work as a call to participate in God's creative transformation of the world, in light of the three principles of creation, incarnation, and redemption, provides exactly that theological vision of work sought by Sayers. This gives a vision of vocation based on a way of working and what one does in work that is connected to the principles of our faith, and that can be used to guide and give meaning to any work.

I do not mean to suggest that transforming the world is a simple thing to do. While work may have value from the spirit in which it is done, this inner spirit is not easily acquired, and knowing where to go is not always clear. Knowledge of vocational framework is not enough. It is difficult to see opportunities and to integrate those principles into the mind-set with which we approach our work every day. The pope describes this as "by inner effort."[24] And effort that is. My father fought this for his entire life and retired bitter from the battle. Like so many others, he lacked the clarity of the framework, the habit of mind, and perseverance in heart to find value in his work, even in the sufferings of it. Lacking these, he also lacked the will to bring his intentionality to it in a way that would have made his work less a source of fruitless suffering and more a labor of valuable sacrifice. To live out our work vocations fully, we need both a theological framework to give us direction

and training in mind and heart that enables us to better see ways to bring
about that transformation, to live out that theory in practice, in good times
and in bad (and constant encouragement in both).

LIVING IT OUT: TRANSFORMING OUR WORK, TRANSFORMING OUR WORLD

Perhaps the best way to combine theory and encouragement is with examples of people who are living out their vocation in the fuller sense called for
by John Paul II and in *Lumen Gentium:* Christian Legal Services' conciliation
ministry, Crown Financial Ministries' Christian financial planning services,
and Robert Enright's research on the psychology of forgiveness. In each case,
the people are not only using their skills for others; they are working to
transform even their profession.[25]

The founders of Christian Legal Services realized that the current legal
system is too confrontational, hardly consistent with a call to love our enemies or with providing a witness of love.[26] As a result, they pioneered the use
of conciliation services as alternatives to lawsuits. This provides people with
a professional service that is needed (the legal resolution of disputes) but
within a Christian context. Crown Financial Ministries organizes financial
planners to use their services to help people free themselves from difficult
financial positions. Financial problems cause people stress, hurt their relationships, and induce them to work so hard they have little time for family
or community, or God. Financial planners dedicated to living out their vocation and trained in Christian discipleship can help people decrease their consumption and improve their finances so they can be free for God. Again, this
provides the needed professional service that cannot be done by a minister,
but within a Christian context to help people see consumption in an eternal
light, and to help them serve God, family, and society more fully. Finally,
recent work in psychology by Robert Enright and others has highlighted
what factors help people engage in positive behaviors such as forgiveness,
and the impact this has on them.[27] This has helped to shift the profession to
consider the importance of factors that help people live more positively (and
consequently has been called positive psychology). In this case, Enright's
Christian framework led him to investigate classical Christian virtues such as
forgiveness, and this has helped transform the field of psychology itself.

To these, many others could be added. *VeggieTales* has brought Christian
messages to children's entertainment. Christian contemporary music (one of
the few sectors of the music industry that has actually seen a profit in recent
years) has demonstrated that quality music can be positive as well. Legatus
supports Catholic business leaders in bringing Christian principles to their

work. The rise of Christian counselors has provided the needed integration of psychological knowledge with understanding of the Christian view of the human person. More broadly, Coalition for Christian Outreach conferences actually train college students in how to acquire this entire mind-set toward their work in any profession.

In all these cases, these workers have gone beyond their positions, beyond using their gifts outside work, to transform their profession and what they do. These people did not think of vocation as a call to a position, but thought about what to do in those positions. I believe that changing our idea of vocation to include the notion that we are called to transform the world as God would have it—and not just to hold some position—allows us to live out more fully the calling we have received.

Our Common Calling to Holiness and Sanctity

William C. Mills

INTRODUCTION

The term *vocation* generally calls to mind a person who is assigned an official service in the church, such as ordained clergy, monastic, religious brother or sister, member of the parish vestry, or some other ecclesiastical service. People often cite Paul's exhortation to the Christian community in Ephesus as a specific example of vocation in terms of church service: "The gifts he gave were that some would be apostles, some prophets, some evangelists, some pastors and teachers, to equip the saints for the work of ministry, for building up the body of Christ" (Eph 4:11-12; see also 1 Cor 12:27-30 and 1 Tim 3). The Christian tradition also knows of other official ministries in the church, such as reader, acolyte, catechist, as well as deacon, priest, and bishop. Throughout time these ecclesiastical roles were rather fluid and either were expanded or contracted depending on the particular needs of the church.

Besides regular service to the church, other people may think of vocation in terms of a career or job; that is, people may have a vocation as a teacher, lawyer, banker, athlete, or stockbroker. However, can we reduce vocation to one's particular or specific job or career? Work is important, and according to the Christian tradition work can be both satisfying and uplifting, and also redemptive. The late Roman Catholic Dorothy Day often noted how one's work can be highly energizing and contribute to the overall work of God in the world.[1]

Furthermore, we might speak in terms of one's role in a family, such as one's vocation as a parent, those with children and those without, or as the vocation of an uncle, aunt, or grandparent. However, this understanding of vocation is also limiting and very specific; it only applies to a select number of persons. What about those people who really don't have a family of their own, such as orphans or single people who live alone?

While many people may speak of vocation in a specific and particular way, such as ministry in the church, careers in the workplace, or even one's marital or family status, there must be a more expansive and inclusive meaning of vocation, one that includes all Christians, no matter what their particular role or function is in a church, family, or community, yet is limiting enough to remain faithful to both the scripture and tradition of the church. I would like to focus on a very primary understanding of vocation that is repeated throughout the scriptures and incarnated and experienced in the lives of Christians. Specifically, I would like to explore the notion of vocation as a common calling toward holiness and sanctity as it is emphasized throughout the scriptures, especially by Paul in 1 Corinthians 1:2: "To the church of God that is in Corinth, to those who are sanctified in Christ Jesus, *called to be saints*, together with all those who in every place call on the name of our Lord Jesus Christ, both their Lord and ours." Paul addresses the faithful in Corinth as saints, or holy ones, which is also echoed in the Letter to the Hebrews 3:1: "Therefore, brothers and sisters, *holy partners* in a heavenly calling, consider that Jesus, the apostle and high priest of our confession"; and in 1 Peter 1:14-16: "Like obedient children, do not be conformed to the desires that you formerly had in ignorance. Instead, as he who called you is holy, *be holy yourselves* in all your conduct; for it is written, 'You shall be holy, for I am holy' ";[2] and finally, in 2 Timothy 1:8-9: "Do not be ashamed, then, of the testimony about our Lord or of me his prisoner, but join with me in suffering for the gospel, relying on the power of God, who saved us and called us with a *holy calling*, not according to our works but according to his own purpose and grace."

This call to holiness is not something to be taken lightly. It is a command from God himself, that we are called to be holy because God himself is holy.[3] The entire scripture testifies to God's holiness and sanctity.[4] Holiness and sanctity is the very foundation on which our life is formed and shaped, and it is through our baptism into Christ and our being raised for new life that we live out our calling to sainthood. We are called not just to be good, not just to be nice, but to be saints. We can fulfill our vocation to become saints because God has sent into the world the Holy Spirit, who gives us the gift of grace to fulfill this high calling. As the Orthodox theologian Thomas Hopko remarks:

> We are all made to fulfill ourselves as creatures made in God's image and likeness for eternal life. And we can do so because God not only creates us with this possibility, and indeed, this command, but because He does everything in His power to guarantee its accomplishment by sending His son and His Spirit to the world.[5]

It is through the outpouring of the Holy Spirit at the feast of Pentecost that vivifies us and sends us out into the world to accomplish God's work which is no less than to bring the good news to the entire world.

The term *holiness*, like vocation, is often misunderstood and generally is taken to refer to holy men and women who are officially recognized as saints, the spiritual giants to whom Christians look for intercessory prayer and for their living witnesses of the gospel: Augustine of Hippo, Francis of Assisi, Claire, Elizabeth Seton, as well as saints of the Orthodox church, Sergius of Radonezh, Seraphim of Sarov, and Herman of Alaska.[6] As officially recognized persons of faith, they have fully exemplified the life of Christ through their unique circumstances, whether as apostles, preachers, martyrs, confessors, ascetics, teachers, soldiers, bakers, theologians, scholars, missionaries, as well as miracle workers and intercessors. Very often the saints seem to be "unapproachable" or "larger than life."[7] However, when reading the hagiographic and biographic stories of the saints we see that, with few exceptions, their lives were quite ordinary. Their holiness and sanctity was expressed through everyday routines of life, whether through preaching and teaching in local parish churches, working and praying in monasteries, serving the poor and needy in cities and towns, or ministering to children, widows, or students. While the saints lived in different cultures, societies, and countries, spoke different languages, and experienced the Christian faith in different ways, they all share one common trait: they always allowed the Lord to work through them, which eventually taught them what holiness truly was—living an authentic life in the precise place where you find yourself in life.

Furthermore, when we begin to dig into their lives, beyond the hagiographic material, we see that the saints were far from perfect, at least in the eyes of many of their followers. Hagiography tends to iron out the wrinkles and remove the warts leaving people looking spotless. However, the saints themselves reveal otherwise. Most saints admit that they were all too human and suffered from great temptations and tribulations, experienced impatience with others, and even lacked faith. One only has to peruseAugustine's *Confessions* or the *Sayings of the Desert Fathers* to see that the saints saw themselves as quite imperfect. Yet, their memory has been kept alive by the church to remind us of the possibility of experiencing the kingdom of God in the present to recognize these authentic lives characterized by striving to follow the supreme commandment of love. While we honor and remember these officially canonized saints as being examplars of the Christian life, what about Paul's message to the church at Corinth, and to us, that we too are *called to be saints*?

Sanctity and holiness is a common vocation for the entire people of God. We all have a calling to live the life of the kingdom of God in our own particular way of life, whether as clergy or lay, married or celibate, with children or childless, and in our relationships with family, friends, and co-workers. I would like to explore this particular understanding of vocation through the writings of the late Orthodox liturgical theologian Alexander Schmemann. Schmemann offers us a nuanced understanding of vocation, one that is derived from the liturgy of the church. Schmemann's main thesis is that the liturgy forms the fabric of our understanding of the Christian faith, and it is through the liturgy of the churchwe learn of our calling to holiness.

ALEXANDER SCHMEMANN: A VOCABULARY OF VOCATION

Alexander Schmemann was born in 1921 in Tallin, Estonia. Soon thereafter his family immigrated to Paris, where he lived until his departure to the United States in 1951. In Paris the Schmemann family joined the growing Russian émigré community, comprised of Russians with various intellectual and social backgrounds including artists, writers, politicians, and theologians, many of whom left Russia on the eve of the 1917 Russian Revolution expecting to return to their homeland after the upheaval had ended. However, for most emmigrants this dream would never be realized.[8]

Schmemann began his studies at the famous Lycee Carnot in Versailles, a military academy for boys. Later transferred to an upper-level *gimnaziia*, the European equivalent of high school, the young Schmemann enjoyed a classical education of literature, music, art, and culture.[9] He later enrolled at the University of Paris and eventually entered the St. Sergius Theological Institute, where he received his theological training and education. While at St. Sergius, Schmemann received the equivalent of a master of divinity degree. He later became a lecturer in church history following in the footsteps of his mentor, A. V. Kartshev. John Meyendorff commented that Schmemann's first love was ecclesiastical history and notes that Schmemann had planned to write a doctoral dissertation on Byzantine theocracy, only later to put history aside in order to study liturgy.[10] However, Schmemann never abandoned his historical studies and rooted his liturgical writings in a historical context. Schmemann also reflected on the historical development of the church in his many articles, books, sermons, and talks.

During his time at St. Sergius, Schmemann met Juliana Ossorgine, who was studying classics at the Sorbonne. Later in 1943 Alexander and Juliana were married and relocated to l'Etang la Ville, a suburb of Paris, where they lived a very austere lifestyle. Schmemann was ordained a priest in 1946 by Archbishop Tikhonistsky and was subsequently assigned to help Father Kyprian Kern with Saints Constantine and Helen parish in Clamart, another Parisian suburb.

On June 8, 1951 Schmemann and his family boarded the *Queen Mary* at Cherbourg, France, and left their native Europe to travel to the United States, where he had accepted a teaching post at St. Vladimir's Orthodox Theologi-cal Seminary, then located in Uptown Manhattan. During his tenure as dean, Schmemann flourished as a scholar, teacher, preacher, pastor, and theolo-gian. Aside from his administrative position at the seminary, Schmemann traveled throughout the United States and Canada giving speeches on college campuses and universities. He also served as an adjunct professor at both Union and General theological seminaries as well as at Columbia Univer-sity.[11] During this period in his career, Schmemann devoted his efforts to writing articles, books, and producing recorded weekly Russian language sermons for Radio Liberty, which broadcast his taped sermons to the Soviet Union during the Cold War.

Schmemann is primarily remembered for his writings on the liturgy, espe-cially the eucharistic liturgy. The Eucharist became the lens through which he envisioned theology and the church, and most importantly, life. It is through the prayers, blessings, and hymns of the liturgical celebration where the church reveals its true nature as the kingdom of God. For centuries Christians have gathered together in order to offer their prayer and praise to God, which is a service of thanksgiving that is offered "for the life of the world and its salvation."[12] When the church gathers for worship, it enters into an encounter with the one true living God, who reveals his holy will to the community of faith through the public reading of scripture, which is affirmed through the common prayers and in the breaking of bread. Thus, the community of faith is engaged in true living theology that is both redemptive and salvific.

For Schmemann, liturgical worship is central to the Christian life; it is through worship that we enter into the reality of the kingdom—the banquet of immortality. This intimate connection between liturgical worship and life is seen in the opening pages of *Liturgy and Life*: "It is my conviction that the Orthodox faith has its most adequate expression in worship and that truly Christian life is the fulfillment of the grace, vision, teaching, inspiration and power that we receive in worship."[13]

Schmemann's critics have questioned his approach to liturgy and have pointed out that he emphasized liturgical worship over spirituality, outreach to the poor and needy, and evangelism. However, when reading Schme-mann's theological corpus in toto, one actually sees an intimate connection between liturgy and life. According to Schmemann, liturgy is meant to be evangelical, in that liturgy always proclaims the gospel to the world around us. As mission, the liturgy is called to transform both the worshiping community and the culture and society in which we live. This missionary and transformative nature of the eucharistic liturgy was the topic for reflection in Schmemann's journal entry in early 1973:

> The Eucharist reveals the Church as community—love for Christ, love in Christ—as a mission to turn each and all to Christ. The Church has no other purpose, no "religious life" separate from the world. Otherwise the Church would become an idol. The Church is the home each of us leaves to go to work and to which one returns with joy in order to find life, happiness and joy, to which everyone brings back the fruits of his labor and where everything is transformed into a feast, into freedom and fulfillment, the presence, the experience of this "home"—already out of time, unchanging, filled with eternity, revealing eternity. Only this presence can give meaning and value to everything in life, can refer everything to that experience and make it full. "The image of this world is passing away." But only by passing away does the world finally become the "World": a gift of God, a happiness that comes from being in communion with the content, the form, the image of that "World."[14]

The liturgy then becomes a mission to the world as the faithful are called to bring the love, joy, peace, and blessedness of the Kingdom to the world, as the risen Lord commanded his disciples: "Go therefore and make disciples of all nations, baptizing them in the name of the Father and of the Son and of the Holy Spirit, and teaching them to obey everything that I have commanded you. Remember, I am with you always, to the end of the age" (Matt 28:19-20). Following our Lord's injunction to continue his teaching ministry, the church of God is called to continue this proclamation of the good news of salvation to whomever has ears to hear. Orthodox Christians are reminded of this command at every baptismal service in which this particular pericope is always read.

Ultimately, the eucharistic liturgy transforms the reality of daily existence, providing the transformation of our life to be the presence of God's kingdom as seen in the following commentary by the Orthodox theologian Michael Plekon:

> The whole of the day, the night, the year, all of time is sanctified in the liturgy. All of human activity is to be transformed: work, play, eating, sleeping. Every point in human life is a moment of God's saving and bringing us back: from our burial and resurrection in Baptism, to Chrismation, or confirmation, to Christian marriage, the anointing of the sick, and the burial of the Christian. Through the Church's liturgy and ordained ministry all of human life, especially material things—bread, wine, oil, water, words, touch—are directed back to what they were created to be—good in God's sight and, in the case of humankind, his very image and likeness. The consequence of this life of God and with God

in liturgy is made explicit. Time becomes the very "sacrament of the world to come," the eschatological icon of God's saving and reclaiming of his fallen creation. . . . Father Schmemann constantly emphasized the paschal or resurrectional nature of the Church, the liturgy, and Christian living, an intense realization within the Eastern Church's experience, exemplified by numerous holy women and men even in our own era.[15]

Thus, the real liturgy begins when we leave church on Sunday morning and go back into the world and share our life with our family, friends, neighbors, and co-workers. The liturgy challenges us to become missionaries of the good news to the entire world in order to see life as transformed in the eyes of God. In other words, we are to live the life of the kingdom in the "here and now," always seeking to incarnate the love, peace, and joy of the kingdom in our daily relationships with friends and family, co-workers and neighbors. We offer our prayer to God on the altar in the church and serve our fellow neighbor in the altar of the world, a theme that Schmemann often commented on in his writings and that is borrowed from the great orator and pastoral theologian John Chrysostom.

John Chrysostom said that there are two altars: one in the church, where we offer the sacrifice of bread and wine for the life of the world and for its salvation; and another in the world, where we offer our dreams and fears, our pain and sufferings, and serve our neighbor. Both altars are required if we are truly following the Lord, since we are not confined to the four walls of the church but the priest sends us out to go forth in peace in order to accomplish God's work, which is none other than to bring his peace and love to the world, to whomever we meet or serve. Chrysostom also referred to this as the liturgy after the liturgy.[16] While we all gather on Sunday morning for the Eucharist, the real test of faith is how we incarnate or encapsulate the command of God to go and serve both him and our neighbor. Perhaps this is why Chrysostom devoted many of his sermons to the service of others.[17] It is through the service of the neighbor that we are transformed into pure love.

However, we learn about our vocation to holiness through worship. The church provides us with this great command to serve our neighbor through the feast days and fasting periods of the church; through the hymns, prayers, and petitions; and through the sermons and scripture readings. This transformative nature of worship was a theme for reflection in one of Schmemann's writings:

> One of Osip Mandelshtam's poems, devoted to the Eucharistic liturgy, the main service of Christian worship, includes this wonderful verse: "Take into your hands the whole world, as if it were a simple apple. . . ." In an apple, and in everything within the world, faith sees, recognizes, and accepts God's gift, filled with love, beauty and wisdom. Faith hears the apple and the world speaking of that boundless love that created the world and life and gave them to us as our life. The world itself

is the fruit of God's love for humanity, and only through the world can human beings recognize God and love him in return. . . . And only in truly loving his own life, can a person thereby accept the life of the world as God's gift. Our fall, our sin is that we take everything for granted—and therefore everything, including ourselves, becomes routine, depressing, empty. The apple becomes just an apple. Bread is just bread. A human being is just a human being. We know their weight, their appearance, their activities, we know everything about them, we no longer know them, because we do not see the light that shines through them. The eternal task of faith and of the Church is to overcome this sinful, monotonous habituation; to enable us to see once again what we have forgotten how to see, to feel what we no longer feel; to experience what we are no longer capable of experiencing. Thus, the priest blesses bread and wine, lifting them up to heaven, but faith sees the bread of life, it sees sacrifice and gift, it sees communion with life eternal.[18]

In the above passage Schmemann outlines his thoughts on all of life as a service of liturgy, for the work of worship is to see everything already transformed and transfigured by the love of God. At its very core, liturgy reminds us that all of life is sacred, that spirituality is found in the everyday objects of bread, wine, and oil and is expressed through the life stages of birth, baptism, marriage, and death. Authentic spirituality is none other than communion with the God of all creation who makes himself known in the breaking of the bread and in the sharing of fellowship with one another (Luke 14:13ff.). Schmemann railed against separating liturgy and life, the church and the world, the world and the kingdom; for Schmemann there is only the life of God and this life is holy, sacred, and good. There cannot be any separation between the world and the kingdom; any separation is merely a reduction of what God had intended from the beginning. The entire Genesis story is about God's love and his sharing that love with all of creation. Therefore, Schmemann can say that all of life has been redeemed, sanctified, and offered up to God through Christ on the cross and celebrated and memorialized in the eucharistic celebration, as the book of Revelation says, "See, I am making all things new" (Rev 21:5).

We might think that Schmemann was simply providing a theological excursus on the liturgy for other academics who are interested in worship as a theological subject worthy of exploration. However, his thoughts on worship are clearly exemplified in the life and writings of Mother Maria Skobtsova, a woman who used her own money to open soup kitchens and flophouses for widows, orphans, and homeless men throughout Paris. While both Mother Maria and Alexander Schmemann lived in Paris during World War II, they lived in very different worlds. Schmemann was teaching church history part-time at St. Sergius Orthodox Theological Institute and assisting in a small parish community in nearby Clamart, while Maria was serving the poorest of the poor in the center of Paris, among the homeless men and women, both Jews and Christians.[19] Despite these differences, Mother Maria is a wonderful example of how we can live out our common calling to holiness through living the liturgy of the church each and every day. Maria's life itself was a liturgy, a work for God but also for her fellow human beings.

MOTHER MARIA SKOBTSOVA: FOLLOWING ONE'S VOCATION, LIVING THE LITURGY

Elizaveta Pilenko was born in 1891 in the Latvian city of Riga. She was raised in a devout Orthodox home and both her parents attended church. Her parents soon moved to the south of Russia near the Black Sea where her father was the mayor of Anapa for a short time, only later to relocate to Yalta, where Elizaveta, or Liza, as she was called, was raised. Liza eventually relocated to St. Petersburg when her father died.[20]

Liza eventually married Dimitri Kuzmin-Karavivev, who belonged to the Social Democrat Party, the extremist wing of the Bolsheviks. During this time Liza's interest in the church waned as she was catapulted into political culture. The time was ripe for change and the young Liza found herself befriended by numerous young men and women her age who were idealistic and were seeking a new identity. However, Liza never became a total unbeliever (atheist) since she still read the Gospels and the lives of the saints, especially after her father's death.[21]

Liza's marriage soon dissolved, but she was pregnant with her daughter, Gaiana. Liza soon moved to Anapa in the south of Russia, where she raised her daughter. Her religious beliefs soon deepened as she turned to God for direction. It was in Anapa that Liza fell in love with Daniel Skobtsova. The two married and Liza quickly became pregnant with a son, whom they named Yura. However, the political situation soon worsened as the Bolsheviks started taking over the country. The Skobtsovas, together with Liza's mother Sophia, emigrated to the West, first through Georgia and then Istanbul, Yugoslavia, and finally to France. It was in Yugoslavia where her third child, Anastasia, was born. In 1923 the Skobtsovas arrived in Paris, where Anastasia contracted influenza and died. Liza was traumatized by the event and grew even closer to God.[22]

It was immediately after Anastasia's death that Liza sought to live a consecrated life as a monastic. Her devotion to the poor and needy in Paris was already evident as she was actively assisting those in need on the streets. However, she felt compelled to do more. Her love for the poor, combined with the untimely death of her daughter Anastasia, opened a door for Liza as she discerned how to combine her devotion to the gospel and to the poor and needy of Paris. Liza did not find traditional Orthodox monasticism to be a viable option, since in the Orthodox spiritual tradition monastics live a cloistered life centered around the daily office, performing manual labor, devoting time to spiritual reading and meditation, and offering hospitality to pilgrims. Liza wanted to live a life consecrated to God, not in the seclusion of a monastery, but in the streets of Paris. She sought advice from Father Sergius Bulgakov, her spiritual father, as well as the local bishop, Metropolitan Evlogy (Georgievsky).[23] Metropolitan Evlogy supported Liza's vocation to the consecrated life and realized that the traditional monastic lifestyle was not flexible enough for her robust and lively personality. Evlogy agreed to tonsure her a nun and allow her to live a monastic life in the streets, what she called "monasticism of the world." In late March 1932 Liza was professed as a nun and was given the name Maria.[24]

Maria's decision to live a consecrated life as a monastic yet in the world may seem extraordinary, especially when one notes that the Orthodox spiritual tradition, unlike that of the Roman Catholic church, has never had religious mendicant orders such as the Dominicans or Franciscans. In the Orthodox Church monastics live a cloistered life centered around both work and prayer. However, Maria saw her life as quite ordinary. She felt compelled to serve the poor and needy in the world. For Maria, there was no other choice; the world was her parish and the people who came to her—the destitute, the orphan, the widow, and the homeless—found solace and peace. Maria would become known for her love of the poor expressed in quite ordinary and concrete ways.

Mother Maria, as she was now called, found her new home at 9 villa de Saxe in Paris, where, with the help of Metropolitan Evlogy, she purchased an unfurnished guest house. Mother Maria welcomed all of those in need: women, children, and homeless men. This was a house of hospitality as she herself wrote in her diary: "The house is roomy, but dusty, grubby, humble, unattractive; yet it is all redeemed by its warm sense of shelter, security, and gratifying huddling together in this salvific Noah's ark, which has nothing to fear from the waves of life's threatening elements, from the horror of rent overdue, of the penury and despair of unemployment."[25] However, this house soon became overcrowded, and Mother Maria had to find a larger one. She eventually found a three-story house at 77 rue de Lourmel.[26] There she created a makeshift chapel and had enough room for more than a hundred guests. Mother Maria was deeply devoted to her new ministry, usually rising early in order to go to the local market and purchase food for the day. She also sought financial donations to help pay for the rent as well as for the utilities, since she herself did not work for money. She would then listen to people's troubles, offering them a prayer or some spiritual direction. Her day lasted long into the night as numerous people sought her out for spiritual advice or a word of encouragement. Her quarters were a small closet underneath one of the staircases in the house. Mother Maria kept as her vision the gospel story of the Last Judgment based on Matthew 25:

The way to God lies through love of people. At the Last Judgment I shall not be asked whether I was successful in my ascetic exercises, nor how many bows and prostrations I made. Instead I will be asked, did I feed the hungry, cloth the naked, visit the sick and the prisoners. This is all I shall be asked. About every poor, hungry and imprisoned person the Savior says, "I": "I was hungry, and thirsty, I was sick and in prison." To think that he puts an equal sign between himself and anyone in need. . . . I always knew it, but now it had somehow penetrated to my sinews, it fills me with awe.[27]

For Mother Maria, holiness was not something contained within the walls of a monastery or even the church, but lived and incarnated in the daily lives of real persons. Her love for the poor, her almost obsession with helping those in need, was exemplary. She often canvassed the area around her boardinghouse seeking out those in need, very much like a mother looking for her children. Yet, her own unconventional lifestyle drew attention from many persons who thought she was odd, especially since she was a professed nun. She wore a tattered and stained habit and was often found drinking red wine and smoking cigarettes with friends long into the night at nearby cafés. She was not enamored by long liturgical services, so she often left early or arrived late to church since she had much work to do, especially as the boardinghouse was soon overcrowded.[28] As the Orthodox theologian Michael Plekon describes her, Maria was not without her critics: "One could criticize the details of her personal life—her hats, the cast-off shoes and food-stained habit she wore, her continued love of Gauloises, smoking usually seen as incompatible with monastic asceticism, her unquenchable passion for debate and discussion with fellow intellectuals and artists. Some found her to have an extremely passionate personality, often given to outbursts of indignation, frustration, and compassion, disturbing to their sense of civility and monastic propriety."[29] Nonetheless, even with her unconventional lifestyle and despite what people thought of her, Mother Maria continued to labor for the poor and destitute, always seeking to love the downcast and downtrodden.

During the Nazi occupation of Paris, Mother Maria found herself burdened with hundreds of homeless Christians, Jews, and Gypsies seeking food, shelter, and comfort. Paris was in shambles; there was little food and no work. Word soon spread that 77 rue de Lourmel was a safe haven. Mother Maria, together with the young priest Father Daniel Klepinin, helped forge baptismal certificates in order to help Jews escape. Rather than looking the other way, Mother Maria went out of her way, even in the face of the enemy, to try to help those in need. It was through caring for the poor and the needy that Mother Maria showed love for the brethren:

A person should have a more attentive attitude toward his brother's flesh than toward his own. Christian love teaches us to give our brother not only material but spiritual gifts. We must give him our last shirt and our last crust of bread. Here personal charity is as necessary and justified as the broadest social work. In this sense there is no doubt that the Christian is called to social work. He is called to organize a better life for the workers, to provide for the old, to build hospitals, care for children, fight against exploitation, injustice, want, lawlessness. . . . The love of man demands one thing from us in this area: ascetic ministry to his material needs, attentive and responsible work, a sober and unsentimental awareness of our own strength and of its true usefulness.[30]

Mother Maria's devotion to the neighbor is seen throughout her life, from tending to the sick and suffering, to purchasing food from the local markets, to offering words of consolation to the unemployed and homeless. Yet, Mother Maria was more than a social activist or political organizer trying to somehow bring a new world order. She was a devoted Christian who saw a great need and tried to do something about it. In other words, her vocation to holiness was concretely expressed through improving the lives of others, even if it was done at the expense of her own personal interests. She always put her own needs and wants second to those of the other person, which was quite remarkable during a time of war when human nature tends to function in survival mode and people tend to look out for their own needs first. Mother Maria saw her entire life as contained between love for God and for the neighbor, which she wrote about in her lengthy essay entitled "Types of Religious Lives," in which she identifies five different types of spiritual lives based on her experience in the church. The last "type" in her essay collection is called the "evangelical type," which refers to the evangelical nature of the gospel as proclaimed by Jesus and preached by the Apostle Paul:

Christ gave us two commandments: to love God and to love our fellow man. Everything else, even the commandments contained in the Beatitudes, is merely an elaboration of these two commandments, which contain within themselves the totality of Christ's "Good News." Furthermore, Christ's earthly life is nothing other than the revelation of the mystery of the labor of love of God and the love of man. These are, in sum, not the true but the only measure of all things. And it is remarkable that their truth is found only in their conjunction. Love for man alone leads us to the blind alley of an anti-Christian humanism, out of which the only exit is, at times, the rejection of the individual human being and love for him in the name of all mankind. Love for God without love for human beings, however, is condemned: "You hypocrite, how can you love God whom you have not seen, if you hate your brother whom you have seen" (1 John 4:20). Their conjunction is not simply a conjunction of two great truths taken from two spiritual worlds. It is the conjunction of two parts of a single whole.[31]

For Maria, the love of God and for her fellow man was the summation of the entire gospel message. She felt that these two commands, or actually one single command, was the heart of the Christian faith. Echoing the words of Paul, even if she had the gift of tongues or of prophecy, if she didn't have love, she was nothing (1 Cor 13). Maria's entire life was a life of sacrificial love. She loved everyone who came to her, whether that person was an orphan, a widow, a Christian or Jew. She did what she could to help other people since she thought that they were sent by God himself. How could she say that she loved God but not the poor who came to her for assistance every day? Maria's life was tied up with love of God and neighbor, which for her was not an extraordinary feat but one that everyone is called to incarnate in their lives. While she lived the life of consecration as a monastic in the Orthodox Church, she saw her larger vocation, her primary vocation, as one of living out the call to holiness through serving the poor and needy in Paris.

In the heat of the summer of July 1942, some 13,000 Jews, nearly two-thirds of whom were children, were arrested and detained at the Velodrome d'Hiver, a sports stadium about a kilometer from Mother Maria's boarding-house at rue de Lourmel. The Velodrome was a holding place for the Jews as they awaited transport to Auschwitz, where many were put to work and then died of exhaustion or were gassed and then put into the crematorium. For three days Mother Maria was allowed access to the Velodrome, where she ministered to the captives, bringing them food, water, and clothes. She even managed to smuggle out children in trash bins.[32]

As the war lingered on, Mother Maria's fate was in the hand of the Nazis. Her good fortune soon ran out as she, together with her coworker Father Klepinin and her son Yura, were arrested and deported to separate detention centers and eventually to different concentration camps—Yura and Father Klepinin to Buchenwald and Mother Maria to Ravensbruck. Both Yura and Father Klepinin died soon after due to the unsanitary conditions at the camp. However, Mother Maria survived almost two more years at Ravensbruck, where she distracted herself from the harsh labor by knitting, writing poetry, leading prisoners in prayer and Bible study, and offering hope and consola-tion to her fellow prisoners.[33] While the conditions at the camp were harsh and inhumane, Mother Maria remained joyful and hopeful, even until the final moments of her life.

The exact details of her final days are uncertain. On March 30, 1945, as the Red Army was quickly approaching, the Germans were exterminating thousands of prisoners every day. Some eyewitnesses said that Mother Maria's number was called while others have said that she voluntarily took the place of another prisoner. As one camp survivor, Jaqueline Pery, wrote, "It is very possible that Mother Maria took the place of a frantic companion. It would have been entirely in keeping with her generous life. In any case she offered herself consciously to the holocaust . . . thus assisting each one of us to accept the cross. . . . She radiated the peace of God and communicated it to us."[34] Whether Mother Maria took the place of another prisoner or whether her number was called, her life and memory will certainly be remembered for generations as a woman who lived a full Christian life, fully free and fully committed to the love of others even in her death.

Mother Maria saw her vocation as following God and seeing holiness in the details of daily life in war-torn Paris. Her limitless love for the poor and needy, her tireless work to assist Jews in escaping France were in response to her understanding of her vocation in life. She lived an authentic life imitating Christ in every way, being poor for those who were poor, being the outcast for those who were outcasts, even sacrificing her own life for the life of the neighbor. Maria didn't simply go through the motions of the Christian faith as many people do, but rather she was the very person who God called her to be. Some say that perhaps Mother Maria was all too real; she didn't adhere to the regular or normal practices of Orthodox monasticism, allowing herself to be free in this world—free from the regimens of formal spirituality in order to live according to the one needful thing, which was to live a life of complete love for the neighbor; free from obscure rules and regulations; free from what other people thought of her. Maria lived out her vocation with humility and patience the best way that she could, without false piety or self-righteousness. Mother Maria was perfectly comfortable being herself and allowing the Lord to use her as an instrument in this world.

CONCLUSION: FULFILLING OUR VOCATION

In an essay entitled "Holiness in the Orthodox Tradition," the late Orthodox lay theologian Paul Evdokimov wrote the following:

> In our time when we speak of "holiness," a kind of psychological barrier goes up. Immediately one thinks of the former giants, hermits and stylites, those hidden away in their cave-cells or perched on their columns so that such "illuminated ones," those "equal to the angels," seem to no longer be consecrated to this world. Holiness appears to be out of date, from an age that has long since passed and now seems alien to the discontinuous forms and syncopated rhythms of modern life. A stylite today would arouse curiosity but would provoke the question of the very purpose of such a great feat. Today a saint seems to be nothing more than a kind of yogi, or put more crassly, one who is sick, maladjusted, in any case no use to us. The same attitude would exile holiness from the cloister, far from human life, as a useless cumbersome object, good only for an historical museum. Even within institutionalized ecclesial religious life, the very thought of striving for sanctity is boring to sincere people. They are bored with archaic ceremonies and services, bored with empty sermons preached in verbally inflated style, bored with the blaring of hollow and meaningless childish songs, bored with community closed in upon itself, the key to its liberation hopelessly lost. . . . Under careful scrutiny it is clear that these religious forms, by their metaphysical indigence and very limited perspective, only function to

make religion appear irrelevant and outdated, an immanence inverted upon itself, empty of any real substance.[35]

Evdokimov's commentary questions the very narrow way that we have chosen to view holiness and sanctity, typically reserving these qualities for the few "larger than life" figures—namely, the men and women who have officially been recognized as saints. Thus, the saints become historical superheroes who have little affinity with how we live life in our day and age. Their lives have somehow been frozen in history to a particular place and time, which very often seems so different than our own. Yet, when we begin to look at their lives and the numerous temptations, trials, and tribulations that they endured, we begin to realize that their lives were not much different than our own. Holiness, then, isn't merely for the few, but for all. The words of Paul echo this conclusion: "To the church of God which is at Corinth, to those who are sanctified in Christ Jesus, called to be saints" (1 Cor 1:2). While we honor and respect the saints as witnesses of the presence of the kingdom of God, we also need to realize that we, too, are called to this same holiness and sanctity.

Mother Maria and Alexander Schmemann reveal to us that one cannot simply reduce holiness to a simple formula, method, or type, to a few rules or regulations regarding prayer and fasting, but rather, holiness is expressed uniquely within each person. In our daily routines of work and family, we incarnate holiness through our daily actions wherever we find ourselves. We encounter our common vocation to sainthood through the liturgy, the worship of the church. Worship gives us the language from which we understand our common calling to holiness. Christians are called to live the liturgy wherever we find ourselves. At the end of the eucharistic service on Sunday we are sent out to do God's work in the world, returning back to church the following week to be consoled, comforted, encouraged, reproved, and admonished to go back out again and serve both God and neighbor. We are fed and nourished on both God's Word and his body and blood, which become our nourishment and source of strength. Through the regular participation of the liturgy we are formed and shaped into the body of Christ, comprised of many members, whose head is Christ (1 Cor 12).

Mother Maria lived the liturgy in her daily life. Although she was not fond of long services, which was the custom in the Russian Orthodox Church during this time, she knew that her vocation was not to remain in the small chapel in her house on rue de Lourmel, but she had to find ways to serve the poor who came to her doorstep. The liturgy challenged her to leave the peace and quiet of her small chapel and serve, as John Chrysostom said, at the altar of the world. Mother Maria did not set out to eradicate poverty from the streets of Paris but saw her life as one of service to the poor, not unlike Mother Teresa would do a few decades later in the streets of Calcutta. All saints both ancient and modern allowed God to work through them, living authentic lives wherever the Lord placed them, whether in cities, towns, or villages, whether clergy or lay, married or celibate. They heard God's call to holiness and lived it as best as they could, in authentic and real ways. Mother Maria did not try to mimic someone else but lived out her calling to sanctity as one who served the poor. Other saints found their lives as teachers, scholars, pastors, bishops, as a path toward holiness as well. Thus, it is in our particular place and time, in our unique station in life, where we encounter the awesome face of God, who comes to us through the face of the neighbor. Holiness is incarnated and expressed in the everyday things of life, including the good and the bad, the warts and the beauty. It is precisely in the various communities of church, work, school, and neighborhood where we meet God face to face in the person of the neighbor as it is so eloquently expressed in the First Letter of John, "for those who do not love a brother or sister whom they have seen, cannot love God whom they have not seen" (1 John 4:20).

The Ethics of Vocation and Military Service

Stephen Butler Murray

The public oftentimes supposes that the issues surrounding vocation are merely ecclesiastical, uniquely suited to a theological vocabulary that would instill value into the particular lifework of priests and ministers. Of course, this is a secular misinterpretation of vocation. A proper understanding may be that vocation is a preordained grace in the form of *vocare*, a God-gifted predisposition toward, talent for, and love of a certain form of work to which one dedicates oneself. Further, one's vocation is not merely a calling to a job, but to a broader, more universal work as a beloved child of God that concerns how one behaves as such in a world that is God's. In this way, one might speak of following and nurturing one's vocation among any number of professions or ways of life, always dependent on whether one feels a certain providential pull toward becoming a priest, a firefighter, a carpenter, a professor, an artist, or a soldier. It is this last vocation—military service—that is the subject of this chapter, specifically, the ethical costs that may be implied in accepting and embracing this vocation.

It is often the case that following our vocation may lead us in directions that confront us with conflicts of interest. When we follow the *vocare* with which God blesses us, we may be drawn toward an engagement with the

107

powers and principalities of the world that we would rather avoid. We may find ourselves called to act in defiance of our ethics and morals as Christians in order to fulfill the duties and obligations that the gift of our vocation demands of us, a situation defined by the Kierkegaardian understanding of the "teleological suspension of the ethical" whereby one's normal ethical demands are subsumed by one's obedience to God. In this chapter, I shall examine the ethical choices involved in following a vocation to military service, a life that promises a potential and commitment to fight and kill in service to one's country. In this way, a military vocation may bring the subject into conflict with his or her Christian ethics for individual comportment and behavior, directly in the face of the commandment "Thou shall not kill."

Let me enter into this topic by acknowledging how I came to be interested in the ethical implications of military service in the first place. I am a systematic theologian by training who serves as a college chaplain at a liberal arts college, and as I have been thinking through the costs that accompany adherence to any ethical system, I concurrently have served in several part-time pastorates with small churches in the Capital District surrounding Albany, New York. At each of these churches, I encountered soldiers and the families of soldiers: soldiers who were in training to go abroad; soldiers who were on leave from Afghanistan or Iraq, but headed back soon; soldiers who had seen combat and who had killed enemy combatants, and now found themselves back in the arms of their spouses and children—a situation that simultaneously was the answer to their prayers and utterly disconcerting in light of all that they had seen and done. It is important to remember that I met these soldiers in the context of church, and so issues of faith and reconciliation were paramount in our discussions.

What I witnessed consistently in my conversations with these soldiers and their families was that in the course of training the soldier underwent fundamental changes to the structure of how he or she thought ethically, and this was especially true among those who went on to see combat and kill enemy combatants. The soldiers who held deeply to a Christian faith upon leaving for service often had developed very different elements of their faith, interweaving their love of God with their love of country and family. In this sense, one could see that their faith had adjusted outside of the boundaries of their previous innocence, and that their faith had adjusted so that they could survive morally compromising corporate conditions and personal actions that could not be reconciled within their previous moral structure. How does a Christian person come to reconcile the teachings of Jesus with the need to kill one's enemy in combat? What does the Christian give up and what does the Christian accept, in the process of moving from civilian to soldier, to combatant, and back again to a life with one's family? What reconcilable and irreconcilable consequences does the Christian soldier believe he has taken on as a result of his time in war? If one understands military service to be a variety of vocation, then what are the ethics of a violent calling?

I will examine three dynamics of the ethical choices that the Christian in the military must make in following his or her vocation. First, I will explore the often twinned motivations of piety and patriotism. In this respect, I shall argue for the importance of the nobility of patriotism in not succumbing to the idolatrous pettiness of mere nationalism. Second, I will discuss the important vocational difference between a life devoted to protection of one's country and a life devoted to killing the enemies of one's country. In the former, one makes a sacrificial commitment to taking utterly regrettable steps in order to fulfill one's vocation. In the latter, one embraces an indefensible ethical stance by which the enemies of one's country are converted into a new reality where they exist as the enemies of God. Third, I will examine the ways in which the ethics of vocation in military service embrace Reinhold Niebuhr's separation of the ethics of the individual versus the ethics of nations, whereby the military serviceperson gives up his or her individual ethics in order to serve the ethical imperatives of the nation.

PIETY AND PATRIOTISM

There is a nobility to patriotism, to the desire to uphold and defend one's country as an ideal that must not succumb to the military might of other countries. Patriotism is what allows a soldier to uphold one's country and one's people as an ideal, rendering a justifiable pride and desire for self-sacrificial service. However, in the politicking that all too frequently accompanies war, we often witness the use of a form of self-glorifying patriotism that dehumanizes the enemy. In this way, the ennobling mantle of patriotism is replaced by a glib nationalism, whereby belief in one's country enables the pursuit of the worst ends for the most feeble reasons.

This sort of petty nationalism typically accompanies the attempts of governments to make war seem noble, to make their soldiers unmeritoriously into heroes, and to define the other side not merely as the enemy, but as evil. In this way, a nationalism divorced from the responsibilities inherent in patriotism offers the Christian soldier the linguistic and ideological tools requisite to a sort of crusade that is not endorsed by the church, but preached and accepted through a conflation of love of God and love of country. This is dangerous ground to tread, whereby one's commitment to faith becomes intertwined and interwoven with the desire to serve one's country. A sort of manifest destiny emerges: the good of the country is the will of God, and thus the enemies of the country are understood as God's enemies. Lisa Sowle Cahill has made it clear that she finds it offensive when politicians use religious symbolism in an ideological way for militaristic purposes, mentioning the operation "Infinite Justice" as a blasphemy.[1]

We in the United States are especially susceptible to this language, for as G. K. Chesterton once observed, America is a nation with the soul of a church.[2] All too often, we Americans are tempted to conflate and confuse Christianity with American civil religion, which is to turn away from the nobility of patriotism and transform the American flag instead into a symbol of idolatry. This is all the more true for soldiers who find themselves in the midst of the unspeakable and the unimaginable, for there may be nothing so effective at the ruination of individual value and meaning than corporate participation in war, where the experience and demands of combat can rip asunder one's previously held worldview. As war shatters the previous commitments of the individual soldiers in the face of intentionally inflicted suffering and death, whether the result of intended harm or a response to the naked aggression that they face, the search for meaning may come in the form of a deviant form of patriotism that is defined by its idolatrous allowances and promises. Such a glib nationalism, cloaked as patriotism, permits one to act in a manner that might otherwise violate one's ethical standards, and holds out the promise of absolution for such violations; an absolution that may never come.

PROTECTING ONE'S COUNTRY VERSUS KILLING FOR ONE'S COUNTRY

When one espouses a militaristic life as a means to protect one's country, one makes a sacrificial commitment to taking utterly regrettable steps in order to fulfill one's vocation. If one becomes a soldier, understanding one's call as composed primarily of destructive dimensions, one embraces an indefensible ethical stance by which the enemies of one's country are converted into a new reality where they exist as the enemies of God. Chris Hedges, the prominent *New York Times* correspondent, speaks of this difference in his book *War Is a Force that Gives Us Meaning*.[3] In an interview with Bob Abernathy on *Religion & Ethics Newsweekly*, Hedges argued that "war is one of the most intoxicating, addictive enterprises ever created by humankind. And the only way to guard against it is finally to understand that, at its core, war is death."[4] What Hedges means by this is that in combat, one reaches a point where one feels that it is better to live for one intoxicating and empowering moment than ever to go back to the dull routine of everyday life. This sort of amoral intoxication provides a sense of purpose, a sense of meaning, a sense of ennoblement, and yet, Hedges argues, it is a meaning that is devoid of happiness.

For those soldiers who find themselves struggling with a sense that what they are doing is appropriate and fits within the constitution of a war that has been advocated by one's country, it again is important not to conflate the justification that a nation provides its soldiers with the justice of God. Soldiers may find themselves in combat undergirded by the demands and support of their country, but without the aegis and justification of the war being just in the perspective of faith and before the ineffable vision of God. Lloyd Steffen articulated this problem recently in *The Christian Century* by juxtaposing the dynamics of faith and politics held by John Quincy Adams and William McKinley:

> "The United States goes not abroad in search of monsters to destroy," Secretary of State John Quincy Adams wrote in 1821. "She is a well-wisher to the freedom and independence of all. She is the champion and vindicator only of her own. If the United States took up all foreign affairs, it would become entangled in all the wars of interest and intrigue, which assume the colors and usurp the standards of freedom. She might become the dictatress of the world. She would be no longer the ruler of her own soul."
>
> Some 80 years later President McKinley, stymied about what to do in the Philippines, went into a late-night, down-on-the-knees prayer session in the White House and emerged with a different vision. It had come to him that he could take all the islands and—"by God's grace" he said—educate, uplift, civilize and Christianize the Filipinos. Having received divine endorsement for an imperial military incursion, McKinley put his worries about empire to rest. "I went to bed," he said, "and went to sleep, and slept soundly." [5]

Steffen, looking at these two paradigms, argues that Adams's warning has gone unheeded, and McKinley's appeal to a long-standing national belief that America enjoys a special or exceptionalist destiny in the history of nations continues to lurk around the edges of many current foreign policy initiatives. The idea that America has received a divinely approved mission to spread freedom, democracy, and capitalist prosperity to the world through its economic and military might persists, and it persists in particular strength among soldiers who search for meaning in the face of that which would threaten to erase all meaning from one's life. By affixing one's individuality to the corporate identity of America, it is possible for the soldier then to call on a strength and endurance that is greater than his or her own. However, summoning such reserves also opens the door to taking on a moral stance that is defined more by the corporate identity of the country than by the ethics of the individual.

If one can hold on to the idea that God specially has enabled one's country to accomplish a specific goal, it is exhilarating to throw oneself into service to realize that goal, no matter the consequences for those that America, and God, stand against. For one who has the assurance that country and therefore God support the war in which one fights, the demands of traditional just war theory do not apply. This conflation of God and country allows a sort of false teleological suspension of the ethical, whereby the responsibilities that are inherent to one's faithfulness to "God and country" trump the typical guidelines of just war tradition—namely last resort, proportionality, reasonable hope of success, and noncombatant immunity. If a soldier believes that in obeying his country he is obeying his God, the call to responsibility of the just war tradition pales in comparison.

THE ETHICS OF THE INDIVIDUAL VERSUS
THE ETHICS OF A NATION

Finally, I would like to examine the ways in which the ethics of vocation in military service embrace Reinhold Niebuhr's separation of the ethics of the individual versus the ethics of nations, whereby the military serviceperson gives up his or her individual ethics in order to serve the necessities of the ethic of his or her nation. One of the ways that Niebuhr is most accessible to the public, in this day and age, is through the considerable fame of his Serenity Prayer:

> God, give us grace to accept with serenity
> the things that cannot be changed,
> courage to change the things
> which should be changed,
> and the wisdom to distinguish
> the one from the other.
> Living one day at a time,
> Enjoying one moment at a time,
> Accepting hardship as a pathway to peace,
> Taking, as Jesus did,
> This sinful world as it is,
> Not as I would have it,
> Trusting that You will make all things right,
> If I surrender to Your will,
> So that I may be reasonably happy in this life,
> And supremely happy with You forever in the next.
> Amen.[6]

I appreciate the efforts of Niebuhr's daughter, Elisabeth Sifton, to remind us that his prayer was written in the context of the Second World War, as a prayer for political wisdom in a time of war. In accordance with Robin Lovin, I appreciate that the serenity for which Niebuhr prayed is "not a matter of getting comfortable with doing nothing, but of doing what we can without being paralyzed by anxiety about where we have to start or blinded by defensiveness about what we haven't done. . . . So there is a kind of political serenity that frees us for change, just as there is a false kind of personal serenity that frees us from it."[7] While the prayer has been appropriated by Alcoholics Anonymous, I wonder if there are members of the military who, when faced by the unfathomable in times of war, find themselves compelled to pray for serenity to accept the things that cannot be changed.

Niebuhr heralded the rise of "Christian realism" in his critiques of Walter Rauschenbusch's Social Gospel movement, defined by its buoyant idealism and pragmatism in the face of America's increasing industrialization and urbanization. A powerful argument coming out of Niebuhr's work was that communities or governments must follow different moral standards than individuals do. At times, governments must do things that would be abhorrent to the ethics of an individual in order to preserve the greater good of individuals that constitute the society that government is constitutionally bound to protect. In *Moral Man and Immoral Society*, Niebuhr presupposes a moral dualism between individuals and groups, making a distinction between individual and group morality due to the group egoism that is an inescapable element of human and political reality. For Niebuhr, individuals are morally sensible in their ability to consider the interests of others and then act on others' behalf when experiencing conflicts between the advantages of others and their own, enabling individuals to be unselfish. However, in a society it is difficult to handle the interest of any group of individuals by means of our rational faculties because groups inherently are the collection of individuals' selfish impulses. This collective egoism becomes more powerful in a social body's moral reasoning than does the individual capacities for unselfishness, for "[i]n every human group there is less reason to guide and to check impulse, less capacity for self-transcendence, less ability to comprehend the needs of others and therefore more unrestrained egoism than the individuals, who compose the group, reveal in their personal relationships." Therefore, "[a]ll social co-operation on a larger scale than the most intimate social group requires a measure of coercion." According to Niebuhr, every group, as every individual, possesses "expansive desires which are rooted in the instinct of survival and soon extend beyond it. The will-to-live becomes the will-to-power," which means that society is then in a perpetual state of war.[8]

In an extension of Niebuhr's thoughts, I argue that members of the military, in times of war, must take on the moral standards of the government that they represent, rather than being held to the moral standards of the individual. In my consideration of this aspect of Niebuhr's ethics, I want to qualify Niebuhr's differentiation between the ethics of the individual and the ethics of the community by saying that such a difference is most applicable in times of duress, such as in times of war or the defense of national security. Otherwise, in nonmilitary settings, to encourage communities to act under different moral standards than those of individuals is to empower individuals within that community to act in unacceptable ways so long as what they do is deemed by the individual to be for the community's best interests. Over time, this would have a corrosive effect on the morality of individuals within society as their justifications for acting outside the boundaries of individual morality shifts toward the less stringent communal morality, a form of morality that must react to certain circumstances with methods what would exceed the boundaries of traditional individual morality. It is important to remember that I am arguing that this sort of morality switch is to be expected or even allowed for soldiers when they are in times of peace, but specifically when they are waging war. Of course, one of the difficulties experienced by soldiers who return home after the fighting has stopped is that they do not know how to reinhabit the moral landscape that they occupied before.

However, among the military, I believe that it is vital to the moral soundness of the individual soldiers that one considers Niebuhr's differentiation between the ethics of the individual and the ethics of the government. In so doing, it is possible for members of the military to articulate a dualistic ethical standard by which they live, one that is appropriate to normal, civilian or enlisted life back home and another standard that bolsters the soldiers during times of war, allowing them the moral latitude to commit actions that normally would bear considerable consequences if committed by individuals in society.

One difficulty of such a dual morality, localized to specific circumstances, is the burden that this sort of divergent, dualized ethic places on the serviceperson who must navigate the feelings of guilt for behaviors that are morally permissible in the circumstances of battle but utterly unacceptable in everyday life. One is able to reconcile oneself with the larger social body of which one is a part, enabling one to embrace the collective group's ethical standards during the wartime. However, how does one reconcile oneself for the same actions in the face of one's spouse, one's children, one's God? How does the military serviceperson articulate the acceptability of deadly actions, whether considered murderous or justifiable, to himself? What are the costs of setting aside one's ethical commitments as a Christian in order to fulfill the responsibilities of patriotic military service to one's country? Must survival in the wake of committing such violent deeds be so raw, so personally contentious?

Faced with the indispensability of committing normally abhorrent deeds during the extraordinarily violent circumstances of war, soldiers find solace in the fact that they are part of a greater body, a military in service to a country that empowers them to act in such a way as is necessary in order to defend the country or make secure the people of the land. Obviously, there are profound differences in what becomes morally defensible under the rubrics of this corporate ethic. For example, while the Christian may be able to justify offensive force that leads to killing another, gross brutality such as the massacre at My Lai obviously offends any moral structure. While the soldier who takes on a more corporate identity may find himself enabled to stretch the boundaries of what his individual morality may allow, this does not begin to imply that a corporate military morality leads to a free-for-all morality tipping the precipice toward anarchy.

One of the theologians that I admire most is Miroslav Volf of Yale Divinity School. Volf is from Croatia, and is so committed to his roots that every year he spends some months back in that war-torn country teaching at a small evangelical seminary. In 2002 he won the prestigious Grawemeyer Award in Religion for his book *Exclusion and Embrace*. Volf focuses in this book on what kind of selves we need to be in order to live in harmony with others. In addressing the topic, Volf stresses the social implications of divine self-giving. He says that the scriptures attest that God does not abandon the godless to their wrongdoing, but God gives selflessly to bring them into communion. We are called to do likewise—"whoever our enemies and whoever we may be."[9] The divine mandate to embrace as God has embraced is summarized in Paul's injunction to the Romans: "Welcome one another, therefore, just as Christ has welcomed you" (15:7).

Obviously, Volf bears some high expectations for how we are to act in the face of adversity. I want to offer a short story that I think displays some real honesty about the costs to ethics in violent times.[10] In the winter of 1993, Volf had finished giving a lecture when Jürgen Moltmann, who had directed both of Volf's doctoral dissertations at the University of Tübingen, stood and asked, "But can you embrace a *cetnik*?" For months, the Serbian freedom fighters called *cetnik* had been sowing desolation in Croatia, herding people into concentration camps, burning down churches, and destroying cities. Volf had just argued that we ought to embrace our enemies as God has embraced us in Christ. So the question was could he embrace a *cetnik*, the ultimate other. For Volf, the evil other. What would justify the embrace? Where would he draw the strength for it? What would it do to his identity as a human being and as a Croat? It took a while for Volf to answer, though he immediately knew what he wanted to say. "No, I cannot—but as a follower of Christ I think I should be able to."

I like that answer. It seems to say that honesty does not require us to act in a superhuman way that betrays our loyalties and personal values. Rather, what honesty really calls us to do is come face-to-face with our God. Honesty is recognizing the ideal of what God would have us be and what God would have us do, even if we cannot reach it. I interpret Volf's directive in this sense: that in the acknowledgment of this honesty, it is possible for the Christian soldier to find peace when confronted by the dually powerful obligations to maintain a Christian ethic and to make painfully difficult sacrifices against those ethics, enabled by the corporate morality that empowers the soldier to act in ways that are normatively indefensible for the individual. The soldier may find himself subject to a different teleology than Kierkegaard implied in his understanding of the teleological suspension of the ethical. Rather than explaining the situation that allows one to violate one's normative ethics for the sake of obedience to God, sometimes, in service to one's country, one violates one's normative ethics for the sake of patriotism. By being honest about one's obligations both to God and to country, it is possible for the soldier to reconcile what God would have him be and have him do with what the soldier's country demands of him and enables him to do in a time of war. While this reconciliation is not easy, it is possible for the Christian soldier, being pulled in two directions at once, to acknowledge the moral forces that are at play. If God's graceful gift of vocation leads the soldier toward a military life, in which violent acts must at times be done in service to one's country, then the soldier is able to find a moral ground on which a teleological suspension of the ethical allows him or her to follow both faith and patriotism. Further, if Christian soldiers understand military service as a form of vocation, maintaining a strong sense of what a vocation demands, then they are less prone merely to follow orders, and more likely to bring their country's demands and God's demands into accord. The Christian soldier is a conscientious soldier, but a soldier nonetheless who must carry out the full duties that come with the vocation of military service.

In short, in ruminating on the place of vocation even in the exigencies of war, Christian soldiers, too, find themselves called by God. While in this difficult situation they might falter or find themselves inspired to attempt greatness, yet it is important that they remain loyal to who they were before the armed conflict began. It is important that, at the end of the time of crisis, one be able to look in the mirror and recognize oneself. For soldiers, a grounding realization is the assurance that they can stand before their families, and have done nothing to distress them or to doubt their support. Ultimately, one must stand before God and not fear God's appraisal of one's actions. The moral imperative of the Christian soldier is to follow the blessings and demands of one's God-gifted vocation, which may involve the compromise, in combat, of one's normative ethics. To embrace one's vocation is to bring the kingdom of God into one's work, and if one's labors lead down a path fraught with ethical challenges, the Christian soldier must then face the very real dilemma of discerning whether one's actions are in service to one's vocation, and thus to God, or in service merely to one's country. For it is only in service to God that the Christian soldier can justify actions that might otherwise seem irreconcilable with the Christian life.

The Call of the Other

A Levinasian Approach to Vocation

Stanley Nevins

INTRODUCTION

Ideas need a language adequate to express their meaning. Lacking such a language, they easily fall out of speech; they lose currency. They become *inert ideas*, as Alfred North Whitehead called them[1]—ceasing both to move us and to be felt.

Such is the case, I believe, with the idea of vocation. Especially among college-age men and women with whom I work, the notion of vocation rarely, if ever, enters into their discourse. They have grown up, it seems, hardly ever hearing the language of vocation, except in the context of careerism or, less likely today than a few decades ago, as a call to the religious life. Few young people have a sense of themselves as being called by something that they feel *freely compelled* to serve. Instead, their lifestyle choices are made on a rationally calculated, instrumental basis.

The aim of this chapter is trifold. In the first place, I will discuss a prevailing language form that appears to be the lingua franca that shapes the vocabulary of so many young people, namely, possessive individualism particularly as expressed in the consumerist ethic. I will show that the centripetal force of the individualist-consumer narrative has the power to turn the self inward and, as a legacy of the modernist notion of the self-determined, independent self, is antipodal to the notion of vocation as it will be developed later in these pages.

Second, I will articulate a language form in which I believe the notion of vocation may be more properly situated. It is the language of the self/other dyad in which the former is understood as constituted by its relation to the call of the other. The vocabulary for this language draws primarily from Emmanuel Levinas, but also from Paul Ricoeur[2] and Charles Taylor.[3] Despite significant differences among these authors, they share a common interest in a decentered self whose identity is not that of a self-constitutive and self-founding subject, but rather of an emerging, intersubjective identity shaped by responsivity to others.

Finally, I will explore what relations may exist between the aims and values of liberal education and the notion of vocation. I will consider how the language of liberal education and the language of vocation intersect, and how they may speak with a common tongue.

MODERN INDIVIDUALISM

Let me begin with the narrative of individualism, a narrative that, since the seventeenth century, has become an ideology that valorizes the individual as an independent, autonomous, and thus essentially nonsocial being.[4] As a first step, we must acknowledge an ambiguity inherent in the term itself to which Robert Bellah has called attention.[5] There are, he says, four types of individualism that lie at the core of American culture: biblical, civic, utilitarian, and expressive.

It is not my intention to discuss these varieties of individualism, but only to note that the common element they share is the highly prized achievement of modern civilization that affirms the dignity and inviolability of individual persons and their rights to choose how to live and to hold and express their own beliefs and opinions freely without fear of political reprisal. However, despite these positive values, Bellah is concerned that the individualist narrative "may have grown cancerous."[6] His concern is that, since the seventeenth century, individualism has become an ideology that valorizes the isolated individual as an independent and thus essentially nonsocial being. As Alain Renaut has put it, "[F]or modern individualism to exist, it is not enough for reality to be conceived as a collection of individualities. Individuality must be posited as *principes*, and the totality, conceived only on the basis of (or through) individuality, as subordinate to it."[7]

Perhaps no one has described the implications of ideological individualism as succinctly as Charles Taylor, who reveals "the dark side of individualism" as a centering on the self that both flattens and narrows our lives, making them poorer in meaning and less concerned with others or society.[8] According to Taylor, individualism furnishes us with a language of self-determining freedom, a language that allows for making decisions by myself and for myself, and consequently, for being responsible only for myself. It is a language in which "doing my own thing" makes sense, a language of a self standing independently of others and saying à la Sinatra, "I did it my way."

The self-isolating individualism Taylor discusses was recognized as developing among the American people as early as 1835 by Alexis de Tocqueville. Tocqueville perceived it as a threat to the new democracy and described it as "a mature and calm feeling, which disposes each member of the community to sever himself from the mass of his fellows and draw apart with his family and circle of friends, so that after he has thus formed a little circle of his own, he willingly leaves society at large to itself."[9] Tocqueville links this developing strand of individualism to deficiencies of the intellect and mistakes of the heart that eventually will merge with egoism.[10] What Tocqueville calls egoism, Taylor calls atomism,[11] a form of self-absorbed individualism that leaves individuals enclosed in their own hearts, content with a freedom responsible only for their own welfare and success. According to this view, the self-determining, self-responsible individual exists only in the first person singular, as one whose center of identity and responsibility has shifted inward, away from others. It is a view that has significant social and political meaning, as, for example, demonstrated by British Prime Minister Margaret Thatcher who claimed, "There is no such thing as society. There are [only] individual men and women."[12]

In his analysis of the dark side of individualism, Taylor employs the term possessive individualism, which C. B. Macpherson introduced in his seminal study, *The Political Theory of Possessive Individualism*.[13] Macpherson's view is that the central difficulty of seventeenth-century individualism lay in its possessive quality. By this he meant its conception of the individual as a proprietor of his own person owing nothing to society. Such a conception allows one to speak of the self in the vocabulary of ownership,[14] whereby a person's skills and capacities are understood to be his possessions and therefore may be used and freely disposed of for a price—in other words, as commodities.[15] This is not a new concept, as those familiar with Marx well know. But it is worth pointing out that Macpherson emphasizes that when human work has become a commodity, market relations so shape and permeate all social relations that it may be called a market society, not merely a market economy.[16] Although it may be difficult to identify aspects of persons that are essential to them as persons, and that even vary by culture,[17] nonetheless it seems counterintuitive to consider that there are features of the human person that can be bought for a price. Macpherson is not concerned to enter the debate about what is or is not commodifiable about the person, but to point out that, in the narrative of possessive individualism, "[e]veryone is a possessor of something, if only his capacity to labor; all are drawn into the market; competition determines what they will get for what they have to offer."[18]

CONSUMERISM

This leads us to a consideration of the consumerist narrative, which is more than the human need to consume the material goods and resources of nature in order to live well and prosper. Consumerism is the dark side of this need. As an expression of possessive individualism that identifies the self as having certain marketable abilities and capacities, which each person is free to sell for a price, the consumerist narrative identifies the self by what it may *purchase* for a price. Possessive individualism and the consumerist ethic both share the common feature of *having* as the essential feature of the self: I sell what I have in order to have what I want. Consumerism is thus a narrative in which the self is represented, according to Joseph Davis, as "mediated by the consumption of goods and services. . . . We know who we are and we judge the quality of our lives through identification with the things we buy."[19] Erich Fromm gives the example of the individual who "defines himself by smoking Marlboro, he determines his being by having this object of consumption. That is his self."[20] By identifying persons in terms of what they can have, the logic of consumerism engenders what John Berger has called "an anxiety which is the fear that in having nothing you will be nothing."[21] It is clear that, like the centripetal force of individualism, consumerism throws the self back on itself. Instead of a centrifugal movement of the individual toward the other, the other is pulled into the self, assimilated and valued in terms of a "captive libido with its tendency to appropriate everything to its own needs."[22]

It would appear that the notion of vocation as having anything to do with responding to the call of the other is unsayable in the language of individualism and its corresponding consumerist ethic. In the latter case, the self exists essentially as a for-itself, but never in the mode of for-the-other, as a response to the call or need of the other. However, what is both interesting and ironic is that somehow the notion of calling or vocation has found currency in the vocabulary of individualism. Consider, for example, such expressions as "One must listen to one's own inner voice," or "Follow the call of one's true self," or "One's true vocation is to follow one's destiny." Such expressions, common today, represent a co-optation of the meaning of vocation, for it is not the call of something other than the self to which one listens and responds, but the call of one's own voice. It is the call of the same to the same, and we remain with a monological self whose self-definition is achieved independently and in isolation from others. It is not surprising, therefore, that Charles Guignon asks us to question what authority or self-transforming power such a call can have when its voice is none other than our own.[23] Gone is the transcendence of the self through a response to the other or to God that is traditionally associated with vocation. This call of the self to itself leaves itself within the sphere of immanence and of its own interiority, thereby "shutting out . . . concerns that transcend the self, be they religious, political or historical."[24]

AN ALTERNATIVE

It must be noted that we not only speak in a language that is familiar to us, but we also hear in that language as well. I wish, therefore, to outline an alternative language that represents the self in a radically different way from the vocabulary of the self expressed in the language of possessive individualist consumerism.

We may begin with Paul Ricoeur, who, in *Oneself as Another*, "suggests from the outset that the selfhood of oneself implies otherness to such an intimate degree that one cannot be thought of without the other." The otherness of the other is not an addition to the self from the outside, as if the self already exists substantively in its own right. According to Ricoeur, "otherness belongs to the very tenor of meaning of the self and to its ontological constitution." On this account the self is not a monological subject but a dialogical self, summoned by the decentering call of the other to come forth from the encapsulated ego to the identity of a responding self. Although Ricoeur insists that the self is inexpungable, he makes a clear distinction between the ego that posits itself and the self that recognizes itself only through relation to the other. Hence he endorses Levinas's assertion that there is "no self without an other to summon it to responsibility."[25] Contrary to the appropriation of the notion of vocation according to the individualist narrative, as the voice of the self calling to itself, it is the voice or call of the *other* that evokes the self as its origin. The self is by being otherwise than for-itself; it *exists* as for-the-other.

In the vocabulary of this language of the self Ricoeur avers, "Never, at any stage, will the self have been separated from its other. . . . [T]he *autonomy* of the self will appear then to be tightly bound up with *solicitude* for one's neighbor and with *justice* for each individual."[26] In short, the response (responsibility) of the self to the call of the other is foundational and constitutive of the self. As Levinas tells us, "No one can stay in himself: the humanity of man, subjectivity, is a responsibility for the others, an extreme vulnerability. . . . [The self] is made of responsibilities."[27] The refiguration of the self in the language of response to the other breaks away from the monological, self-regarding call of the self to itself of the individualist narrative. It situates the self in a position of extreme vulnerability and openness to all since, as Levinas insists, "the voice of the other is a call to universal care and universal justice—*Tikkun olam*: repair the world."[28]

Perhaps it is Derrida who clarifies the language of vocation best when he reminds us that "the singularity of the self is not the individuality of the thing that would be identical with itself, it is not an atom. It is a singularity that dislocates or divides itself in gathering itself to answer the call of the other whose call somehow precedes its own identification with itself"[29] In other words, to speak of the self in terms of vocation does not forsake the singularity or autonomy of the self. Rather, it opposes the isolation of a self-founding subject that is constituted independently of relation to the other. Responding to the call of the other abandons the notion of individualist independence, which refuses any relational limits on the self; it does not, however, eschew the notion of the singular autonomy of the self that is constituted by the response "Here I am" to the other's call. Autonomy is not compromised by care for another. The call of the other is the challenge for a response that defines a person's autonomy in a unique manner. No one can respond as I do. Hence, the self in terms of vocation is a

> shattering of indifference [to the other]—even if indifference is statistically dominant—[it is] a possibility of one-for-the-other, that constitutes the ethical event. When human existence interrupts and goes beyond its effort to be—there is a vocation of an existing-for-the-other stronger than the threat of death: . . . posing from the start the I as responsible for the being of the other; responsible, that is, unique and elect, as an I who is no longer just any individual member of the human race.[30]

It should be pointed out that although the self exists only in a responsive relation to the other, the self may isolate this primordial relation by intention so that the relation becomes impersonal, as in the case of individualism and consumerism. But the intentional separation of the self from relation to the other does not annul the relation: it refuses it. Consider the following passage from Levinas: "Why does the other concern me? What is Hecuba to me? Am I my brother's keeper? These questions have meaning only if one has already supposed that the ego is concerned only with itself. In this hypothesis, it indeed remains incomprehensible that the absolutely outside-of-me, the other, would concern me."[31] But it is precisely this hypothesis that Levinas puts into radical question. Even though I may say "No" to the other, I am the one who is responsible for refusing him or her; my refusal does not imply a nonrelation. In the case of individualism, the other is just not my business or concern. As Ricoeur says in *Oneself as Another*, "[T]o be sure, despite the affirmation of life's interiority in relation to itself, the self is essentially an opening onto the world, [and] its relation to the world is indeed . . . a relation of total concern—everything concerns me."[32]

The difference between the individualist and the Levinasian narratives of the self is that the former positions the self as a free, self-responsible unit essentially separate from others, whereas for Levinas, the self is, from the start and all the way down, already responsible for the other by "a responsibility that empties the ego of its imperialism and egoism."[33] The self of individualism is a subject, separate and distinct from the other as object. In contrast, in the vocabulary of Levinas, "The self is a *sub-jectum*: it is under the weight of the universe, responsible for everything."[34]

VOCATION AND LIBERAL EDUCATION

Long ago Aristotle noted that the meaning of words depends on the habits of the listener; we expect the language we are accustomed to and anything beyond this, he said, seems strange and unintelligible.[35] My experience confirms that many of the students I teach speak in the vocabulary of their culture, which has instructed them in the language of self-regard and self-interest. But if the language to which young people are accustomed is that of possessive individualism and the consumerist ethic, how will they understand vocation as anything other than vocationalism or careerism? Will not speaking of a call to respond to the needs of others for compassion and care and for forgiveness and justice seem strange and unintelligible to them?

As a professor in a university inspired by the tradition of liberal education, I must ask: What can my institution or any other liberal arts college do to expose students to a form of discourse about the self that would open them to the experience of vocation, of being called by the other? Perhaps as a first step, liberal institutions must be clearly and forthrightly countercultural in their mission statements, advertisements, and public relations, and in the sacredness evident in their regard for the value of education, not only as a private virtue but as a public virtue as well. They must speak to students in a language different from what the media, their peers, and their parents may tell them about the purposes of liberal education and about themselves as human beings and their relations to others. Wittgenstein says that the limits of my language are the limits of my world.[36] Therefore, a liberal education must offer students a more inclusive language about themselves that reveals to them the primordial relation of care and responsibility for others which Levinas calls the "human fraternity itself."[37] While it may be impractical to abandon the utilitarian concerns of students and their parents altogether, the university need not organize itself around those concerns. Students must be transformed by a liberal education into persons of enlarged sensibilities, capable of discerning the qualities and relations in life that transcend the pursuit of self-interest only. To accomplish this, the university must be a place where students may hear, perhaps for the first time in our society, "an invitation to disentangle themselves, for a time, from the urgencies of the here and now and . . . listen to the conversation in which human beings seek to understand themselves."[38]

Both the language of liberal education and the language of vocation ask us not to take our world as the only world, and also to recognize that human motivation is not exhausted by self-interest alone. Liberal education is more than the propositional knowledge that tends to define the different disciplines in the minds of students; it is a process that frees the self from itself and opens it to wider, more expansive, and different perspectives. It enlarges the self to what is other than the self—to other languages, other cultures, other values, other epistemologies, and other worldviews. The liberal university must be a place where students can meet the diversity of others among their companion learners and among their teachers. Liberal education is education of the self in the experience of otherness.

A liberal institution must educate for the professions in a way that rescues the professions from the for-oneself of careerism. Students should be guided slowly into career choices and not merely in terms of their interests and abilities alone, but also by exposure to the needs of others to which their professions may respond. Students, besides being asked to reflect carefully on their interests and abilities, can also be asked to ponder where the voice of the other is in those professions they are considering. To whose need for service or justice are students responding as they contemplate business, law, medicine, or teaching? A liberal education that speaks in the vocabulary of vocation will interrogate not only the *what* of these professions, but the *who* —who speaks for those served by the professions in such a manner that one feels summoned to respond with the commitment of talent, time, indeed, one's life? A liberal education will teach students to see a face in the profession of their choice and a corresponding responsibility, and not a dollar sign only. As I mentioned earlier, education is a public virtue as well as a private virtue. Hence, a liberal education, in both its curricula and its pedagogy, intends the formation of a certain type of person who is prepared for service to others by the development of critical and reflective skills, a facility with language, depth of knowledge, and enlarged moral sensibilities.

Finally, institutions committed to a liberal education will endeavor to create not only a curriculum and a pedagogy, but a community culture that will make it possible for students to move beyond the acquisition of information, through a mastery of knowledge and skill to a kind of wisdom that will guide them "to live well with and for others in just institutions"[39] in the universal religious sense of being servants of one another.

Part Three

VOCATION AND THE UNIVERSITY

The University, the Quest, and Student Culture

Thomas Hibbs

In 1907, not long after a devastating earthquake leveled San Francisco, W. E. B. Du Bois gave a commencement address to students at a public school in Washington, D.C., on Saint Francis of Assisi as a model for civilization. Such a "strange catastrophe," Du Bois observes, "gives the whole world pause." The silent pausing in the face of unfathomable destruction does not easily lead to articulate speech. Du Bois's suggestion is not the first one that would likely have come to mind, either to the students before whom he spoke or to the citizens of San Francisco. Du Bois proposes that we reflect on the roots of civilization and the ends of education embodied in the life of the saint and prophet after whom the city by the bay was named. Son of a merchant, Francis profited from the burgeoning capitalist economy of his time; a "glorious vista of wealth and laughter and gay abandon" characterized his youth. Wealth, laughter, and the joy of living are goods, not evils. But Francis lived in a world where poverty, misery, and sorrow abounded, and it is to his great credit that he could not ignore these realities. Instead of the merely self-referential desires of the small souled, Francis had a great passion for which his own joy and laughter would not suffice. "Something," writes Du Bois, "would be lacking—a dark void of crying want stretching forth out

127

of the shadowy valley and up the tremulous sides of the great wide hills, crying till souls must listen, even in their laughter, your soul and mine, the soul of Socrates and Christ, and the soul of St. Francis of Assisi."[1]

Why, Du Bois asks, should we ponder the life of a medieval saint? Why go so far back in time to understand where we are today? By fixing in our memories the life of Francis, we will come to appreciate a certain "attitude toward wealth and distinction and the need and place of human training to emphasize this attitude."[2] What was Francis's attitude?

Francis understood that there were material and bodily needs and that satisfying these needs was a good. But he was also convinced that there were "greater wants," for "human service and sympathy," for "knowledge and inspiration," for "hope and truth and beauty." And Francis also understood the tension between the great and the greater wants. To satisfy spiritual starvation requires some degree of renunciation of material goods. Education certainly involves the cultivation of a sense of relative importance of these different wants and goods. But education is principally about what Francis's life was about at its core: a quest to "read life's riddle and tell the world its true unraveling." Francis faced the same human condition we face, and he posed the questions each of us must ask, "What am I? What is this world about me? And the word and I—how shall we work and laugh together?"[3]

Of course, Francis's solution to life's riddle was not achieved merely by rational reflection; instead, it was the result of the transforming experience of being called by Christ and his church, of being transformed into the body of Christ to such an extent that even before he received the stigmata, the signs of crucifixion in his very flesh, he was called by contemporaries a "second Christ." Francis was not a starry-eyed flower child, but a devoted servant of Christ, who led a life full of sacrifices in the very midst of which he heard Christ's call everywhere, especially in nature, in the poor, and in the sacraments. Not weekend retreats to the mountains but holy poverty and endless prayer were the means by which he was able to call the sun brother and the moon sister. This was his way of reforming the church and civilization.

It is sobering to compare Du Bois's and/or Francis's vision of civilization and the ends of education with the account of contemporary college life in Tom Wolfe's recent novel, I Am Charlotte Simmons (2004). Charlotte Simmons, a gifted if sheltered young girl from a religious family living in a small town in the Blue Ridge Mountains, is a first-year student at the fictional Dupont University in Pennsylvania, an elite Ivy League sort of university with a superb sports program. Wolfe discovers a student world where the weekend never ends, where the greatest competitive spirit is exhibited in the pursuit of taut tummies and in Olympic-style drinking bouts, a carnival atmosphere in which nearly everything other than academics dominates the lives of students. The precocious, if naive, Charlotte, who expects college to be about the exalted life of the mind, is the vehicle through whom Wolfe tries to communicate the shock of the contemporary mores of campus life. Wolfe has great fun, perhaps too much fun, describing Charlotte's first experience in a coed bathroom: "The vulgarity, the rudeness, the virtual nudity—people parading around in towels, and drinking. . . . How was she supposed to live like this?—stripped of all privacy, all modesty. . . . This was Dupont."[4]

Beyond her initial experiences in coed bathrooms, what especially appalls Charlotte are the sexual mores of college students, for whom "hooking up," casual sexual encounters with acquaintances, has all but replaced dating. As Wolfe notes, this practice contributes to the dorm life phenomenon known across the country as being "sexiled," the experience of being blocked from access to one's dorm room—for hours, days, or weeks at a time—while a roommate "hooks up" with a partner.

Wolfe's take on university life is prurient and one-sided, but much of what he describes finds confirmation in more balanced, if less dramatic, studies of contemporary college life—for example, in the writings of *The New York Times* columnist David Brooks. In his astute book on contemporary culture, *On Paradise Drive*, Brooks describes the students at today's universities as "organization kids," who fill their days with activities designed to gain them success as society currently defines it. Today's students embody many virtues: they are industrious, tolerant, and affable. This generation of students "doesn't see itself as a lost generation or a radical generation or a beatnik generation or even a Reaganite generation. They have relatively little generational consciousness." They are "not trying to buck the system; they're trying to climb it."[5]

Although his observations overlap Wolfe's, Brooks sees something more and other than what Wolfe sees. Brooks detects in students a longing for something more than what universities supply in the way of services and paths to career success. Students are not merely interested in money or success narrowly conceived. Brooks puts the problem in terms of a question: "How do you organize your accumulations so that life does not become just one damn merit badge after another, a series of resume notches without a point? . . . [Students] hunger for the solution. But that is the one subject on which the authorities are strangely silent."[6]

Do those inside the university see the problems Wolfe and Brooks identify? Well, yes. In his much discussed piece in *Harper's* in 1997, "On the Uses of Liberal Education: As Lite Entertainment for Bored College Students," Mark Edmundson, a popular and well-published English professor at the University of Virginia, laments the positive teaching evaluations he receives from his students, who consistently praise him for being entertaining, sympathetic, and hip. Edmundson worries that the entire enterprise of teaching is now under the power of students' "cool consumer worldview."[7] The problem is not just that student life has become unmoored from academic life, but that the latter is quickly being transformed to meet the standards and expectations of the former.

Even as the typical classroom experience—in cavernous lecture halls with professors who are rarely available to students—remains largely impersonal, universities lavish increased attention on meeting the creature comfort needs of students in the form of better exercise facilities, greater internet and cable TV options, and fancy dining opportunities. The university thus serves, rather than counters, the dominant cultural assumptions of today's students; worse, it reinforces the easygoing skepticism and detached irony that popular culture fosters in them, the jaded sense that life contains no great adventures and makes no great demands on them. The emphasis on comfort and entertainment reinforces the students' sense that they are consumers to whom the university supplies services. Edmundson sees what Brooks sees: intelligent, compliant, pleasant, and conventionally ambitious students. But he also finds them to be a "touch depressed."[8] He notes that students stumble in response to the question, Who are your heroes? For all their ambition, they lack a sense of something greater than themselves worthy of admiration and imitation.

One of the problems here may well be the decadent formation of the moral imagination of our youth. The real danger with the nihilistic celebration of violence and sadomasochistic sexuality that permeates so much of the culture of film, music, and video games is not that exposure to it will produce a generation of Columbine killers, but that it will atrophy the moral imagination of our youth. The alternative is not a nostalgic return to a pristine world of the mid-twentieth-century American sitcom. In his perceptive book *Nightmare of Main Street: Angels, Sadomasochism, and the Culture of Gothic,* Edmundson argues that our culture is trapped in a dialectic between facile transcendence, evident in films such as *Forrest Gump* that offer happy endings achieved by the avoidance of difficulty and complexity, and debased Gothic, a pervasive, unrelenting, and unredeemable sense of evil evident in the popular genre of contemporary horror.[9] Behind every serene neighborly face there lurks a monster, where (in films such as *Seven* and *Silence of the Lambs*) goodness is bankrupt but evil, well, evil is interesting, even artistic. Of course, the demonic antiheroes who transcend our petty conventional codes of good and evil can sustain our interest, and keep us terrified, for only so long; audiences quickly become jaded by the surface aesthetics of evil, the competition of one serial killer, really one filmmaker, after another to one-up his or her predecessor in the number and complexity of slayings and maimings. Thus does contemporary horror almost inevitably degenerate into camp and self-mockery (see *Scream,* etc.). Having abandoned goodness, we find that we cannot take evil very seriously either.

We are saddled with an impoverished vocabulary of good and evil and an increasingly truncated sense of the narrative possibilities for our lives. We lack stories of redemption that embrace and transcend the horrors of our time. Edmundson detects in his students an enormous appetite for popular culture, an eagerness to discuss the relationship between academic subjects and pop culture. But he laments that this appetite and aptitude among students rarely leads them to pursue academic subjects for their own sake or for the sake of self-transformation. They are odd inhabitants of Plato's cave, intrigued by coming to a better understanding of the images projected on the wall but with little motivation to seek, or little belief in, the realities beyond the cave. This, I would argue, is the idolatrous tyranny of popular culture in our time. Into the vacuum of formative moral education in the lives of most teenagers, popular culture—by which we mean almost exclusively the Hollywood culture of movies, TV, video games, and music—enters to fill the gap. But many of the most popular Hollywood products are self-consuming artifacts; their only model of human excellence is the skimming ironic mode of detached, clever humor about pop culture itself. Thus, culture no longer points beyond itself but becomes involuted, specializing in the self-canceling insights of those who are in on the endless litany of allusions to its own constructs. This is as true of the humor on popular sitcoms from *Seinfeld* to *Friends* as it is of what we take to be our hippest filmmakers like Tarantino.

We are not unaware of the dilemma. Some of our frustration and uneasiness with our culture, evident in the popularity of such films as *The Matrix, Dark City, Memento*, and *The Truman Show*, reposes in a worry that much of what is presented to us as real is but a construct. Our despair is that we are inclined to doubt that there is anything beyond the constructs. The astonishing popularity of reality TV provides ample testimony both to our longing for the real, the immediate, the unscripted and to the way the really real forever recedes from our grasp. Self-lacerating violence, which can of course be channeled outward toward others, can be a result of such a despairing sense of unreality. As the line from the song goes, "when everything feels like the movies, you bleed just to know you're alive."[10]

But how would we begin to provide an education that engages such a culture without succumbing to it? an education that is deeply countercultural and radical, not in the sense of simply taking up a stance of protest or hostility toward the culture, but radical in its etymological sense of returning to the roots of culture and civilization, to the principles and virtues someone like Du Bois discovers in the life of Francis? an education that would allow us to "read life's riddle and tell the world its true unraveling"?

Of course, there is not just one way of unraveling this riddle. And while universities would want to have a variety of models represented, any university will and should embody some take on these questions, some mission statement. This is important not just for the university itself but also for the landscape of higher education and institutional diversity. We certainly should not fall prey to nostalgia about the university. As Andrew Delbanco notes, the "liberalizing trajectory of higher education" in the second half of the twentieth century has opened the doors for many who were previously shut out because of race, ethnicity, or gender. It has also allowed for the founding of many small religious liberal arts colleges. As in every human story, Delbanco adds, "there is loss as well as gain." The loss, as he sees it, concerns the question "what students ought to learn once they get to college" or even "why they are going at all." In nearly a quarter century of teaching at Harvard and Columbia, Delbanco writes, "I have discovered that the question of what undergraduate education should be all about is almost taboo." He goes on to note that the greatest freedom is allotted to those few American students who attend a traditional liberal arts college, where "intellectual, social, and sexual freedom" is assumed to be an inalienable right. Delbanco wonders whether "behind the commitment to student freedom is a certain institutional pusillanimity"—a market-based fear of how requirements of any sort, anywhere on campus, might shrink the applicant pool and thus trigger a decline in the university ranking in the *U.S. News & World Report* annual evaluation of colleges.[11]

The critics of universities, whether they be conservatives or liberals, often trade in half-truths and easy caricature. On the right, there is a tendency to trace what ails the university to the dominance of professorial liberalism, to the invasion of academe by political correctness and speech codes. Surveys, much in the news of late, confirm what we already knew, namely, that political liberals far outnumber political conservatives on university faculties. The real problem with the conservative view is that, by focusing exclusively on the restoration of free speech, by equating the classroom and the marketplace of ideas, conservatism has little to say about the proper purpose and aims of a university.

Meanwhile, on the left, the tendency is to see the university as succumbing to the forces of market capitalism and thus producing students who are no more than clever consumers. But the Left misses the way liberal secularizing tendencies in the university have created a vacuum on the question of mission and student vocation. Once the religious mission perishes, it is not clear what resources universities will draw on to inspire students to have a vision of the world larger than themselves. It is striking that none of the authors mentioned above—not Wolfe, not Brooks, not Edmundson, and not Delbanco—advert to the role religious colleges might play in supplying precisely what they identify as the chief lack in the contemporary university. This is not to say that what they want cannot be done apart from religion; the first schools in antiquity were philosophical, not religious. But it is not clear what in the current climate can provide an exalted and inspiring vision for students.

Where Right and Left seem to diverge sharply in their analysis of what ails education, I would argue that the chief obstacle to fostering an exalted vision for students is a too little noticed and almost always unintentional conspiracy between a certain strain of academic postmodernism and popular, consumer capitalism. As Brooks notes, the indeterminacy of truth, the sense of language itself as an endless series of provisional constructs, is perfectly suited to the ethos of the achievement-oriented capitalist. After all, why should the achiever want to make enemies or waste time in angry conflict? Why should the time-maximizer struggle to find that thing called Absolute Truth when it is more efficient to settle for perception? Why should one get involved in the problematic rigor of judging? Easygoing tolerance is energy-efficient.[12]

One wonders whether this mode of interaction with the world and others is not also one of the reasons that today's students are, as Edmundson observes, a "touch depressed." The deadly combination for the soul is a purely capitalist conception of the person as producer/consumer with the Hollywood-inspired vision of the individual as spectator.

In his remarkable new book on Hollywood, *The Whole Equation,* celebrated film critic David Thomson focuses squarely on the problematic ethics of the moving, visual image. Thomson is at once immersed in, fascinated with, and horrified by Hollywood. Unlike most contemporary critics of the entertainment industry, Thomson locates Hollywood's questionable influence on the culture, not in the late twentieth century with the rise in explicit violence and sexuality, but in its glory days. What is unusual and highly instructive in Thomson's way of construing the moral question is his focus on the very nature of film and its effect on audiences, on the mode of its presentation and reception. He focuses on the "enormous . . . tidal pull toward new dreams" and the consequent and far-reaching "romantic transformation," wrought by the influence of film and TV in the twentieth century.[13]

As viewers, he asks, are we "watching heightened things—great danger, great desirability, intense loveliness—without being tied by the responsibilities that attach to real onlookers?" "We are," he suggests, "like voyeurs, spies, or peeping toms." In contrast to literature, which actively engages the imagination to probe the "meaning behind events," film involves the "fetishization of appearance." Film is less about glimpsing hidden meaning than about "what happens or appears next." It thus suffers from "the crushing restriction of visibility."[14] That's actually not a bad way of putting Socrates' lesson concerning the inhabitants of the cave.

Form here reflects or produces (it's unclear which way Thomson thinks the causal line runs) a corresponding ethical content. He compares the nineteenth-century novel—which offered an education of the passions and tried to help individuals discern whom to marry and what virtues assist in the maintenance of marriage—with twentieth-century film, and its gratification of fantasy, its "parade of dreams."[15] Now, one might object to numerous features of Thomson's argument. It seems to me that his contrast between films and novels is a bit overdrawn. It was, after all, in nineteenth-century novels such as Flaubert's *Madame Bovary* that the demise of marriage and the celebration of fantasy first occurred. But even if he overstates his case in certain respects, what he has to say about the differences in the form of presentation and the mode of reception of novel and film is astute.

In this context, he offers some perceptive reflections on the classic romantic comedy *His Girl Friday* (1940), a film that features a divorced couple recovering their marital commitment and that is often seen as a Hollywood reaffirmation of marriage. But Thomson wonders whether, in this film, love is contingent upon the "endlessly renewable fantasy of breaking up" so that the characters "can find each other again." Have they, he asks, "divorced just to ensure the need for a fresh wooing?" Here Thomson puts his finger on the crucial ethical question regarding Hollywood, indeed regarding film itself as a cultural artifact. Hollywood film, "the professional craft of pretending," comes to the fore just as our sense of identity becomes "destabilized by the slippage of religious belief." Hollywood offers its own "images to worship," as it reveals "rather ghastly fake gods."[16] The new model for humanity becomes the actor, with his infinite variety.

If in its infancy Hollywood offered certain dangerous temptations to American citizens, the situation seems hardly to have improved in recent years. At least in older films, there was something grand and moving about the world of film. Thomson is, however, skeptical as to whether today's youth feel the "stealthy rapture" of film, or are "inclined to take it seriously."[17]

What is or might be the stealthy rapture of film? It is the sense that a new world is opening up before our eyes, that, however much we might not directly articulate it, we are being moved by a story, by characters in which we ourselves are in some measure invested, that we might discover or rediscover some truth about ourselves. In Walker Percy's *The Moviegoer*, the main character, Binx Bolling, a stockbroker and film fan who enjoys coastal drives in his MG and seducing his secretaries, has the intermittent sense that there is or could be something more to life. When this happens, he embarks, however briefly, on a quest:

> What is the nature of the search? You ask.
>
> Really it is very simple, at least for a fellow like me; so simple that it is easily overlooked.
>
> The search is what anyone would undertake if he were not sunk in the everydayness of his own life. This morning, for example, I felt as if I had come to myself on a strange land. And what does such a castaway do? Why, he pokes around the neighborhood and he doesn't miss a trick.
>
> To become aware of the possibility of the search is to be onto something. Not to be onto something is to be in despair.
>
> Movies are onto the search, but they screw it up. Their search always ends in despair. They like to show a fellow coming to himself in a strange place—but what does he do? He takes up with the local librarian, sets about proving to the local children what a nice fellow he is, and settles down with a vengeance.[18]

Partly inspired by his habit of moviegoing, his addiction to celluloid fantasy, Binx has a glimmer of the quest. He is not in complete despair, since, as

Kierkegaard defines it in the epigraph to this novel, ". . . the precise character of despair is this: it is unaware of being despair."[19] Thomson thinks that contemporary film is even less likely to produce or inspire characters like Binx. The mysteries present in great filmmaking have migrated further to the margins of the industry, which itself has moved steadily in the direction of attracting a young audience for whom camp, irony, endless motion, novelty, and spectacle are the real draws. Audiences now seem enraptured by the "capacity of the visible to exceed reality," rather than illumine it. As Thomson notes, TV has all but replaced film as the source of shared cultural stories. The TV world proclaims that there are all sorts of things happening to which you do not have "to pay attention" and in which you have no responsibility to "take part." On this issue, Thomson leaves us with a pressing pedagogical question, a question with which today's parents and educators have especially to grapple. How many of us have had any "education in the nature of moving imagery, its grammar, its laws or lawlessness, or how the naïve viewer is expected to distinguish news from fantasy, art from deception"?[20]

From Percy to Thomson, the worry about our current popular culture has much to do with the sheer passivity it induces in spectators. Training in the logic of images, in various art forms, and in advertising and political propaganda would also need to foster a spirit of questioning in youth. But this habit of questioning requires training, which itself must be informed by some sense of hope that the questions will lead somewhere, that we can, as Du Bois describes Francis, "read life's riddle and tell the world its true unraveling."[21] Narratives constructed out of nothing more than the spectacle of the prurient or the violent—or what is increasingly the case, prurient violence—these foster in youth a jaded cynicism and sap the soul of eros, as it was understood by Socrates and Francis, a longing for wholeness, for beauty, truth, and goodness. Eros is evident precisely in the instability Du Bois notes between the desirable and the yet more desirable.

One can be made aware of the tension between the desirable and the more desirable, as happened in the lives of Augustine and Francis, through the shattering realization that the pursuit of success, honor, money, pleasure, and fame—all the artificial needs conventional society and (in our time) the advertising industry persistently tell us we can't live without—are but husks and shadows of true happiness. There is a great scene early in Augustine's *Confessions* where as an ambitious and already successful young man he is on his way to give a speech in praise of the emperor.[22] Along the way, he meets a drunk beggar who earns his drink by happily wishing everyone well. Looking back on this, Augustine compares himself, filled with pride, self-concern, and anxiety, unfavorably to the beggar whose vices are more innocent and whose happiness is less filled with apprehension and disquiet. Not known for his wit, Augustine frequently uses humor to undermine the seriousness with which adult preoccupations, the games of grown-ups who have forgotten that they were once children and are oblivious of the true measure of things. As Pascal would quip centuries later, "A trifle consoles us because a trifle upsets us."[23]

A related awakening in the souls of Augustine and Francis concerns the insight that material reality is not all there is. In a quite different context, Thomson speaks of the crushing restriction of visibility, the tyranny of being stymied from probing beneath or beyond the surface, the inability to discover anything more than a series of events, wherein the only intelligible question is not a why question, but what happens next. (Or, as Jerry Seinfeld has commented on the male addiction to the remote control, "Men don't want to know what's on TV; they want to know what else is on.") To make the distinctions Thomson suggests we need to make—between news and fantasy or art and deception—would entail a conception of truth distinct from wish fulfillment or mere fantasy. In his book, *Truth and Truthfulness*, the late Bernard Williams, philosopher and atheist, and perhaps the most renowned British moral philosopher of the last half of the twentieth century, argues that what ails the university, particularly the humanities, is the institution's declining commitment to the virtues of truthfulness. Indeed, students are apt to see our society as caught in the grips of a crisis of truthfulness. They are cynical about politics because they see it as nothing more than deceptive spin; they are distrustful of corporations and churches because they see them as prone to self-interest and self-protecting deception, as in the Enron scandal and the child sex-abuse crisis in the American Catholic Church.

For Williams, truthfulness involves the virtues of sincerity, a habit of "fidelity, loyalty, or reliability," and accuracy, "desire for truth for its own sake—a passion for *getting it right*."[24] This is not to say that the achievement of truth is easy or ever complete or that we should ever quit engaging opposing positions. Indeed, university education is less about reaching peremptory answers than it is about developing habits of inquiry that equip students to make ever further progress by learning how to ask the next relevant question in whatever subject they happen to be studying. Williams's fine book stumbles a bit at the end when he poses the question, What in our time will inspire the sort of confidence that we need both to sustain hope in democracy and in the virtues of truthfulness? One of the paradoxes of our current situation, noted in John Paul II's encyclical *Fides et Ratio*, is that it may be religious institutions of higher learning that keep alive the mission of the university as the forum for the pursuit of truth, in both its complexity and anticipated unity.[25]

In a recent piece in the *Chronicle of Higher Education* entitled "One University under God," Stanley Fish notes the increasingly intellectual interest in religion, even on secular campuses. Fish notes that the old cultural assumption, especially prevalent in academe and the media, that we could "quarantine the religious impulse in the safe houses of the church, the synagogue, and the mosque" is coming undone. And he wonders whether the university is in a position to take seriously what is fast becoming the most important topic in the cultural and intellectual life of Americans. In so doing, he makes an important distinction: "It is one thing to take religion as an object of study and another to take religion seriously. To take religion seriously would be to regard it not as a phenomenon to be analyzed at arm's length, but as a candidate for the truth."[26]

Religious universities are likely to be attractive in the present marketplace of higher education precisely because they can do a better job of fulfilling what some students want from a university—rigorous discussion and debate about the big questions. I must confess that I am made uneasy about certain ways in which the old boundaries can come undone—for example, the ways in which creationism has come to replace serious science in some public schools or the way education itself can be reduced to a mere instrument of religious piety and become a form of catechesis or apologetics. As much as they may receive sustenance and inspiration from churches and contribute to them, a university is not itself a church. Nor does a professed commitment to the truth of the gospel or even to the unity of truth commit an individual or a university to any immediate sense of how things precisely fit together. Premature unification can be as disastrous to the intellect or to faith as can prolonged specialization. As Newman himself wrote:

> We know, not by a direct and simple vision, not at a glance, but, as it were, by piecemeal and accumulation, by a mental process, by going round an object, by the comparison, the combination, the mutual correction, the continual adaptation, of many partial notions, by the employment, concentration, and joint action of many faculties and exercises of mind. Such a union and concert of the intellectual powers, such an enlargement and development, such a comprehensiveness, is necessarily a matter of training . . . of discipline and habit.[27]

Of course, what Fish describes as the quarantining of religion can happen and does too often happen at religious universities, including Catholic universities. The specialization and fragmentation of the disciplines fosters the belief that theological matters fall exclusively under the purview of the theology or religion department or, what is even worse, that theology is not a matter for the academy at all, perhaps best left to the exclusive control of campus ministry or balkanized centers for the study of religion. Most depressing of all is the creation on Catholic campuses of centers of Catholic studies. This has the effect of reinforcing the most immature assumptions in our students, namely, that religion is to be neatly compartmentalized from the rest of life and that it really does not have much to do with the subject matters the university demands that we approach with intellectual seriousness. Like most persons in our culture, many of our students come to college thinking they already know all there is to know about God or even that there isn't anything there to be known. Religious universities should attack this complacency, a complacency that afflicts believers and unbelievers, liberals and conservatives.

It is instructive that as perceptive a teacher as Edmundson should describe his students as a "touch depressed." Beneath student cynicism about education, there is a kind of despair, a sense that, even were they to devote themselves to learning, it would not be worth it, that there is no great truth to be discovered, no great transformation to be experienced.

As writers from Plato to Tolkien have pointed out, our creaturely existence is characterized by wonder. Wonder strikes a balance between presumption and despair, between an overly confident certitude that we already have all the answers and a self-defeating skepticism about whether there is any truth to be found anywhere. As the Catholic philosopher Josef Pieper eloquently puts it, "Along with *not-knowing*, and *not-giving-up*, wonder is also . . . joy, as Aristotle said. . . . In this juncture of *Yes* and *No* is revealed the 'built-in' *hopefulness* of wonder, the very structure of hope, which is peculiar to the philosopher and to human existence in general."[28] Now this all sounds, well, it sounds wonderful. Who could object to joy or wonder? But what Pieper proposes is far from easy. For Pieper, the cultivation of wonder—and sadly after the first few years of life, it does need to be cultivated—requires the habit of receptive silence, of attentive listening to things, persons, and God. As Iris Murdoch observes, this openness to the world is a species of love, which she defines as "the painful realization that something other than myself exists." It requires practices of "unselfing."[29] Silent solitude is difficult and we flee it like death. Pascal captures this rather nicely when he describes young people's lives as "all noise, diversions, and thoughts for the future. But take away their diversion and you will see them bored to extinction. Then they feel their nullity without recognizing it, for nothing could be more wretched than to be intolerably depressed as soon as one is reduced to introspection with no means of diversion."[30] One way to put the challenge to our universities is to ask how silent they are. And what is the quality of our silences? There is no such thing as mere silence; it is always understood in relation to speech. And there are different types of silence, empty and full, sad and joyful. What sort of silence do we cultivate in our classrooms, our dorms, and our churches? There is the silence of bored students and bored faculty—we might call this Ferris Bueller silence. But there is also the full and active silence that leads to the formulation of an innovative hypothesis or the next relevant question, the hypothesis or question that can be an occasion for the shared experience of insight, the sort of moments for which teachers teach. It may seem quixotic even to raise the issue, but what sort of silence, if any, is there in our dorms? One of the greatest challenges facing universities today is to break down the division between student life and academic life. And what is the character of the silence in our worship and prayer? Prayer can itself be nothing more than idolatrous chatter. Do our liturgies foster silence where the encounter with the presence of God, where communion with the unseen God, is marked by the silent acknowledgment of His absence and otherness?

As Augustine eloquently states, the silent listening to the world opens us to the Word through whom all things have been made. Toward the end of his *Confessions*, he writes that "if the very soul" were to grow "silent to herself" and listen to created things,

> all these would say, "We did not create ourselves, but were created by Him who abides forever"—and if, having uttered this, they too should be silent, having stirred our ears to hear him who created them; and if then he alone spoke, not through them but by himself, that we might hear his word, not in fleshly tongue or angelic voice, nor sound of thunder, nor the obscurity of a parable, but might hear him—him for whose sake we love these things—if we could hear him without these, as we now strain ourselves to do, we then with rapid thought might touch on that Eternal Wisdom which abides over all.[31]

Calling Students to
Transformation

Charlene Kalinoski

What does it mean to be a student? A student studies and, of course, a student learns. Why? There are many reasons commonly cited: to serve the world, his or her country, society, community, and family; for self-realization and personal fulfillment; and to make a better living after graduation. The vocation of student is so commonplace that we usually take it for granted and leave it unexamined. But should we? Gilbert Highet wisely said, "It is a serious thing to interfere with another man's life."[1] Indeed, it is a serious matter for educators to influence the minds and hearts of their students, who will forever be affected by their labors in the classroom.

When I went to the library of the college where I teach to consult what scholars and sages have to say about the vocation of student, I discovered that there are many more books and articles written on education or teaching than there are on what it means to be a student. Most of the books and articles I found on being a college student were short on theory and long on such practical advice as academic success tips, how to get the most out of one's education, and how to prepare to make a graceful transition after graduation to the "real world" or graduate school. In many ways, this is not surprising. We all know that a college education is a commodity in our society, and that students typically need a "decent job" after graduation in order to provide for their legitimate needs and to repay their student loans. The young man or woman possessing a college degree or degrees also desires a superior job, since it is the gateway to a more desirable house, car, or lifestyle in general. While self-fulfillment may be found in community projects and activities, it is largely material in nature and concerns having a good life in the temporal sense. When higher education is so directly tied to the goal of material well-being or to the secular philosophy of the good life, which is increasingly hedonistic, the lofty yet achievable goal of education as an experience that deeply transforms is severely undermined. Higher education, however, has nobler ends. College professors often pursue the teaching profession in order to shape future generations and even the world through their efforts in the classroom. While contemporary colleges and universities certainly educate their students in various disciplines and afford them the opportunity to become better thinkers, writers, and speakers as well as to widen their worldview, I'm not convinced that most students feel "transformed" as they walk across the graduation platform to be awarded their undergraduate degrees; I would argue, rather, that they feel "confirmed," and not in any religious sense.

Are undergraduate students asked to ponder the vocation of student seriously and deeply, to discern their callings as a student, and to what they are being called in life? Probably not. It is true that students take classes on a large array of subjects, are afforded many experiences designed to enrich their education such as study abroad, and are the beneficiaries of services such as those that help them improve their study skills and identify prospective internships. But confronting students directly with the challenge of addressing their vocation as student and their life callings is not a regular feature of campus life. It is assumed that students will ponder these issues on their own, which some do to a degree, no doubt. Integrating this exercise into their undergraduate experience is another matter entirely, and represents quite a challenge for educators, one that we may not be prepared to undertake immediately. However, if this were done successfully, students could be "transformed" by spiritual experience rather than merely "confirmed" in a secular philosophy of the good life. Faith-related institutions of higher learning have a decided advantage over their secular counterparts in this regard. It is commonly thought that the academy is purely the realm of "Athens," and not "Jerusalem." It can be argued, though, that "Jerusalem" can deepen the "Athens" experience for our students and transform them in ways "Athens" alone cannot.

We are fortunate to live in a society in which opportunities for postsecondary education are plentiful and relatively affordable to many. Because we value education highly and are largely literate, we tend to forget what it is like not to know how to read or write, or to live in a nation in which education is not universally available. I recently read *Los de Abajo*, Mariano Azuela's

1915 novel about the Mexican Revolution, with an upper-level Spanish class. This novel, whose title literally means "Those from below"—that is, the "lower ranks of society"—reminded my students and me of such circumstances. In the early stages of the revolution, the protagonist, Demetrio Macías, a *campesino* or peasant, and his band of soldiers fight against the corrupt regime of President Porfirio Díaz. As the revolution advances, its leaders tragically come to fight against each other to determine who will lead Mexico. Demetrio Macías is a magnificent soldier, but as the politics of the conflict become more complex, it is apparent that he no longer understands the war he is fighting. Only one of his soldiers, Luis Cervantes, has attended university. Demetrio's illiterate soldiers note the difference between Luis and them. They muse: " 'In truth, people who know how to read and write understand things.' And the two sighed sadly, 'How great it would be to know how to read and write.' " As further rifts develop between the revolutionaries, Demetrio's superior general asks him on which side he will fight. Demetrio is confused and cannot answer. After some deliberation, he says: "Look, don't ask me questions; I'm not schooled. You know that all you have to do is say to me, 'Demetrio, do this and then this.' That's all there is to it."[2] My students took particular note of this passage in the novel and were unsettled by it. How could the brave and clever Demetrio not know what to do? Why couldn't he give General Natera a more reasoned answer? Yes, the education we have been privileged to receive since early youth, and probably take for granted because it is so expected and "normal," does shape us in dramatic ways; without it we would truly be different people and we would find it far more difficult to understand and function in the complex world in which we live.

Unlike Demetrio Macías, contemporary educators and students have many educational opportunities and access to much information—so much information that we are saturated by it. In this information age it is increasingly important to separate what is significant from what is not; one can get lost easily in the ever-growing forest of data. It has been said that "[i]n the sixteenth century, it was possible to have read every book ever printed . . . [and that] [t]he number of books published between 1945 and 1970 alone equaled that issued during the entire 500-year period between the invention of the printing press and the end of World War I."[3] From the benchmark of the current year, we can estimate that the number of books produced since 1970 has greatly exceeded those published from 1945 to 1970, most likely doubling or tripling that number.

Argentine writer Jorge Luis Borges seems to allude to a state of information overload in his short story "The Library of Babel," from his famed collection *Ficciones*. Borges was a lover of books and libraries and once worked in a municipal library in Buenos Aires as a humble cataloger; he later became the Director of the National Library of Argentina. His fictional library is a vast, fantastical place. The narrator of his story states, "The universe (which others call the Library) is composed of an indefinite, perhaps infinite, number of hexagonal galleries." The library is rigorously organized: "Five shelves correspond to each one of the walls of each hexagon; each shelf contains thirty-two books of a uniform format; each book is made up of four hundred and ten pages; each page of forty lines; each line of some eighty black letters." The library of Babel contains all books, which provokes a feeling of "extravagant joy," for "men felt themselves lords of a secret, intact treasure. There was no personal or universal problem whose eloquent solutions did not exist—in some hexagon." In spite of the library's immense holdings, the knowledge it contains does not satisfy the narrator, who longs to find a book that will explain all the others. Borges himself was not religious in any conventional sense, a characteristic that the narrator of his story appears to share. It is interesting, however, that the narrator, one of the librarians of Babel, has "journeyed in search of a book; perhaps the catalogue of catalogues." He adds:

> To me, it does not seem unlikely that on some shelf of the universe there lies a total book. I pray the unknown gods that some man—even if only one man, and though it have been thousands of years ago!—may have examined and read it. . . . May heaven exist, though my place be in hell. Let me be outraged and annihilated, but may Thy enormous Library be justified, for one instant, in one being.[4]

Borges's short stories, like Shakespeare's sonnets, send the mind racing in search of meaning through fields that are especially lush. "The Library of Babel" is a short, complex narrative that defies facile interpretation, but for this reader it functions as an apt metaphor for our age, the information age.[5] Like the librarians of Babel, we point with pride to the vast amounts of information we have collected, organized, and cataloged. Information and meaning, however, are separate categories, and vast amounts of information don't necessarily yield understanding, particularly understanding in any teleological sense. The title of Borges's story isn't promising. The reference to Babel suggests the elusiveness of real insight and understanding, while the narrator of the story indicates an attitude of resignation to it. This modern fable may raise the question in some readers' minds of whether such resignation is the only response to an increase in information that threatens to bury rather than liberate us. Do we educators fail to engage the issues that are ultimately the most important ones?

In his recent book, Harold Bloom asks, *Where Shall Wisdom Be Found?* The title of the work is intriguing. It is remarkable that a prominent scholar values wisdom and searches for it openly. Bloom says his work "rises out of personal need, reflecting a quest for sagacity that might solace and clarify the traumas of aging, of recovering from grave illness, and of grief for the loss of beloved friends." *Where Shall Wisdom Be Found?* is both a personal reflection and a scholarly work. In part its value resides in its audacity: "Whether pious or not," Bloom states, "we all of us learn to crave wisdom, wherever it can be found."[6] So, where shall we look? Can wisdom be found in the contemporary academy? Professors are highly trained hunters and gatherers of information; students are our apprentices. Our expeditions are often thrilling, and wisdom no doubt is found along the way, but we usually do not acknowledge it. There are no academic trophies awarded for wisdom. As our students come to colleges and universities to be educated, we may well ask if wisdom is a fitting goal of this experience. Although wisdom would be a difficult outcome to measure, we should encourage our students to seize it when they find it.

Can we find the word *wisdom* mentioned in the mission statements of our colleges and universities? In conducting an informal survey of the mission statements of twenty-one colleges and universities in the state of Virginia, I discovered the word in only one of them, that of Bridgewater College.[7] In a recent essay in the *Chronicle of Higher Education*, Harry R. Lewis, a professor of computer science and former dean of Harvard College, wonders if Harvard has lost its way because "Harvard teaches students but does not make them wise." Lewis suggests a new course, arguing, "The university's leaders must believe in the process of self-discovery, and they must articulate that belief."[8] The absence of wisdom is apparently beginning to be noted in contemporary higher education, even in secular institutions. Education is not just about mastering subjects; it also entails the values and insights needed to help one navigate through life personally and professionally. Why have many in higher education forgotten this?

Demetrio Macías and his raggedy band of soldiers would have benefited not only from some formal education but also from wisdom, the type that could guide them through difficult and unfamiliar circumstances. Although Demetrio and his men take up the cause of freedom and justice, they lose their way morally. Spoiled by their military successes, they feel empowered to kill indiscriminately, to rob, to violate, and to destroy property. The public they believed they were liberating comes to abhor and to fear them. For instance, when the band of soldiers enters the town of Juchipila, one of Demetrio's soldiers notes how different their reception is from the ones they received at the beginning of the war: "When we used to arrive in town, they would ring the church bells for us, and the people would come out to greet us with music and flags. They would say 'Viva!' and even set off fireworks." To this observation, Demetrio adds, "They don't love us anymore." Another soldier replies, "But why should they, my friend?"[9] It is clear that the townspeople realize that the soldiers are fighting not for the collective cause of Mexican freedom but for themselves, and so they are feared.

The sad truth is that Demetrio and his soldiers were essentially brave and decent men. As was the case in many revolutions and conflicts before and after the Mexican Revolution, their moral and ethical standards were lost in the fog of war, to the detriment of others and themselves. Luis Cervantes, the university-educated soldier in Demetrio's small army, also participates in many of the cruel excesses of the group. The condition of having been educated to whatever extent is not a guarantee against inhuman behavior, as we well know. Demetrio Macías and his soldiers lose their way morally in the throes of revolution; our moral values are similarly "fogged" even though we live in times of relative peace. We also are living through a revolution of sorts, but one that is more social in nature and that is driven by science, politics, economics, and culture among other forces. Revolutions are inevitable, and they often bring good effects and positive change. History provides us with abundant evidence, however, of the senseless destruction and suffering that also accompany them. What can higher education do to help us and our youth through this and future revolutions? It can do quite a lot, but it needs to do more than educate in the sense of transferring knowledge; it needs to impart wisdom in the form of institutional values, which should also have their place in the classroom.

In Borges's "Library of Babel," the librarians search feverishly through the labyrinthine and seemingly infinite corridors until they exhaust their lives. The narrator, worn out by his journeys through the library, prepares for his own death. "Once dead," he states, "there will not lack pious hands to hurl me over the banister; my sepulcher shall be the unfathomable air: my body will sink lengthily and will corrupt and dissolve in the wind engendered by the fall, which is infinite."[10] The modern academy has some characteristics in common with the library of Babel. Contemporary scholars, like the librarians of Babel, peruse the shelves of libraries and those in cyberspace in search of knowledge that is ultimately incomplete. Many in the academy amass information about a universe that for them is ultimately meaningless. Aren't we training our students to do the same until they, like us, are hurled over the banister, so to speak?

The library of Babel, by its very name, evokes associations with multiplicity and fragmentation. Education should be about wholeness, integrity. In *The Many Faces of Virtue*, Donald DeMarco writes that "our unity of personality demands the integration of its parts." His reflection on the virtue of integrity goes on to state, "But the integrity that is perhaps most basic to a human being is the one that binds one's *being* to one's *behavior*, *endowment* to *achievement*, or *giftedness* to *response*."[11] The vocation of student or the call to learning involves discerning what really matters, what is truly meaningful. Learning should aspire to be more than the accumulation of knowledge in the form of course units or hours, opportunities for service, or special educational experiences such as study aboard. For education to aspire toward integration and wholeness, there needs to be a well-articulated framework of values to work from and within. In the opinion of this writer, church-sponsored higher education has a decided advantage over its secular counterpart, which tends toward multiplicity and fragmentation. Christian higher education may be limiting or reductive in the eyes of its critics, but it aspires to wholeness, the sort that binds a student's education to his or her individual calling. It acknowledges that every person has a special calling entrusted to him or her by God. Secular higher education cannot make this claim and so places value on open-endedness, the freedom not to have to choose.

One of the paradoxes of Christianity is that it promises freedom precisely to those who make choices. One is liberated by choosing not to do what one often feels most compelled to; this has always been Christianity's challenge. To be a Christian means giving up behaviors and attitudes that are often those embraced by society. Finding one's true freedom by not giving in to one's desires and by ignoring perceived social norms is a new, untried concept for many in our society, especially those who are unchurched or poorly churched. Certainly, the discovery of one's vocation and the subsequent living of it is a vital part of the Christian concept of freedom.

The life of Saint Benedict offers some uncomfortable, yet still valuable insights into higher education. According to Pope Gregory the Great's account of his life, Benedict, the son of a prominent patrician family, was "sent . . . to Rome for a liberal education." Benedict did not respond favorably to his new environment. The narrative reads, "When he found many of the students there abandoning themselves to vice, he decided to withdraw from the world he had been preparing to enter; for he was afraid that if he acquired any of its learning he would be drawn down with them to his eternal ruin." [12] This is not a ringing endorsement of liberal education, which has a long tradition in many colleges in the United States and throughout the West. We must remember, of course, that modern liberal arts institutions were often founded by religious orders such as the Benedictines, or by denominational churches. As we in the West live in an age in which traditional religious values are embattled, perhaps we have forgotten why colleges and universities sprung out of Christianity. I don't think the answer is simply because they were founded in a "more religious" period in our collective history. The founders of these institutions intended to provide the wholeness in the students' educational experience that would otherwise be lacking in a curriculum that was solely dedicated to the liberal arts. Knowledge of the liberal arts is liberating, but more so when encompassed by the liberating effects of Christianity.

The *Allegory of the Liberal Arts*, a painting by the Italian Renaissance artist Biagio D'Antonio da Firenze (c. 1445–c. 1510) depicts personifications of the seven liberal arts arranged on a mountain that is towerlike in appearance. [13] At the top of the mountain sits a prelate, symbolizing "theology." A classically styled golden door provides entrance to the mountain, implying that some but not all will pass its threshold to make the ascent. Above the mountain are heavens consisting of spheres that contain the moon, the planets, and the stars, reflecting the universe as it was conceived by Aristotle and Ptolemy. In accordance with medieval Christian thought, God sits enthroned above all, encircled by angels in the empyrean sphere. [14] Biagio D'Antonio da Firenze's depiction of learning contrasts vividly with Borges's library, a tower of hexagons that reaches ambitiously but blindly into the universe, serving ultimately as a monument to the knowledge stored within it, but nothing more. For me the two towers, those of Biagio D'Antonio da Firenze and Jorge Luis Borges, serve as allegories of higher education. Students have a choice: do they wander the hexagons of the library of Babel or do they attempt to ascend a mountain benignly watched over by God himself? Will they elect wholeness or multiplicity? Will they aspire to integration or will they settle for its opposite?

One of the problems with higher education in the United States is that the critical difference between secular and church-related institutions is not more clearly articulated or understood. The latter offer their students the possibility not only of knowledge, but of wholeness—that is, seeing others, the world around them, and themselves through the "luminous eye(s)" of faith, to borrow a phrase from Ephrem (c. 306–373), one of the Syriac Fathers.[15] If church-related colleges are to aspire to such a lofty but worthy goal, they are going to have to be serious and purposeful about presenting Christian values, and about challenging the criticism that this system of values will limit students with the notion that it will expand and enrich them.

As we know, students often enter colleges and universities without a firm idea of what they will study or where they are headed in life, which can be the cause of considerable anxiety to them and their parents. The wholeness or integrity that DeMarco writes of is, once again, one that "binds one's being to one's *behavior, endowment* to *achievement,* or *giftedness* to *response.*"[16] The calling of the student to wholeness involves the patient and careful discernment of individual callings, which requires a level of personal and especially spiritual awareness. Discerning one's calling is a lifelong process, but one with which the Christian tradition has much experience. Church-related higher education can bequeath this legacy to its students, getting them off to a good start on the project of their lives. Reminding students they are created in the image of God and have been given talents to share with the world for the greater good is a very reassuring message in our anxiety-ridden world. The Christian tradition presents a system for understanding and embracing life and all it contains from its beginning until its end.

Turning to practical matters, how can the Christian academy do this? There are many opportunities for meaningful reflection on vocation and personal wholeness in first-year advising groups and seminars, in senior capstone courses, or in other general education courses. Cocurricular activities can be enlisted in the project in addition to academic ones.

The call of the student to wholeness is also a call to understanding one's cultural heritage. Indisputably, the Judeo-Christian tradition is a foundational pillar of Western civilization; not to have solid knowledge of it places one at risk of a profound separation from the collective past. How can one truly appreciate many works of literature, art, or music if one does not understand and sympathize with the system of religious values in which they were created? While it is true that this religious heritage has been undermined and rejected by many over the course of several centuries, it remains inextricably woven into the Western experience.

The Spanish writer and philosopher Miguel de Unamuno is a good example of a modern skeptic. He wanted to embrace Christianity but had difficulty making the leap of faith. His personal spiritual crisis is a frequent theme in his works. In the novel *St. Manuel the Good, Martyr,* the main character is a priest who, like Unamuno, respects Christianity but doesn't believe in eternal life. Although Don Manuel suffers a spiritual crisis, he wants his parishioners to have a firm and robust faith. Unamuno finished the first edition of this work in 1930 as political and social tensions were building that would soon erupt into the Spanish Civil War. His character, Don Manuel, alludes to the conflict of ideologies present at that time. He says "If there is a new society in which there are neither rich nor poor; wealth is fairly distributed; and everything belongs to everyone, then what? Don't you think that life's tediousness will surge forth even more forcefully from the general well-being?" Don Manuel understands that the restless human spirit will not be satisfied by political or social solutions alone, and he wisely fears the violence that civil conflict can entail. He preaches, therefore, "Resignation and charity in everyone and for everyone."[17] Don Manuel attempts to protect his parishioners from the competing ideologies of their time by urging them to live Christian lives. It seems that Unamuno himself feared the consequences of a de-Christianized society, in spite of being a skeptic. Sadly, his worst fears were realized when war broke out in 1936; he died a few months later.

Jorge Luis Borges, like Unamuno, also recognized the dangers presented by aggressive ideologies. His short story "Tlön, Uqbar, Orbis Tertius" is an indictment of Nazism and other human-made political systems that promise utopias but result in earthly hells. In his story, Borges invents his own ideology, that of Tlön. The narrator of the story says, "Ten years ago, any symmetrical system whatsoever which gave the appearance of order—dialectical materialism, anti-Semitism, Nazism—was enough to fascinate men. Why not fall under the spell of Tlön and submit to the minute and vast evidence of an ordered planet?"[18] The Judeo-Christian tradition, unlike Tlön's ideology and the many "isms" of the nineteenth and twentieth centuries, is not manmade but asserts that it is revealed. Within this tradition, one of its elemental stories, that of the Fall of Adam and Eve, serves as a permanent reminder of human frailty, that human beings are easily led astray and confused. As the verb *to educate* means "to lead forth," the church-related academy does so by educating within the system of Christian values. If students are to aspire to wholeness with regard to their individual callings, they need to be led forth to knowledge within the framework of the Judeo-Christian tradition and its values. Attending to this call is the distinct mission of church-related institutions of higher education, which transform students as they educate; within their walls wisdom can be found.

The Catholic University Contribution and Formation of Catholic Teachers

Deborah Wallace Ruddy

A couple of years ago, Helen Alvare, a prominent Catholic lawyer and spokesperson on a range of controversial issues such as abortion, euthanasia, capital punishment, and feminism in the church, gave a lecture to undergraduates on vocation. She spoke compellingly about work as a vocation and about the integration of faith with professional life. She urged students on various preprofessional tracks to become the best in their fields and then, having achieved excellence by worldly standards, to place it all in the service of Christ and his church: "[P]ursue your disciplines as if they are an end in themselves and then surprise everybody and turn that intelligence to the service of Christ."[1] This recommendation—first become a professional, then learn theology and live out your vocation in service to Christ—set me to thinking about Catholic school teacher formation.[2]

In this essay, I intend to examine critically this "values-added" approach in Catholic school teacher formation.[3] In this approach, the distinctively Catholic elements of education are "added" to the standard teacher preparation requirements established by local and national accrediting agencies.[4] By examining this approach, I hope to diagnose some problems in Catholic teacher preparation and point the way toward more creative, interdisciplinary work that can forge a better integration of the Catholic teacher's faith formation with his or her professional preparation.[5]

I will begin by reviewing briefly some current "signs of the times" in Catholic schools, their teachers, and teacher formation programs. Next, as the current cultural and demographic shifts in Catholic education today raise the issue of Catholic identity, I will focus on some key aspects of Catholic education, namely, Catholic anthropology and the human vocation. The Catholic understanding of the human person can serve as one illustration of how Catholicism offers a rich and compelling vision of education that can lead to the strengthening and initiating of programs and courses targeted specifically at Catholic school teacher formation. Third, I will mention some ways that Catholic universities today can respond to the specific needs of Catholic school teacher formation. In sum, this chapter aims to provide some conceptual clarity about how a distinctively Catholic approach to education might shape Catholic teacher preparation programs from the ground up, rather than maintaining standard teacher preparation and supplementing it with Christian approaches to the field. Given the lack of current scholarship on the topic of Catholic school teacher formation, this study aims to be introductory with the goal of spurring continued research, dialogue, and collaboration among philosophers, theologians, and education scholars.

SIGNS OF THE TIMES

Catholic primary and secondary education has undergone myriad changes over the past fifty years or so. Most notable for my purposes is the shift to a predominantly lay teaching staff, which has taken place alongside the secularization of teacher education programs at Catholic colleges and universities. John L. Watzke, an education scholar, writes:

> Although the shift from religious and clergy to a lay teaching force has unfolded since the 1960s, there has been no national plan for this transition, no systematic program to form lay teachers for work in Catholic schools, and an increasing reliance on public education as a model for the professional preparation of teachers for these schools.[6]

In 1950 over 90 percent of Catholic school teachers were in religious orders. Today 95 percent of the teaching staff are laypeople, most of whom (85 percent) are Catholic.[7] When Catholic school teachers were largely religious and clerics, their religious communities provided the faith context for their studies and their teaching. Their communal lives had an intentional focus that nurtured religious, intellectual, and moral formation. While many lay teachers have found creative and fruitful ways to integrate faith and work, the formation challenges remain largely unresolved.

Today there are a variety of needs met by Catholic schools—namely, passing on the faith to the next generation, breaking the cycle of poverty, providing a corrective or alternative to the public school system, and giving suburban parents an alternative to private nonreligious schools. It has been observed, though, that Catholic schools are unsure about how distinctive they really are and whether there is a unifying vision for them among Catholic educators.[8] The diversity of needs met by Catholic schools, as well as the increasing number of non-Catholics and poorly catechized teachers and students within those schools, gives greater urgency to questions of Catholic school teacher formation and identity. One common concern expressed by bishops and education leaders alike is that students and teachers are unformed in the essentials of the Catholic faith.[9]

By the close of the Second Vatican Council in 1965 and in the years immediately following it, as the Catholic school teaching staff shifted dramatically from a religious to lay teaching corps, a second major shift occurred: most Catholic postsecondary schools of education, facing financial and enrollment pressures, moved away from their original missions of educating teachers for Catholic schools.[10] They broadened their educational task, marketed themselves to a wider range of students interested mostly in public school education, and put in place programs that focused primarily, if not exclusively, on meeting state certification requirements. Catholic schools themselves began hiring many teachers without any notable Catholic dimension to their teaching preparation.

Prior to Vatican II, particularly from the 1930s to the 1950s, many education students at Catholic colleges and universities took a substantial number of theology and philosophy courses as part of a broad liberal arts program that oriented them to a Catholic vision of education. Mario O. D'Souza, professor of religion and education at the University of St. Michael's College in Toronto, observes that "[i]n the era just prior to the Second Vatican Council, Catholic education literature and teacher preparation programs considered education to be a primarily philosophical process, governed by a theology of education."[11] Catholic university schools of education taught about the distinctively Catholic approach to education, which implicitly relied on philosophy, for example, to provide an account of the human person and on theology to give a complete account of the human condition and destiny. There also existed a lively discussion among Catholic university professors of humanities and education about a Catholic philosophy of education. Over these decades, several books treated key characteristics of a Catholic view of education and compared these characteristics to secular approaches to education such as materialism, progressivism, scientific realism, and experimentalism.[12] For the most part, these works were apologetic and sought to demonstrate the fallacies of these modern approaches to education. Some acknowledged the positive contributions of new pedagogical ideas,[13] but most were set on showing the gulf between a Christian and secular view. Although this stance of mistrust and wariness too often failed to truly dialogue with the best in current educational thought, there was nonetheless a community of notable scholars devoted to philosophical and theological inquiry about education which has since waned.

Although scholarship in Catholic educational theory moved increasingly away from philosophy and theology in the 1950s and 1960s, drawing more heavily on psychology and other social sciences, there was nonetheless a substantial cross-fertilization between philosophy, theology, history, and education.[14] John L. Elias, a professor of religion and education at Fordham University, illustrates the dissipation of this cross-fertilization with the example of changes at Fordham:

> At one time there was a Division of Philosophy and History of Education, in which a course in the Catholic philosophy of education was taught. Professors John Redden, Francis Ryan, and John Probst taught and wrote on the subject. In the 1950s the Jesuit educator John Donohue taught a similar course. But in the mid-1960s the department was abolished, and history and philosophy courses moved within the new urban education program. A course on Catholic philosophy of education was no longer offered.[15]

In the years following Vatican II, this Catholic philosophy of education itself faded from the academic scene.[16] John L. Elias writes:

> The study of the philosophy of education—undertaken by treating various schools of philosophical thought—was largely displaced by analytic philosophy, a study of issues, and more recently by a study of the subdisciplines of philosophy. The analytic philosophers gradually outnumbered all other philosophers of education in meetings of societies and in published articles.
>
> By the 1960s the analytic philosophy of education had become the predominant mode of philosophizing in the English-speaking world. This mode was opposed to all normative and synthetic approaches to philosophy that attempted to prescribe that education should be based on certain assumptions about the human person, human society, and the educational enterprise. Analysts subjected educational language, slogans, arguments, and policies to careful scrutiny in applying principles of logical positivism and ordinary language philosophy. These philosophies tended to reject all metaphysical views, such as presented in neo-Thomism, and other normative and metaphysical philosophies.[17]

In general, by the 1970s philosophy of education was no longer a major subject area in most education programs.[18]

Today the majority of students in most Catholic college and university education programs will teach in public schools. These programs, largely separate from the grounding and synthesizing influence of philosophy and theology, now function more independently, as do most other university disciplines. Yet the design of an education major comes largely from external pressure in the form of accrediting organizations determining the best preparation for public school teaching. The all-encompassing demands of these accrediting bodies is not rigorously questioned, so education programs at Catholic colleges and universities are nearly indistinguishable from their secular counterparts, except that their students may have a few philosophy and theology courses as part of their undergraduate core requirements.[19] In their student teaching, Catholic school teachers are prepared for teaching in a variety of educational settings, but without a particular focus on, or sometimes even mention of, Catholic schools.[20] One may ask, on whose terms are Catholic schools determining teacher preparedness?

John Watzke has recently completed several studies of current trends in teacher education programs at Catholic colleges and universities. He explains that the majority of the faculty in such programs have no experience in Catholic schools. In his study he notes that many faculty members regarded preservice teaching experience in Catholic elementary or high schools as "professionally limiting."[21] Given the common perception in Catholic higher education that secular teacher preparation is the best preparation for teachers entering multiple contexts, Watzke presents a compelling challenge, arguing for the effectiveness of an alternative teacher education program, Alliance for Catholic Education (ACE), sponsored by the University of Notre Dame, that is intentionally focused on a comprehensive and integrated preparation of teachers for Catholic education.[22]

The ACE program is unique in its design. First, faculty are focused on teaching education topics in light of Catholic Christian faith so that students are guided in a certain habit of mind whereby the life of faith and its intellectual dimensions are integrated with the topics and methods of their education studies. Teachers, for example, explore the idea of leadership as service with "Christ the teacher" as a model; the meaning of teaching as a God-given vocation permeates the program as a whole; and the significance of educating "the whole student" morally, intellectually, and spiritually is explored in-depth. Moreover, teachers are encouraged to help their own students become aware of the way God calls each of us in a personal way to a particular kind of work. ACE members also live together in community for two years, praying together regularly, sharing meals, and discussing their personal and professional lives together. The experience of both spiritual and professional support deepens their teaching commitment and the understanding of teaching as a unique and noble calling. Support from mentor teachers who understand and give witness to Catholic education also has a profound effect on the professional and personal development of new teachers.[23] The multipronged approach of the ACE model seems most effective in addressing the tendency toward compartmentalization more common in programs that simply "add" theology or liturgical experiences to standard education courses.

In recent years several Catholic colleges and universities have begun institutes or established courses or tracks that are designed specifically for Catholic school educators. The "values-added" approach is followed by many of these initiatives—students fulfill their professional requirements, and theology courses are "added" to their professional preparation. In some cases there are formation experiences such as retreats and liturgies that enhance the students' faith formation, but integration between faith and the content of education is still lacking. Two experiences of mine at the University of St. Thomas have shown me the need for this integration and the challenges it poses to today's academic culture of specialization.

For the past five years I have taught an interdisciplinary course at the University of St. Thomas called "Christian Faith and the Education Profession," which fulfills a third-level theology core requirement and is part of a core course series called "Faith and the Professions."[24] Most of the education students in the class, who are juniors or seniors and interested in teaching in Catholic schools, have never been introduced to a Christian understanding of vocation or to some of the fundamental connections between the Catholic intellectual tradition and the field of education. Claims to the unity of knowledge, the complementary relationship between faith and reason, and the universal aspiration to truth all have implications for how we learn and how we teach. Without the habit of thinking comprehensively about one's faith, education students planning to teach in Catholic schools find it hard to see the relevance of their faith for their education studies. Without these connections there tends to be a rather superficial grasp of the Catholic schools' aims of suffusing Christian faith throughout the curriculum[25] and of educating the "whole student."[26]

For the past six years, I have also been involved with the Murray Institute, a partnership between the schools of education and divinity of the University of St. Thomas and the Archdiocese of St. Paul-Minneapolis.[27] Since 1992, the institute has been seeking to address Catholic school teacher formation needs in light of the shift from religious to lay teaching staff. Through both degree and non-degree programs, the institute provides tuition-free education in courses that enhance professional competencies and theological formation. The institute has generally followed the "values-added" approach, although the faculty are increasingly seeing the need for more deliberately integrative subjects and programs that connect theology and education. As both an instructor and committee member of the Murray Institute, I hear Catholic school teachers and principals commenting that their theology courses are personally enriching but remain theoretical, abstract, and disconnected from their everyday work of teaching and administrating in a Catholic school.[28] While grateful for the personal edification received from courses such as "Christian Theological Tradition" or "Foundations of Biblical Interpretation," these teachers and principals often remain unclear about how such topics inform their subject matter, their pedagogy, or their administration.[29]

In their Catholic social teaching course, for example, teachers learn about how the incarnation gives new meaning to principles like human dignity, solidarity, and justice. But when asked to create Catholic social teaching lessons for their students, these teachers tend to switch gears and treat Catholic social teaching principles in nontheological, purely humanistic terms, seemingly unaware that the distinctly Christian dimensions go unmentioned in their lessons. There is a personal/professional separation in the teachers' own lives, perhaps, and the courses get channeled into these compartments. Certainly, Catholic social teaching draws from both theological and philosophical language to reach a wide audience, but it was striking to see the difficulty teachers have in integrating the theological into concepts that were more familiar to them from secular contexts. How can Catholic school teacher preparation overcome this split between the personal and the professional, which relegates faith matters to the private sphere? Such a habit of mind seems to be cultivated or, at least, reinforced in the standard teacher preparation process.[30]

One challenge in Catholic school teacher preparation is to move beyond relatively general treatments of terms such as human dignity, social justice, and vocation—which in a vague form receive general approval within most education circles—in order to provide a more robust account of these concepts in a Christian context. Connecting, for example, Catholic social teaching concepts with core tenets of faith such as the incarnation and the Eucharist can provide an integrated approach to the social mission of the church. This is all the more important given the current needs of Catholic school students. A 1998 Vatican document on education makes the following observation:

> [A] vague sort of generosity is characteristic of many young people. Filled with enthusiasm, they are eager to join in popular causes. Too often, however, these movements are without any specific orientation or inner coherence. It is important to channel this potential for good and, when possible, to give the orientation that comes from the light of faith.[31]

One reason for this gap has to do with what William F. Losito, a professor of educational philosophy, observes about the current dearth of scholars who are interested in these integrating questions:

> [T]here is no community of Catholic intellectuals pursuing a coherent agenda of inquiry to serve as a significant resource for educational leaders who are grappling with the formulation of a sacred vision for education in a secular, pluralistic society. . . . [A] community of Catholic intellectuals has not emerged devoted to philosophical inquiry about education that finds its wellspring in the Catholic intellectual tradition.[32]

How then can a Catholic framework be integrated into topics in education courses? Without such a community of scholars and the curricula that could flow from this community, I suspect that Catholic teachers will continue to adopt rather schizophrenic habits of mind, giving secular explanations for concepts that have rich Catholic significance and thereby compromising the distinctive character of Catholic education and its evangelizing mission.[33]

While efforts like those of the Murray Institute are laudable and show a marked improvement from the recent past, this kind of formation of Catholic school teachers still fails to take seriously the intellectual character of faith in engaging professional knowledge. When Catholic school teacher education programs rely on theology courses and faith-formation programs to *supplement* secular professional education, the theology and professional components often run along parallel—and therefore nonintersecting—paths. As a result, teachers-in-training do not learn how to bring their theological knowledge to bear on their competencies in education. To avoid this two-path phenomenon, there needs to be a more intentional integration of a Catholic view of education with the rest of the curricula of teacher education. This is a new task that cannot be accomplished by looking back with nostalgia hoping to recover a supposed golden age of Catholic education and teacher preparation. Catholic schools and teachers are in a new situation today, and while drawing from the past is essential, something new is needed. This new integration will raise a variety of unexplored questions. What is the relationship, for example, between the theological aims of a Catholic school and the pedagogical methods taught in a secular education program? If the theological preparation remains extraneous to most of the curricular and pedagogical lessons in education, then it is no wonder that the religious mission of Catholic schools is only superficially engaged or confined to religion class.

In light of the current situation of Catholic schools and Catholic school teacher preparation, the need for developing a comprehensive Catholic education theory could not be more pressing. Drawing on the rich heritage of Catholic thought on education, a contemporary Catholic education theory will need to be based on the synthesizing disciplines of philosophy and theology but also to draw on the psychological and social sciences as well. Fostering real partnerships with faculty in theology, philosophy, history, the social sciences, and education will be a challenge in the highly specialized atmosphere of higher education today. Perhaps by turning to the foundational education topic of the human person the relevance of this much needed interdisciplinary scholarship will become clear. The church's reflection on education has always emerged from a philosophical and theological understanding of the human person. Due to the dynamic character of our humanity, we need guidance and instruction to cultivate our human capacities and to become fully human. This dependence on others to teach us provides the primary rationale for education in the Christian tradition. More-over, the delicacy and importance of this task of helping others to develop their humanity in light of God is the principal reason for teaching being viewed as a noble calling within the Christian tradition. Teachers who live out their work as a vocation witness to a life of integrity for their students and help their students understand themselves as persons called by God to a particular path that leads to the fullness of their humanity.

CATHOLIC ANTHROPOLOGY AND VOCATION

In this next section, guided by the thought of Jacques Maritain, I will exam-ine a Catholic understanding of the human person, the vocational nature of teaching, and the relevance of both for a distinctly Catholic teacher forma-tion program. Maritain, one of the foremost Catholic, neo-Thomist philoso-phers of the twentieth century and a prominent voice in the development of a Christian philosophy of education,[34] wrote two classic works on education: *Education at the Crossroads* (1943) and *The Education of Man* (1962).[35] Several scholars have noted that Jacques Maritain's work on education has been one of the few notable modern efforts to put forth, in a general but systematic way, a Catholic view of education.[36]

Laying out a distinctly Catholic vision of education, Maritain held that education cannot be properly studied apart from philosophy and, ultimately, theology. He begins *Education at the Crossroads* with the assertion that the chief task of education consists of shaping the individual person, who is called to become fully human. He critically observes that his contemporaries know about "primitive man, or Western man, or the man of the Renaissance, or the man of the industrial era, or the criminal man, or the bourgeois man, or the working man, but they wonder what is meant when we speak of man."[37] In other words, we rightly want to know how history, social environ-ment, nationality, and gender shape a particular human person or group of persons, but our most fundamental identity, our human identity, escapes us.

When philosophy and theology are not integrated into teacher education programs, teachers and students do not address the question of human iden-tity at its deepest level. As a result of this gap in understanding and forma-tion, teachers are ill-prepared for helping students take on the difficult but important task of "becoming who [they] are,"[38] namely, human beings. Mar-itain writes:

> [E]ducation needs primarily to know what man is, what is the nature of
> man and the scale of values it essentially involves; and the purely scien-
> tific idea of man, because it ignores "being-as-such," does not know
> such things, but only what emerges from the human being in the realm
> of sense observation and measurement.[39]

Maritain does not want to diminish or dismiss the social, historical, and physical characteristics of human identity, but he does argue that these qualities ought to be understood in light of commonly shared human qualities that are intrinsic to all people. The starting point, then, for Maritain's Christian philosophy of education is the study of the human person. Only when we know who human persons are can we decide how they learn, what kind of society enables them to flourish, and what institutions support them. Maritain believed that a Christian understanding of the human person could be rationally argued and developed such that a wide range of religious and non-religious people could be inspired and shaped by it. Other Christian (or non-religious) colleges and universities may find deep resonances with Maritain's approach, but for the purposes of this paper I will focus on the relevance of Maritain's Christian anthropology for Catholic school teacher formation and preparation.

Maritain argues that a humanized education must attend to the soul of the student. He writes:

> [W]hat is of most importance in educators themselves is a respect for the soul as well as for the body of the child, the sense of his innermost essence and his internal resources, and a sort of sacred and loving attention to this mysterious identity, which is a hidden thing that no techniques can reach. And what matters most in the educational enterprise is a perpetual appeal to intelligence and free will in the young. Such an appeal, fittingly proportioned to age and circumstances, can and should begin with the first educational steps.[40]

Maritain's emphasis on the attentiveness that teachers need to have toward each student means that personalized education is essential to honoring each child's dignity. This call to close interaction between teacher and student poses a serious challenge for Catholic schools unable to afford low teacher-student ratios. At the very least, it seems, Maritain's vision calls for an awareness of the importance of individual attention. He writes, "A person possesses absolute dignity because he is in direct relationship with the realm of being, truth, goodness, and beauty, and with God, and it is only with these that he can arrive at his complete fulfillment." For the human person has a divine calling integrally bound up with life here and now, but also transcending it. Maritain's view of the person draws from both Greek and Jewish understandings of human beings. The Greeks held that we are intelligent creatures whose highest capacity is the ability to reason, while Judaism saw human beings as called to enter freely into personal relationship with God. Building on these two views, Maritain adds that Christian revelation shows us that the person is "a sinful and wounded creature called to divine life and to the freedom of grace, whose supreme perfection consists of love."[41]

Without explicitly developing the theme of vocation, Maritain sheds light on this Christian notion by pointing out that our most personal and profound calling to divine life is a universal calling: "The Gospel was to lift up human perfection to a higher level [than Greek philosophy]—a truly divine one—by stating that it consists in the perfection of love and, as Saint Paul put it, of the freedom of those who are moved by the divine Spirit." Maritain clarifies that the freedom of this supreme calling is not "a mere unfolding of potentialities without any object to be grasped." Rather, we move toward an end or objective, however partially grasped, and this end measures and rules all that we do, "not materially and by means of bondage, but spiritually and by means of liberty." In other words, we grow more deeply into our human vocation as we submit to a truth higher than ourselves. Thus, Maritain says that "no one is freer, or more independent, than the one who gives himself for a cause or a real being worthy of the gift."[42]

Relating the human vocation to education, Maritain explains that the human person is dynamic, endowed with intelligence and free will, but also incompletely formed. In contrast to animals who automatically move toward the fulfillment of their nature, the human person relies more heavily on the accumulated wisdom of a tradition, individual effort, and instruction for the full realization of his or her capacities and purpose. He writes:

> Due to the very fact that he is endowed with a knowing power which is unlimited and which nonetheless only advances step by step, man cannot progress in his own specific life, both intellectually and morally, without being helped by collective experience previously accumulated and preserved, and by a regular transmission of acquired knowledge.[43]

Thus, the teacher, as an authoritative guide, helps students engage the Judeo-Greco-Christian civilization so as to lead them closer to the truth that they naturally seek. Because we human beings are charged with the duty of "becoming who we are," this need for instruction and the "duty" to become fully human, Maritain argues, is the fundamental rationale for education.[44] In other words, we are educated into our human vocation.

Maritain also makes an important Thomistic distinction between two aspects of the human person: individuality and personality. Individuality is rooted in matter and refers to the more physical aspects of one's existence, which are tangible, visible, and measurable—ethnic background, cultural environment, genetic traits, and so on. Personality, on the other hand, is the more important but elusive dimension of human existence, which can be overlooked because it requires a subtle attentiveness on the part of the teacher. A student is a person according to the spiritual subsistence of his or her intellectual soul. The *person* is rooted in the innermost essence (the spiritual soul).

Maritain accuses the educational practitioners of his day of mistakenly emphasizing the individuality of students more than the richer, nobler dimensions that relate to human personality and sociality. Maritain's contemporaries sought to liberate the inner vitality of the student by stressing

individual inclinations, an approach that, for Maritain, is potentially problematic because it can lead to a disordered catering to those tendencies that
· are in the student by virtue of matter and heredity.[45] This emphasis on "individuality" can be seen today when teachers identify qualities rooted in a student's ethnic identity as his or her most distinctive qualities. Certainly, ethnic
qualities are important to identity, and individual inclinations are important
for the teacher to attend to, especially for gaining the interest of a student in
a particular topic. Yet, attention to individuality without greater stress on
personality can lead to a pandering to the student's more selfish and individ-
ualistic tendencies at the expense of deeper identity development.

In clarifying the proper role of church, school, and family as educational
agents, Maritain distinguishes between the natural and supernatural ends of
the human person. These two integrally connected ends of the human person, hierarchically ordered, clarify the proper role of church, school, and
family. The precise role of the school is to contribute to the natural end of the
human person by educating the intellect and refining the faculty of reason.[46]
The human person is fundamentally made for truth and searches for it
instinctively, but needs guidance. The human intellect, however, is not an
isolated capacity. The intellect has a spiritual dynamism, Maritain explains.
Human reason naturally moves toward ultimacy, the fullness of truth. Our
intellectual powers move us beyond the limits of reason. Conversely, the
dynamism of faith moves toward intelligibility and the understanding of
what is believed. The movements of reason and faith toward each other
express the inherent relationship between the intellectual and the religious,
between thinking and believing, that reflects the unity and integrity of the
human person. The ultimate purpose of the school—intellectual knowledge—is intimately bound up with the final end or calling of the human person—union with God.[47] While Catholic school teachers may readily agree
with the Catholic maxim that faith and reason are not contradictory but complementary, many would likely find their own work enhanced by a deeper
understanding of how the integral relationship between faith and reason is
evident in the inner dynamism of the human person.

Based on this understanding of human ends and the purpose of the
school, teachers can be assured that fundamentally they do not need to
implant in students a desire for truth, but should *awaken* in students the deep
attraction to the truth that is within them. Maritain notes, for example, that
while at first a system of reward and punishment may be necessary to moti-
vate students, the goal of education is to build on natural inclinations and
inspire students so that they tend toward the truth by attraction rather than
simply obligation or duty. In order for a teacher to attend to the move from
external to internal motivations, there needs to be a certain intellectual and
affective sympathy with the student and an intuition about his or her person
and native, God-given human capacities. Thus, while many education students today would be aware of the importance of moving from external to

internal motivations for learning, it is discussion about inherent human qualities—the relationship between intellect and will, emotion and imagination—that enables the prospective Catholic school teacher to understand how the shift from the external to the internal is critical in the life of faith, not just for the students' retention of knowledge. Moreover, in contrast to some contemporary education theories that have a constructivist vision, stressing the construction of knowledge rather than the receiving of it, Maritain presents an understanding of the person in relationship to truth such that students do not *create* truth but *discover* it. Hence, a certain docility and receptivity are necessary for a student to draw closer to truth. Contemporary progressive educators may look askance at the cultivation of such dispositions in students.

Although Maritain does not directly address the education of Catholic school teachers, his thought has implications for their formation and vocation. The first task of the teacher, for example, is to have a philosophically and theologically informed understanding of the student as a human person. Maritain writes:

> The educational task is both greater and more mysterious and, in a sense, humbler than many imagine. If the aim of education is the helping and guiding of man toward his own human achievement, education cannot escape the problems and entanglements of philosophy, for it supposes by its very nature a philosophy of man, and from the outset it is obliged to answer the question: "What is man?"[48]

Before learning education theory or teaching skills, for instance, the Catholic school teacher must be able to have a rationally and religiously grounded grasp of the student's humanity. This grounding enables teachers to understand the most fundamental purpose of their work, and ultimately, what is at stake in teaching. Maritain insists that while the social sciences can tell us important things about the human person, the person is *more* than what these disciplines can measure and observe.

Because of the prevailing individualism in today's culture, future Catholic school teachers need an understanding of the social nature of the human person. *By nature*, the human person finds fulfillment in and through communion with others and, ultimately, with God. Maritain writes, "Man finds himself by subordinating himself to the group, and the group attains its goal only by serving man and by realizing that man has secrets which escape the group and a vocation which is not included in the group."[49] In other words, social commitments are not simply matters of convenience or duty, but are integral to the human vocation. Thus, knowledge is not given for individual power and material prosperity or even an individualized view of salvation, but for "a fuller understanding of and communion with [humanity] . . . to serve and be responsible for others."[50] Catholic education's pursuit of the ultimate end or calling of the person goes hand-in-hand with the bettering of our communal human life here and now. The Second Vatican Council's call for the universal right to education, for instance, stresses the importance of education in enabling men and women to participate in social and political life: "For men, as they become more conscious of their own dignity and responsibility, are eager to take an ever more active role in social life and especially in the economic and political spheres."[51] In sum, there is an integral connection between this world and the next, between social transformation in history and our ultimate call to union with God. Such an integration of education's relationship to the historical and the transcendent is foreign to more mainstream progressive education, which focuses on education for this world to the exclusion of the next.

Through a philosophically and theologically rooted awareness of the human person, the Catholic school teacher is able to serve her students with insight. Understanding the nature of the human person not only clarifies the primary rationale for education; it also deepens a teacher's understanding of why certain educational theories and practices matter while enabling more critical consideration of certain mainstream education maxims about the goals of education. Moreover, a grasp of Christian anthropology reveals the true nobility of teaching as a profession and the true significance of teaching in service to the human vocation. Human integrity and flourishing—now and in the world to come—depend on good education, which, in turn, depends on good teachers. The Vatican II Declaration on Christian Education, *Gravissimum Educationis* (1965), reminds us:

> Teachers must remember that it depends chiefly on them whether the Catholic school achieves its purpose. They should therefore be prepared for their work with special care, having the appropriate qualifications and adequate learning both religious and secular. They should also be skilled in the art of education in accordance with the discoveries of modern times. Possessed by charity both towards each other and towards their pupils, and inspired by an apostolic spirit, they should bear testimony by their lives and their teaching to the One Teacher, who is Christ.[52]

While the council rightly called for Catholic school teachers to be prepared with the best of religious and secular knowledge, the dynamics of teacher preparation as it currently stands needs to be more carefully explored and developed. Truly integrating the religious and secular components of Catholic school teacher formation and preparation calls for a more deliberate effort to think through how contemporary educational theories and practices complement and, in some cases, conflict with a Christian approach to education. Maritain's vision of the human person is but one example of how a Christian philosophy of education has direct implications for the theoretical and practical components of contemporary education programs. Perhaps this cursory illustration of these implications can serve as a catalyst to a much needed interdisciplinary development of a Catholic educational theory that can incorporate more fully the insights of modern educational theory and practice as well as the insights of psychology and the natural sciences. Such an updated Christian theory of education could serve as a framework for students preparing for Catholic school teaching. What, then, can Catholic universities do to meet this pressing need of Catholic school teacher formation and preparation?

TEACHER EDUCATION AT CATHOLIC COLLEGES AND UNIVERSITIES

Catholic colleges and universities that take up the challenge of creating effective Catholic school teacher formation programs will necessarily forge a new integration between the humanities, particularly theology and philosophy, and the psychological and social sciences, so as to strengthen the intellectual, spiritual, and professional preparedness of the Catholic school teacher. But this integration will involve asking some difficult and delicate questions related to university faculty and curricula: How do the aims and values of the education program cohere with the Christian idea of vocation, which goes beyond the understanding of work as utilizing personal talents and bringing personal fulfillment? How can we find common or complementary points of integration between professional preparation and Catholic formation, without glossing over differences and opposing ideas? How do we approach areas of tension between a distinctly Catholic approach to education and the implicit worldview and habit of mind imbedded in the education theories of teacher preparation programs? How is the primary interpretive lens or defining framework for most education programs today at variance with the Catholic vision of education? This last, more theoretical question is particularly relevant in light of the recently noted shift in schools and departments of education from the practical to the theoretical. For the past few decades, perhaps reflecting the absence of a theoretical grounding, education programs have stressed preparing not simply "technicians" but "educators" who go beyond the practical side of teaching to embrace certain educational theories.[53] While the recognition of dependence on theory is encouraging, the kind of theory that frames education practice can be at variance with what Catholic schools propose.

Consider, for example, a recent study of the highest-ranking schools of education by David M. Steiner, chair of the Department of Administration, Training, and Policy Studies at Boston University's School of Education, and his research assistant, Susan Rosen. The study, recently highlighted in a *New York Times Education Life* article, revealed a certain ideological bias influenced by Dewey's tradition of progressive education. It has been noted that such foundational topics as understanding what constitutes an educated person are not addressed. Likewise, classical sources, such as Plato and Aristotle, are not drawn on but figures such as John Dewey, Jean Piaget, Henry Giroux, and Howard Gardner figure prominently. *The New York Times* reporter Anemona Hartocollis cites Steiner's conclusion: "[T]he general posture of education schools . . . was countercultural, instilling mistrust of the system that teachers work in."[54] A Catholic teacher education program would certainly challenge the "hermeneutic of suspicion" as a starting place for engaging students, the educational system, and society at large. Catholic anthropology's stress on human dignity is rooted in the conviction that human beings are "in direct relationship with the realm of being, truth, goodness, and beauty, and with God."[55] Yet, even with such differences, there are likely to be areas of shared concern between the mainstream educational critique of "the system" and the vague aspirations to "social justice" noted by Steiner.[56]

In an interview with Hartocollis, Steiner summarizes his understanding of top schools of education: "There is a vision here, and it's all just one vision. It is a synthesis of what we call the progressivist vision and the constructivist vision" [defined as the theory that it is better for children to construct knowledge rather than to receive it]. Steiner continues, "The counterview has an equal and much longer tradition—the responsibility to engage the student, but to engage the student as the authority."[57] While Maritain agreed that engaging the student personally is important to education, he worries that this can be taken too far: "Modern pedagogy has made invaluable progress in stressing the necessity of carefully analyzing and fixing its gaze on the human subject. The wrong begins when the *object to be taught* and *the primacy of the object* are forgotten, and when the cult of the means—not to an end, but without an end—only ends up in a psychological worship of the subject."[58] Perhaps a certain skepticism about fostering student receptivity in teacher education is due to confusing receptivity with passivity whereby students are expected merely to absorb and regurgitate ready-made formulas. In the Catholic Christian tradition, fostering the habit of receptivity is by no means passive but calls for a humble attentiveness to reality. Receptivity is critical to Christian education, for not only is knowledge earned by discursive engagement with external stimuli but insights are given to students innately through their own God-given desires. This less conventional path to real knowledge is essential to Christian education.

Education faculty at Catholic colleges and universities ought to be aware that there can be a certain "split mind" evident among prospective teachers of Christian faith who may be caught in the tension between learning certain helpful educational practices and resisting the accompanying ideologies that animate faculty and undergird certain pedagogical techniques. Perhaps opening up greater discussion for why certain education practices are encouraged would help students to see that there can be different reasons for the same teaching practice. For example, encouraging students to respect one another's opinions can be based on the teacher wanting her students to appreciate each child's natural connectedness to truth. It can be rooted in a fundamental optimism about the person's relationship to truth. Another teacher might encourage respect for individual opinion based on a more skeptical view that each opinion is equally valid since there is no objective truth but only different subjective views.

CONCLUSION

Given the pressures on many Catholic schools merely to survive, reflections on Catholic identity and teacher formation may seem a luxury. Certainly, a Christian philosophy of education discussed prior to the Second Vatican Council is harder to justify in the contemporary academic atmosphere where metaphysics is under attack and universal philosophical theories are suspect. Thinking about how to strengthen the Catholic approach to education, particularly in the formation of our teachers, is a real challenge. I have tried to show that Catholic universities are uniquely able to meet the current needs of Catholic school teacher formation. But to do this we need to acknowledge the inadequacy of preparing Catholic school teachers with the standard teacher education curriculum and the addition of theology courses.

I have focused on the need for developing a Catholic theory of education that draws from the church's philosophical and theological tradition and brings it forward by incorporating the insights of the psychological and social sciences, as well as twentieth-century phenomenology and existentialism. I expect that a clearer, more persuasive vision of Catholic education, truly lived out in our schools, will capture the broader Catholic community (that has a weakened commitment to Catholic education) and be an uplifting force for public and private schools as well. Catholic colleges and universities can further this task of an integrated approach to the professional preparation of teachers so as to *enhance, challenge, and learn from* the secular models.

As the U.S. Catholic bishops remind us, teachers play a critical role in the formation of Catholic school identity.[59] Bishop Wilton Gregory, speaking at the one-hundredth anniversary of the National Catholic Educational Association in St. Louis, posed this challenge to Catholic educators: "Without qualified leaders, teachers and catechists, we cannot expect our programs to be successful." He added, "This will require cooperation between the leadership of schools, religious educators, and colleges and universities. If we do not prepare those who will take the place of our current leadership in this vital ministry, who will?"[60] To meet this challenge we need to draw on the full potential of the Catholic intellectual tradition so as to develop teacher preparation programs that will comprehensively form teachers who know the difference that Christian faith makes in the vision and everyday practices of Catholic education. The theoretical and practical challenges are many. Yet, I hope that this paper contributes to clarifying the need for interdisciplinary work in the area of Catholic education theory. Catholic teacher formation has an impact on the very substance of mainstream education curricula, for it is comprehensive and thus needs to be carefully and thoroughly delineated by scholars in the humanities and social sciences working together.

The Art of Teaching and the Christian Vocation

Jeanne M. Heffernan

INTRODUCTION: MULTIPLE SENSES OF VOCATION

In recent years, the secular and religious press alike have paid increasing attention to the intersection of faith and learning. Whether the subject is a sociological survey of evangelicals in higher education or a history of the decline of denominational identity in prestigious schools, the topic of religious commitment and the academy is ever present.[1] Among Christian academics, in particular, the past ten years have witnessed an extended conversation about the role of Christian faith in the life of the university, from the shaping of curricula to the hiring of faculty to the tenor of campus culture. I would like to add to this conversation by reflecting on the art of teaching in light of the Christian vocation.

When I was young, vocation had a rather narrow meaning, namely, a call to the religious life. It was a meaning that I (being immature and having a fairly uneven catechesis) understood in a largely negative sense: you can't get married. Thankfully, my understanding of religious life—that it is fundamentally a "yes" and not a "no"—and my understanding of vocation more broadly has developed. In fact, I think it is one of the richest concepts in the Christian life.

In this essay, I will explore that richness—that is, the multi-layered meaning of vocation—as it relates to the teaching profession. Appealing to the Catholic tradition, I understand vocation to mean at least three things. First, in its primary sense, it is a calling from God to the life of Christian discipleship formally initiated in the sacrament of baptism. Second, it is a calling from God to a particular state in life—whether ordained, religious, or lay—that constitutes the distinctive shape this discipleship will take. Third, it is a calling to live out the first and second aspects of vocation in the particular work that has been committed to us.

I am increasingly aware of the vital dependence of the second and third senses of vocation on the first. Whether one is a priest or religious or married Christian and, atop that, whether one teaches, practices medicine, or engages in a trade, the baptismal calling is primary; it is the touchstone for the rest. My focus here will be on the vocation of the lay Christian working in the academy and will not distinguish more finely among the states in life.

I'd like to turn our attention first to baptism and describe an insight I had during the Easter vigil at my parish. The 2005 Lenten season was an especially hard one for me, and for various reasons by the end of it I was tired and my senses felt deprived. The deprivation continued into the triduum, right up to the start of the vigil mass. As I slowly entered our dark church—no light to give my poor eyes consolation—I still carried a certain heaviness about me. But then, I took a deep breath and my nostrils were flooded with the scent of Easter lilies, tulips, and hyacinth that I could not yet see. Something stirred within me; yes, my senses and spirit were coming back to life. Then the Easter candle entered, announcing the Christ, Our Light. And from one candle to another the once dark, then dimly lit, church became ablaze with light. The sense of awakening, of anticipation, and even eagerness in the congregation was palpable. Among the catechumens, who had awaited this night for many months, it was even greater. Then came their moment, the moment at which they might have wondered with T. S. Eliot's wise men, "Were we led all that way for Birth or Death?"[2] To which Paul responds, "Both," since we who are baptized into Christ are baptized into his death, buried with him so as to be raised with him by the Father and so walk in newness of life (Rom 6:24). Never before had those words of Paul to the Romans registered so deeply with me.

I found myself simply amazed at baptism, both at its simplicity and its magnitude. Using the humblest of material elements, it yet means nothing less than life and death. The words of the celebrant say it all:

> The God of power and Father of our Lord Jesus Christ
> has freed you from sin
> and brought you to new life
> through water and the Holy Spirit.
> He now anoints you with the chrism of salvation,
> so that, united with his people,

> you may remain for ever a member of Christ
> who is Priest, Prophet, and King.[3]

The only particular thing I knew about those catechumens was their Christian name. I did not know whether they were married or single, whether they intended to enter religious life, whether they were plumbers or professors. I simply knew that once they were not but now they were Christians and that their lives had changed radically and forever; whatever else they did, from that moment forward, they now shared in the identity and work of Christ as priest, prophet, and king. This is a momentous commission. And it occurred to me after the vigil that it applies to me—a cradle Catholic—no less than to the newly baptized.

But what does it mean to share in what the Catholic Church calls the *muneris Christi,* the offices of Christ? The rite of baptism with its rich symbolism of purification—think of the waters of baptism, the white garment of Christian purity—makes it clear that Christians have the singular and life-unifying purpose of holiness. But the anointing with the sacred chrism differentiates this purpose, for we grow in holiness by partaking in the distinctive mission of Christ as priest, prophet, and king—which, as John Henry Newman observes, was a momentous convergence of offices: never before had a single individual received such an anointing. "Melchizedek, for instance, was a priest and a king, but not a prophet. David was a prophet and a king, but not a priest. Jeremiah was priest and prophet, but not a king. Christ was Prophet, Priest, and King."[4] And yet, as Eusebius of Caesarea marveled, while Christ uniquely fulfilled these roles, he did so in such a way as to empower his disciples to follow in his stead.[5] Thus, the least among the baptized enjoy a gift denied even the greatest figures in salvation history before Christ: they participate in his three holy offices.

How do we understand this participation? Vatican II's *Lumen Gentium,* in its reflections on lay participation in the mission of Christ, articulates an answer.[6] In Christ's priestly mission, he offers spiritual worship for the glory of God and the salvation of the world; in our priestly capacity, we have the extraordinary privilege of likewise lifting up all that we are and all that we do—our relationships, our work, our play, our hardships—as a sacrificial offering to God through Jesus. In doing this, the Council insists, we are doing nothing less than "consecrat[ing] the world itself to God."[7]

Having been obedient unto death, Christ also enjoys a kingly office. He is Christ the King, and he desires that all of creation be renewed under his reign. In stirring words, the Council Fathers declare that "Christ has communicated this royal power to His disciples [to us] that they might be constituted in royal freedom"[8] so as to conquer the reign of sin within our hearts and spread the kingdom of God.

As the great prophet, Christ proclaimed the kingdom of his Father, by "the testimony of His life and the power of His words"[9]—each of which, as Newman put it, "authoritatively reveal the will of God and the Gospel of Grace."[10] We share in this prophetic mission when we give witness to the faith, "announcing . . . Christ by a living testimony as well as by the spoken word" in the ordinary circumstances of the world; this witness of word and example, in keeping with the great prophetic tradition, will identify and denounce evil, proclaim the requirements of justice, and, as the Council puts it, "enlighten those who seek the truth."[11]

While the most direct expression of this mission is found in explicit evangelization, I would submit that we, in our own way as professors, also exhibit the prophetic-teaching office, because we are about seeking and communicating truth. So approached under the light of faith, the teaching of every subject takes on theological meaning. One might query, "Even mathematics at a state university?" Yes. As Simone Weil with characteristic surprise proposes:

> The solution of a geometry problem does not in itself constitute a precious gift, but the same law applies to it because it is the image of something precious. Being a little fragment of particular truth, it is a pure image of the unique, eternal, and living Truth, the very Truth that once in a human voice declared: "I am the Truth." Every school exercise, thought of in this way, is like a sacrament.[12]

This is a particularly clear way our first and third vocations are related. And it is only in light of that baptismal vocation to holiness that our third vocation, expressed in our academic work, can be rightly ordered. For what our baptism makes clear is that God is our existential ground; it is in him that we find our identity—not in our university, not in our departments, not in our disciplines or publications, not *even* in our teaching. Our identity most fundamentally comes from Christ. As Pope John Paul II affirmed so simply and powerfully, "Jesus Christ is the answer to the question posed by every human life."[13] And if we do not call this to mind—often—our work will become an idol, or as Augustine phrased it, a counterfeit reality.

Newman understood something of this temptation and described it with characteristic clarity, and his example illustrates the interdependence of the three *munera*; the prophetic-teaching function can only be understood and rightly exercised in company with the priestly and kingly offices. Observing that philosophers of great renown, "whose words are so good and so effective, are themselves too often nothing more than words," he diagnoses the heart of the problem: their lives are disconnected from their art, and their art is disconnected from their faith. They teach but do not believe and live what they profess. Of these men Newman pointedly asks, "Who shall warrant for their doing as well as speaking? They are shadows of Christ's prophetical office; but where is the sacerdotal or the regal? Where shall we find in them the nobleness of the king, and the self-denial of the priest?" Newman's answer is sharp and direct (and might apply to us no less than to Victorian gentlemen). Nobility and self-denial, he laments, are not to be found among them. "On the contrary," he writes, "for nobleness they are often the 'meanest of mankind'; and for self-denial the most selfish and most cowardly. They can sit at ease, and follow their own pleasure, and indulge the flesh, or serve the world, while their reason is so enlightened, and their words are so influential." This worldly greatness is for Newman so despicable because it is a distortion of something so noble: the teaching office of Christ. In the face of such a distortion, Newman despairs, "What shall we say to men like Balaam, who profess without doing, who teach the truth yet live in vice, who know, but do not love?"[14]

Newman's words hit home. As I have experienced this temptation, I have found it very disturbing. For when I forget who I am in my baptism, when I forget my Christian name, as it were, then I become defined not by who I am but by what I do. And as a junior nontenured faculty member, I can attest that the temptations, though perhaps banal, are nevertheless real and ugly, and they distort my whole vision. Colleagues become competitors; students become ciphers; courses become vehicles for crass self-display. And like Newman's worldly philosopher, I become disconnected from what I teach and believe. It's a grim scene.

But then there is grace—the Lord's gentle voice reminding me that my calling as a teacher is but a reflection of my calling as a disciple and that to fulfill both vocations my professional life must be, in the words of *Lumen Gentium*, "elevated from within by the grace of Christ."[15] So I—we—must enter the academy as baptized people called to renew the world. Moreover, as academics, we partake in a special way in the prophetic-teaching office of Jesus, meeting the university where it is, now, and trying to bring to it the light of Christ. What might this mean?

MAKING ALL THINGS NEW: A CHRISTIAN VISION OF EDUCATION

Whenever I survey the scene in higher education and consider the role that Christians are to play in it, I immediately turn to my intellectual heroes for wisdom. Let me call these people "signposts in a strange land," borrowing the title of Patrick Samway's volume on Walker Percy.[16] Among their number I would include such diverse thinkers as Wendell Berry and John Paul II and Cardinal Newman. The signposts tell us that something is amiss. They alert us to the fact that, yes, we inhabit a strange land. But what makes the land—our land, the land of the academy, not to mention the larger culture—strange? I think that our land is strange because it is too flat—its surface has been reduced, leveled, so that what were once mountains are barely molehills. Or, better, what are mountains are now *reckoned* as molehills. We've got a topographical map that is askew.

How so? Well, if Wendell Berry is right, and I think he is, we've taken our map from the wrong surveyors. The academy's most illustrious mapmakers are reductionists; their equipment is suited to studying small bits of earth, but they presume to measure the whole world with it, to compass the horizon using a microscopic lens. Chief among misguided mapmakers, for Berry, is Harvard sociobiologist E. O. Wilson. Wilson is a very clever scientist; this Berry grants. But he's a poor philosopher, theologian, and political theorist. Does Wilson claim these areas of expertise? Not exactly. But he presumes to speak on all of them because his method is imperialistic: it conquers every territory of knowledge and becomes its master. In Wilson's own words, "all tangible phenomena, from the birth of stars to the workings of social institutions, are based on material processes that are ultimately reducible to . . . the laws of physics."[17]

That matter is subject to the laws of physics is not the problem. What is objectionable is the notion that everything tangible is reducible to and determined by the laws of physics. Wilson's reductionism is thoroughgoing; there is no room here for a nonmaterial explanation of anything in our experience. Even meaning itself succumbs to the cold clutches of scientific reductionism. As Wilson reveals, "What we call *meaning* is the linkage among the neural networks created by the spreading excitation that enlarges imagery and engages emotion."[18] Berry rightly points out that "this idea is explicitly imperialistic, and it is implicitly tyrannical. Mr. Wilson is perfectly frank about his territorial ambitions. He wishes to see all the disciplines linked or unified—but strictly on the basis of science."[19] With meaning reduced to molecules, the profoundest insights of all the disciplines are imperiled. Contrasting the world of Shakespeare's *King Lear* with Wilson's laboratory, Berry notes that only in the former is there a genuine place for the miraculous and mysterious.

But then how has Wilson been able to concoct such a scheme? What has happened here? For Berry, the fact that Wilson can seriously propound the theory of "consilience" and the fact that he has been richly rewarded for doing so with accolades and a prestigious post in the academy testifies that the university is lost. It has no meaningful unity, but is fragmented, split into different territories, each speaking hyper-specialized languages. As Berry argues in "The Loss of the University," there is no common tongue with which to communicate, no forum within which to discuss—and defend—one's ideas.[20] Thus, safely distant from theologians and Christian literary scholars, an E. O. Wilson can say that, Milton's own testimony notwithstanding, *Paradise Lost* owes nothing to God's inspiration. Without challenge, Wilson is allowed to rest in what E. F. Schumacher called "a methodical aversion to the recognition of higher levels . . . of significance."[21]

Now this is not a problem in the natural sciences alone; so many of our disciplines fall prey to a similar reductionism. This is the predicament of the modern university. But it was not always so; this radical fragmentation of knowledge is a relatively recent thing. As H. J. Massingham has observed,

"Modern knowledge is departmentalized," whereas, he continues, "the essence of culture is *initiation into wholeness,* so that all the divisions of knowledge are considered as the branches of one tree, the Tree of Life whose roots go deep into the earth and whose top is in heaven."[22]

Here is an alternative, and I think recoverable, vision of learning. This vision is guided by what the medievals called *adaequatio rei et intellectus:* the principle that the understanding of the knower must be adequate to the thing to be known. To put it simply, there are different ways to know different things; and there are different ways to know the same things. Take a book. Let's say the Bible, a first edition King James at that. Now, a physicist can tell us a great deal about the atomic particles of its parchment; a chemist about the carbon remaining in its pages; a linguist about its distinctive verbal forms; a religious historian about the social and political context of its creation. Yet, none of these has comprehended its meaning; each has added to our understanding, yes, but none is adequate to the full reality of the object; the proper bounds of the disciplines prevent this.

This is why we have universities, ideally communities of learners who complement one another's work in an effort to understand the whole. The recovery of the liberal arts taking place in many of our colleges and universities is a step in the right direction. Baylor's Interdisciplinary Core, Pepperdine's Great Books Program, and Notre Dame's Program of Liberal Studies come to mind in this connection. Even in secular universities, the study of the liberal arts promises some protection against reductionism. To put it positively, the liberal arts in and of themselves can begin one's initiation into wholeness.

Consider this scenario. A nonbelieving student with an empirical, pragmatic bent enrolls in a state university. He declares a chemistry major, loads up on natural science courses, and quickly refines his grasp and practice of the scientific method; its precision profoundly shapes his habit of mind. Flush with his newfound knowledge, he examines everything—even his girlfriend—according to its chemical components. (This, of course, gets him in trouble!) But in the following semester, he begins to satisfy his general education requirements with courses on British literature, Western civilization, and art history. Suddenly, he's taken aback. The tools that had served him so well in the lab offer little assistance in interpreting George Herbert or understanding Augustine's *Confessions* or accounting for the paintings of Giotto. Herbert evokes in him a fascination with language—with the way in which finite forms gesture toward transcendence. Augustine prompts a new and strange self-examination. Giotto whets his appetite for beauty. All of this is mysterious to him, and he can't reduce it to the proportions of chemistry. He has experienced intimations of something beyond. And, like the unforgettable Binx Bolling in Walker Percy's *The Moviegoer,* he undertakes a *search*; he has thus begun the initiation into wholeness.

What may deliver him into a fuller wholeness? The light of faith, our baptismal gift. It is the leaven his liberal arts studies need in order to rise to new heights, for a Christian perspective markedly changes learning. What might it mean to view education, and specifically higher education, from a Christian perspective? I think it entails at least two things: a certain orientation toward learning and a sense of the proper breadth of education.

A CHRISTIAN ORIENTATION TOWARD LEARNING

A Christian orientation toward learning, as I see it, is an openness to the truth that is marked by wonder and gratitude. James Taylor, in his remarkable book *Poetic Knowledge: The Recovery of Education*, describes wonder as "an emotion of fear, a fear produced by the consciousness of ignorance, which, because it is man's natural desire (good) to know . . . is perceived as a kind of evil."[23] Ignorance is a kind of deprivation, the awareness of which produces fear. Think of walking into a great study filled from floor to ceiling with beautiful books and at once feeling surges of anxiety and excitement and desire. We know that we don't know the riches the books contain; we're daunted by this fact, and yet we're drawn to the books just the same; we want to know. As Taylor reckons, this is what Plato and Aristotle understood as wonder, *the* existential starting point of philosophy.

Plato and Aristotle illuminated much about the experience of wonder and the birth of philosophy in the soul; they were great teachers. But it seems to me that what we learn from the Judeo-Christian revelation adds immeasurably to our orientation toward learning, because we know from God's self-disclosure to the Jews and, even more, from his incarnation in Christ that the unmoved mover of the ancients is actually a personal God—so personal that we call him Father—who created the world out of generosity, who considered his creation very good, and who so loved the world even after it rebelled that he sent his only Son to die for its salvation. This prepares us, it seems to me, to approach the learning process not only with wonder but also with profound gratitude. Everything about our Christian story should encourage this, for we see from start to finish that self-giving love is the very ground of existence; it is the deepest truth about the world. It is out of this love that we have been *given* everything—from the creation of the world to its salvation. And the proper way to receive a gift is in gratitude. Thus, the Christian can affirm what Socrates expressed so well about education in Plato's *Republic*, namely, "the object of education is to teach us to love what is beautiful"—to which she will add, "and to be grateful to her heavenly Father for it."[24]

Christian revelation also informs us that the context within which all learning takes place is a great drama. Think about these biblical themes: the way of life versus the way of death; truth in contest with falsehood; the forces of light arrayed against the powers of darkness; heaven and hell. Human life is charged with supernatural meaning, meaning that transcends the bounds of time and history. As Pope John Paul II explains in his encyclical *The Gospel of Life:*

> Man is called to a fullness of life which far exceeds the dimensions of his earthly existence, because it consists in sharing the very life of God. The loftiness of this supernatural vocation reveals the *greatness* and the *inestimable value* of human life even in its temporal phase. Life in time, in fact, is the fundamental condition, the initial stage and an integral part of the entire unified process of human existence. It is a process which, unexpectedly and undeservedly, is enlightened by the promise and renewed by the gift of divine life, which will reach its full realization in eternity (cf. 1 John 3:1-2). At the same time, it is precisely this supernatural calling which highlights the *relative character* of each individual's earthly life. After all, life on earth is not an "ultimate" but a "penultimate" reality; even so, it remains a *sacred reality* entrusted to us, to be preserved with a sense of responsibility and brought to perfection in love and in the gift of ourselves to God and to our brothers and sisters.[25]

If we understand life as a sacred reality, entrusted to us, we will insist that education remain faithful to the supernatural dimensions and destiny of the human person. Our thoughts about education will begin, as Jacques Maritain's did, with a consideration of the essence of man. "Man," in Maritain's words, "is a person, who holds himself in hand by his intelligence and his will. He does not merely exist as a physical being. There is in him a richer and nobler existence; he has spiritual superexistence through knowledge and love." Thus, contra E. O. Wilson, Maritain insists that man "is in some way, a whole, not merely a part; he is a universe unto himself, a microcosm in which the great universe in its entirety can be encompassed through knowledge. And through love he can give himself freely to beings who are to him, as it were, other selves; and for this relationship no equivalent can be found in the physical world."[26]

A SENSE OF THE BREADTH OF EDUCATION

Man is "in some way, a whole, . . . a universe unto himself," and education should be commensurate to this stature; this is the second insight a Christian perspective offers. Education must reflect the height, depth, and breadth of human experience, attending to the body, soul, and spirit, to time and eternity. It must, in short, guard against reductionism. It should not attempt to understand the human experience according to the epistemological constraints of any one discipline, nor should it focus on a narrow and limited goal, such as "career preparation."

Instead, as Wendell Berry passionately argues, education should be about the making of a good human being, that is to say, a fully developed person.

And it does so by engaging the student in broad, basic studies that enable us to understand the whole, the cosmos. A curriculum should be faithful to the multifaceted nature of reality, from subatomic particles to the heights of religious mysticism. From a Christian perspective, this makes sense, since God reveals his wisdom and love through the book of Revelation and the book of Nature; faith and human reason both yield truths that originate with the Author of Truth. As Ambrose of Milan affirmed, "Anything true, by no matter whom said, is from the Holy Spirit." The unity of truth lends dignity to the investigation of all of reality—sacred and mundane—as all reality bears the stamp of God's creative love. In the words of John Henry Newman, "All that is good, all that is true, all that is beautiful, all that is beneficent, be it great or small, be it perfect or fragmentary, natural as well as supernatural, moral as well as material, comes from Him."[27]

Hence, in fidelity to our prophetic office, that is, the teaching office into which we were commissioned at baptism, we should insist that all of God's truth receive attention. There should be, in other words, a Christian impulse to offer an expansive, unified curriculum, grounded in the conviction that approaching life and learning through a dedication to the liberal arts illumined by faith provides the surest initiation into human wholeness. Cultivating this kind of wholeness, which is to my mind the work of Christian humanism, runs against the reductive impulses so pervasive in our culture—in the academy, politics, medicine, and economics. A Christian humanism consciously resists this reductionism—and in a prophetic mode exposes its limitations—all the while insisting, instead, on seeing things whole.

CONCLUSION: UNITING FAITH AND LEARNING IN THE CLASSROOM

Having touched on the way in which Christian faith transforms one's vision of education, I would like to conclude by saying a few words about how our first and third vocations—or how faith and learning—might come together in the classroom, as I think they ought. For genuine Christian faith permeates the whole life of the believer—at work, at play, when busy, when at rest, in high celebration and in ordinary time. To be a Christian is, in short, an identity, not a role.

Thus, given the comprehensive nature of our faith and our baptismal vocation to sanctify the world, "as from within like leaven,"[28] it is fitting that our Christian identity would affect our professional lives as teachers, for our most basic commitments permeate all we do. To divide faith from teaching would bifurcate our lives, and a bifurcation of that magnitude—dividing what we do from who we are—leads to a kind of schizophrenia. The attempt to integrate faith and learning in the classroom guards against this division. Or, to state it positively, it affords us the opportunity to live as whole, integrated people.

The foregoing reflections have concrete implications. I would like to mention four that have been important to me, and as I discuss them I am mindful that each of these implications will take on a different shape or aspect, depending on one's discipline, temperament, and classroom setting. Yet, I would maintain that they are applicable in some way to each of us. As John Paul II expressed so well in *Christifidelis laici:* "There is an urgent need in various schools, whether Catholic or not, for teachers and professors among the lay faithful to be true witnesses of the gospel, through their example of life, their professional competence and uprightness, their Christian inspired teaching, preserving always—as is obvious—the autonomy of various sciences and disciplines."[29]

The first implication of my thesis above is this: To integrate faith and learning in the classroom means that I must be a person of both faith and learning because they work together. The light of faith illumines the intellect, and the cultivated mind penetrates more deeply into faith. As a Christian teacher I have found that the more I cultivate the spiritual life, the more open I am to the wisdom of my discipline and to sharing that wisdom with my students; likewise, the more faithful I am to my scholarly work, the richer my appreciation of God's purposes in the world. This connection makes sense, given that Jesus reveals himself to be "the way, and the truth, and the life." This suggests that truth is personal, not simply propositional, and that if I am more deeply connected to the personal source of truth, I will likely be a better seeker and communicator of truth in all its dimensions. This also suggests that my truth-seeking has to be informed by a distinctive moral disposition, carefully attuned to the subtle temptations of the academic world. On my best days, I want to imitate Cardinal Newman, aspiring to his authentic Christian humanism—once described as "a union of intellectual curiosity and achievement with the humility and charity of the truly religious man."[30]

The second practical implication is that I would seek to incorporate faith into the course material. In this I am blessed to work at an institution, and more specifically in a department, that not only allows but also encourages such integration. The integration of faith into the coursework includes broadening the scope of questions raised and the range of resources to which I appeal. I will, for instance, pose theologically informed questions to my students and will expose them to the insights of Christian intellectual traditions. As a teacher of political theory, I integrate faith and learning by challenging students to penetrate the heart of a thinker's anthropology and by inviting them to assess its adequacy in light of religious wisdom. Bringing the theological perspective into play expands the parameters of the discussion in fruitful ways. For instance, after reading Aristotle's quite compelling account of happiness in book 1 of the *Ethics,* I will present a quite different view taken from the reflections of an American Jesuit missionary to Russia, Walter Ciszek, who spent more than twenty years in Soviet prison on account of his religious convictions. As the students and I puzzle over the two accounts, I consistently find that incorporating a distinctly Christian perspective into the discussion leavens the loaf, makes it rise to higher dimensions—the dimensions of the soul, suffering, and eternal life—than would be reached otherwise.[31]

The third implication I take from the principles sketched above is that as a Christian teacher, I need to pray for my students. This is not a practice I have perfected by any means, but I think it is worthwhile. In those times when I do pray for my students, I approach the enterprise differently; the difference is subtle but real. I find that when I pray for my students, I am humanized by the practice, freed just a bit from what is for me *the* occupational hazard of teaching: egotism. I am better able to view the task as subject-centered, not self-centered, and I measure the effectiveness of classroom time less by the positive or negative personal reaction of the students and more according to how well they appropriated the material. Not only does praying for my students humanize me; it humanizes them in my eyes. I am more able to perceive their dignity and less prone to instrumentalize them.

Praying for my students in the context of the daily liturgy offered on campus is a special privilege and, in its way, an expression of the teaching office. As Yves Congar notes, "Teaching through witness is not given through words alone; often its more effective form is that of belief translated quite simply into life, with no attempt at persuasion." The faith, he continues, is given prophetic witness through the celebration of the sacraments, especially the Eucharist. If Congar is right, then when we—as faculty—participate in this celebration, we "testify to the mysteries, showing them forth before those who are willing to take notice."[32] It seems to me that the quiet witness shown by professors who interrupt the busyness of their day to worship the Lord sends a subtle yet important message to "those who are willing to take notice," including, I suspect, not a few of their students. I have found that that message, which is to say the testimony of my discipleship, is more powerful—because more real and integrated—when I lift my students up in prayer in the simple daily masses in our campus chapel. It is when I do this that I am able to see my profession as a vocation, a particular kind of service to which I have been called.

Finally, I have found that integrating faith and learning in the classroom is assisted by not only praying *for* the students, but *with* them. Teaching at a university like Villanova makes this possible. Following the lead of several of my mentors at Notre Dame, I begin either each class or the semester with a brief prayer and invite the students to join me if they wish. I have come to view this as a privilege and a blessing, and it's a practice that has been well received by the students. In setting my teaching in the context of prayer, I find that in a very concrete way I integrate my professional role and my Christian identity, bringing together the callings I have received both to be a disciple and to be a teacher and thus honoring at once the priestly, prophetic, and kingly dimensions of my baptismal anointing.

Notes

Introduction

1   All translations from the Bible in this chapter are from *The New American Bible* (Iowa Falls, Iowa: World Bible Publishers, 1970).

2   Ignatius of Antioch, *Early Christian Fathers*, ed. and trans. Cyril C. Richardson (New York: Touchstone, 1995), 104, 105.

3   Augustine, *The Confessions*, trans. John Ryan (New York: Image Books, 1960), 200 (book 8, chap. 11).

4   Kierkegaard writes, "What our generation lacks is not reflection but passion." Søren Kierkegaard, *Fear and Trembling*, ed. and trans. Howard Hong and Edna Hong (Princeton: Princeton University Press, 1983), 42n.

5   Kierkegaard writes, "Would it not have been better, after all, if he were not God's chosen? What does it mean to be God's chosen? Is it to be denied in youth one's youthful desire in order to have it fulfilled with great difficulty in one's old age?" *Fear and Trembling*, 18.

6   Kierkegaard, *Fear and Trembling*, 21.

7   Kierkegaard, *Fear and Trembling*, 38–40, 50, 43.

8   Kierkegaard, *Fear and Trembling*, 41.

9   Dietrich Bonhoeffer, *The Cost of Discipleship*, trans. R. H. Fuller (New York: Touchstone, 1995), 58.

10   John Henry Newman, "Divine Calls," in *Parochial and Plain Sermons* (New York: Ignatius Press, 1997), 1579.

11   Martin Luther, "To the Christian Nobility of the German Nation," in *Three Treatises*, trans. C. M. Jacobs (Philadelphia: Muhlenberg, 1943, 1960), 16.

12   Martin Luther, "The Gospel for the Early Christmas Service," trans. John G. Kunstmann, *Luther's Works*, vol. 52 (Philadelphia: Fortress, 1974), 36.

13   Miroslav Volf, *Work in the Spirit: Towards a Theology of Work* (Oxford: Oxford University Press, 1991), 105.

14   *Gaudium et Spes*, in *Vatican Council II* (Northport, N.Y.: Costello, 1992), 943.

15   For example, see *Decree on the Apostolate of Lay People*, in *Vatican Council II*, 768.

16   Volf, *Work in the Spirit*, 107.

17   Volf, *Work in the Spirit*, 108–9.

18   Parker J. Palmer, *Let Your Life Speak: Listening for the Voice of Vocation* (San Francisco: Jossey-Bass, 1999), 3.

19   Frederick Buechner, *Wishful Thinking: A Seeker's ABC* (San Francisco: HarperSanFrancisco, 1993), 119.

20   Sharon Daloz Parks, *Big Questions, Worthy Dreams* (San Francisco: Jossey-Bass, 2000), 48.

21   Parks, *Big Questions*, 49.

22   Michael Novak, *Business as a Calling: Work and the Examined Life* (New York: Free Press, 1996), 39.

23   See Saint Thomas Aquinas, *Summa Theologica*, pt. I, question 12, notably art. 11.

24   See Aquinas, I–II, Question 8, art. 1.

25   Tim McGraw, "Live Like You Were Dying" (Curb Records, 2004).

26   Mitch Albom, *Tuesdays with Morrie* (New York: Doubleday, 1997).

Fulfilling Your True Nature

1   *Joan of Arcadia*, "Out of Sight," first broadcast 1 October 2004 by CBS, directed by Rob Morrow, written by Stephen Nathan.

2   See, for example, "Does *Joan of Arcadia*'s Theology Ring True?" *Beliefnet*, 11 November 2004, http://www.beliefnet.com/story/61/story_6170_1.html, and Heidster et al. "Who Is God?" Listserv message, 14 April 2005, http://www.joanofarcadia.com/forum/showthread.php?t=590.

3   I am indebted to Dr. Michael Miller for first suggesting this point to me.

4   Bill Keveney, "Joan Mixes Faith, Family into Compelling TV," *USA Today*, 8 September 2004; Lynette Rice, "Holy Roller: *Joan of Arcadia* Is a Heaven-Sent Gift for CBS and Its Fetching Young Star—and an Act of God for Its Creator," *Entertainment Weekly*, 7 November 2003, 36; "*Joan of Arcadia* Has Intelligent Quirkiness," MSNBC.com, 22 November 2004, http://www.napoli.msnbc.com/id/4430498/print1/displaymode/1090.

5   Gillian Flynn, "*Joan of Arcadia*: The Lord Is Joan's Shepherd, and Her Religious Drama Shall Not Want for Ratings in Its (Slightly Edgier) Second Season," *Entertainment Weekly*, 10 September 2004, 92; Michael Hill, "God Speaks, Viewers Watch," *Washington Post*, 9 November 2003; "*Joan of Arcadia*: It's Still a Godsend," NYDailynews.com, 19 November 2004, http://www.nydailynews.com/entertainment/v-pfriendly/story/254139p-217617c.htm.

6   Nancy Haught, "Channeling God," *Oregonian*, 29 September 2004; Mark Matlock, "Does Joan Have It Right?" *Christianity Today*, November/December 2004, 28; Gabriel Garnica, "*Joan of Arcadia* Is Wolf in Sheep's Clothing," 10 October 2003, http://www.catholicexchange.com/vm/index.asp?vm_id=2&art_id=20747; Elliot B. Gertel, "*Joan of Arcadia*: The Latest TV Show to

Cheapen—and Abuse—Religion," 17 December 2003, http://www.jewish-worldreview.com/elliot/gertel_joan_of_arcadia.php3.

7   Kate Arthur, "Joan Slips," *The New York Times*, 25 April 2005; Rick Kissel, "Sophs Hit Their Stride," *Variety*, 5 December 2004, 24; Alex Strachan, "*Joan of Arcadia* Is on a Real Downer," *Leader Post* (Regina, Saskatchewan), 15 October 2004.

8   Rati Bishnoi, "Save Our Shows: Hold 'em or Fold 'em? *Joan* Fans Look to a Higher Power," *USA Today*, 2 May 2005; "Fans of *Joan* Are Hoping for a Miracle," *Chicago Tribune*, 30 May 2005; Maureen Ryan, "It's Time to Pray for the Return of *Joan*," *Chicago Tribune*, 22 April 2005.

9   David Bauder, "CBS Puts Match to *Joan of Arcadia*: Decision Leaves Fans Baffled," *Houston Chronicle*, 31 May 2005; "Demographics Win Out over Quality Television," *Los Angeles Times*, 12 June 2005: C3; Tim Goodman, "Unforgettable? Apparently Not for Many Shows," *San Francisco Chronicle*, 2 May 2005: C1.

10   Charlotte Triggs, "*Joan of Arcadia*: The First Season," *People*, 16 May 2005: 47; Jill Vejnoska, "The DVD Effect," *Atlanta Journal*, 3 May 2005. On the enthusiastic fan reaction to the DVDs, see, for example, AmSmile et al., "Season Two DVD News!!" Listserv message, 10 February 2006, http://amtam.ipbhost.com/index.php?s=7860e5c1963c49117f434d3f4e307b16&showtopic=11054.

11   Robert P. Laurence, "Heaven Sent," SignonSanDiego.com, 22 February 2004, http://www.signonSanDiego.com/uniontrib/20040222/news_m1a22jon.html.

12   Mary Warner, "TV's *Joan of Arcadia* Generates a Cult Following," *National Catholic Reporter*, 30 April 2004, 15.

13   *Joan of Arcadia*, "Pilot," first broadcast 26 September 2003 by CBS, directed by James Hayman and Jack Bender, written by Barbara Hall.

14   *Joan of Arcadia*, "The Fire and the Wood," first broadcast 3 October 2003 by CBS, directed by James Hayman, written by Hart Hanson.

15   *Joan of Arcadia*, "The Devil Made Me Do It," first broadcast 14 November 2003 by CBS, directed by James Hayman, written by Hart Hanson.

16   *Joan of Arcadia*, "Death Be Not Whatever," first broadcast 7 November 2003 by CBS, directed by Peter Levin, written by Barbara Hall.

17   "Does *Joan of Arcadia's* Theology Ring True?"

18   "*Joan of Arcadia* Has Intelligent Quirkiness."

19   For example, the official CBS *Joan of Arcadia* Web site features "diary entries," clearly meant to appeal to female teenage viewers, written in the character Joan's voice. See "Joan's Diary," CBS.com, 6 April 2005, http://www.cbs.com/primetime/joan_of_arcadia/diary/20050406.shtml#.

20   James Fabiono et al., "The History of Luke and Grace," Listserv message, 27 November 2004, http://amtam.ipbhost.com/index.php?showtopic=6442; Maureen Ryan, "*Joan of Arcadia* Fans Are True Believers," *Chicago Tribune*, 5 June 2005; Laura Sheahen, "*Joan of Arcadia*: Talking Back to God," Beliefnet 10 February 2005, http://www.beliefnet.com/story/154/story_15423.html.

21   Laura Sessions Stepp, "An Inspired Strategy: Is Religion a Tonic for Kids? You Better Believe It, Say Teens and Scholars," *Washington Post*, 21 March 2004; Namaste et al., "Who Is God?" Listserv message, 14 April 2005, http://www.joanofarcadia.com/forum/showthread.php?t=590; Saramaria2 et al., "If You Could Be God on JoA," Listserv message, 13 January 2005, http://amtam.ipbhost.com/index.php?showtopic=6937.

22   *Joan of Arcadia*, "Bringeth It On," first broadcast 31 October 2003 by CBS, directed by Joy Gregory, written by David Petraca.

23   Teresa Blythe, "Watching *Joan of Arcadia:* A Mini Study Guide to Discussing the Show," n.d., http://www.pcusa.org/today/joan/guide1-6.htm.

24   *Joan of Arcadia*, "The Uncertainty Principle," first broadcast 12 December 2003 by CBS, directed by Helen Shaver, written by Joy Gregory.

25   *Joan of Arcadia,* "St. Joan," first broadcast 21 November 2003 by CBS, directed by Martha Mitchell, written by Randy Anderson; *Joan of Arcadia,* "Dive," first broadcast 10 December 2004 by CBS, directed by Martha Mitchell, written by David Grace; *Joan of Arcadia,* "Touch Move," first broadcast 10 October 2003 by CBS, directed by Josh Brand, written by Barbara Hall; *Joan of Arcadia,* "State of Grace," first broadcast 6 February 2004 by CBS, directed by Steve Gomer, written by Joshua Ravetch; *Joan of Arcadia,* "Queen of the Zombies," first broadcast 14 January 2005 by CBS, directed by Graeme Clifford, written by Joy Gregory.

26   If the show had continued into a third season, the depiction of God's call might have changed significantly. In the finale of the second season, God warned Joan that she would face her biggest challenge yet and hinted that Joan would be doing battle with evil—a rather different project than "fulfilling your true nature." The question, what does it mean to be called by God? very much shaped this particular episode. Joan pondered God's call, wondering why God had chosen her for this task. Joan also remembered that God (dismissed as an "imaginary friend" by her family) appeared to her when she was a young girl. Meanwhile, Helen's friend Lilly, a former nun, discussed the nature of God's call in the most traditional sense of a vocation for ministry. See *Joan of Arcadia,* "Something Wicked This Way Comes," first broadcast 22 April 2005 by CBS, directed by James Hayman, written by Barbara Hall.

27   Nancy Franklin, "Down to Earth," *New Yorker,* 13 October 2003, 110.

28   *Joan of Arcadia*, "The Fire and the Wood"; *Joan of Arcadia*, "Recreation," first broadcast 16 January 2004 by CBS, directed by Elodie Keene, written by Barbara Hall; *Joan of Arcadia,* "Anonymous," first broadcast 30 April 2004 by CBS, directed by Steve Gomer, written by David Grace; *Joan of Arcadia,* "The Gift," first broadcast 14 May 2004 by CBS, directed by Martha Mitchell, written by Stephen Nathan.

29   *Joan of Arcadia,* "The Fire and the Wood."

30   *Joan of Arcadia,* "Double Dutch," first broadcast 20 February 2004 by CBS, directed by Alan Myerson, written by Tom Garrigus.

31   James Cone, *God of the Oppressed*, 2nd ed. (Maryknoll, N.Y.: Orbis Books, 1997); Gustavo Gutierrez, *A Theology of Liberation: History, Politics, and Salvation* (Maryknoll, N.Y.: Orbis Books, 1988); Ivan Petrella, *The Future of Liberation Theology: An Argument and Manifesto* (Aldershot, N.H.: Ashgate Publishing, 2004); Jon Sobrino, Paul Burns, and Francis McDonah, *Jesus the Liberator: A Historical-Theological Reading of Jesus of Nazareth* (Maryknoll, N.Y.: Orbis Books, 1994).

32   Germain Grisez and Russell Shaw, *Personal Vocation: God Calls Everyone by Name* (Huntington, Ind.: Our Sunday Visitor, 2003), 11.

33   Gordon Smith, *Courage and Calling: Embracing Your God-Given Potential* (Westmont, Ill.: InterVarsity, 1999); Palmer, *Let Your Life Speak,* 10.

34   Perhaps the most widely known book on this topic is *The Purpose-Driven Life* by Rick Warren. This book gained nationwide attention in March of 2005 when an escaped prisoner and murder suspect took an Atlanta woman, Ashley Smith, hostage and Smith calmed and apparently convinced the gunman to turn himself in by reading him passages from War-

ren's book. Warren urges readers to forgo selfish endeavors and devote themselves to furthering the work of evangelical Christianity via worship, ministry, evangelism, fellowship, and discipleship. Yet Warren, like some of the aforementioned authors, seems to argue that fulfilling one's individual call from God will automatically benefit the Christian community. See Rick Warren, *The Purpose-Driven Life: What on Earth Am I Here For?* (Grand Rapids: Zondervan, 2002).

35   Os Guinness, *The Call: Finding and Fulfilling the Central Purpose of Your Life* (Nashville: Word Publishing, 1998), 46.

36   C. Thomas Anderson, *Becoming a Millionaire God's Way* (Mesa, Ariz.: Winword Publishing, 2005), and Kirbyjon Caldwell and Mark Seal, *The Gospel of Good Success: A Road Map to Spiritual, Emotional, and Financial Wholeness* (Wichita, Kans.: Fireside, 2000). See also, for example, Tracey Armstrong, *Becoming a Pioneer of Success: God's Plan to Help You Win in Life and Business* (Shippensburg, Pa.: Destiny Image Publishing, 2004). For a brief discussion of this trend, see Andria Y. Carter, "Get Right, Get Rich: Books Preaching the Theology of Prosperity Grow in Popularity," *Black Issues Book Review* 1 (September 2005): 70–74. I am grateful to Alyson Monaghan for first suggesting this point to me.

37   Bruce Wilkinson, *The Prayer of Jabez* (Sisters, Ore.: Multnomah Publishing, 2000). On the growth of this market, see Phil Kloer, "Words to Live By," *Atlanta Journal*, 3 June 2004, and Carol Eisenberg, "America's Old-Time Religious Revival: More People Reaching Out for Spiritual Guidance," *Washington Post*, 25 April 2005.

38   Michael D. Beenethum, *Listen! God Is Calling! Luther Speaks of Vocation, Faith, and Work* (Minneapolis: Augsburg Fortress, 2003); Robert Hudnut, *Call Waiting: How to Hear God Speak* (Downers Grove, Ill.: InterVarsity, 1999); Roslyn Karaban, *Responding to God's Call: A Survival Guide* (San Jose, Calif.: Resource Publications, 1998); R. J. Leider and D. A. Shapiro, *Whistle While You Work: Heeding Your Life's Calling* (San Francisco: Berrett-Koehler, 2001); Gregg Levoy, *Callings: Finding and Following an Authentic Life* (New York: Three Rivers Press, 1998); Edward Little, *Ears to Hear: Recognizing and Responding to God's Call* (Harrisburg: Morehouse Publishing, 2003); Gary Morsch and Eddy Hall, *When There's No Burning Bush: Following Your Passions to Discovering God's Call* (Grand Rapids: Baker Books, 2004); Sharon Daloz Parks, *Big Questions, Worthy Dreams;* Doug Sherman and William Hendricks, *Your Work Matters to God* (Colorado Springs: Navpress, 1987); Volf, *Work in the Spirit.*

39   Marsha Sinetar, *Ordinary People as Monks and Mystics: Lifestyles for Self-Discovery* (New York: Paulist Press, 1986), 59.

40   *Joan of Arcadia*, "Do the Math," first broadcast 2 April 2004 by CBS, directed by Rob Morrow, written by Antoinette Stella; *Joan of Arcadia*, "Pilot"; *Joan of Arcadia*, "Touch Move"; *Joan of Arcadia*, "The Election," first broadcast 22 October 2004, directed by Rob Morrow, written by Ellie Herman.

41   James Poniewozik, "Losing God's Religion: *Joan of Arcadia* Ducks Some Divisive Issues of Faith, but Its Miracle Is Finding the Drama in Ordinary Life," *Time*, vol. 162, no. 14, 3 November 2003. See also Ken Tucker, "Heaven Help Us: The Gods Must Be Crazy to Make CBS's *Joan of Arcadia* This Season's Unexpected Hit," *Entertainment Weekly*, 31 October 2003, 63; Patrick McCormick, "In the Name of the Father, the Son, and the Cafeteria Worker," *U.S. Catholic*, February 2004, 48.

42   Poniewozik, "Losing God's Religion," 74.

43   Theodore Heibert, "Theophany in the Old Testament," in *The Anchor Bible Dictionary,* ed. David Noel Freedman (New York: Doubleday, 1992); Jeffrey J. Niehaus, *God at Sinai: Covenant and Theophany in the Bible and Ancient Near East* (Grand Rapids: Zondervan, 1995); Bernard Robinson, "Moses at the Burning Bush," *Journal for the Study of the Old Testament* 75 (1997): 107–22.

44   Robin Blaetz, *Visions of the Maid: Joan of Arc in American Film and Culture* (Charlottesville: University Press of Virginia, 2002), 22.

45   Jen Waters, "Joan of Arc Leaves Indelible Mark: Christian Saint Inspires TV Show," *Washington Times,* 20 May 2004.

46   Thomas Skill et al., "The Portrayal of Religion and Spirituality on Fictional Network Television," *Review of Religious Research* 35 (1994): 251–67; John Patrick Foley, "Why Not More Programs like The Waltons?" in *Religion and Prime Time Television,* ed. Michael Suman (Westport, Conn.: Praeger, 1997).

47   Mark Pinsky, *The Gospel according to The Simpsons: The Spiritual Life of the World's Most Animated Family* (Louisville, Ky.: Westminster John Knox, 2001).

48   Tim Goodman, "Priest Is a Pill Popper Who Chats with Jesus: Controversy, Anyone?" *San Francisco Chronicle,* 6 January 2006; Gail Pennington, "TV Seeks Religion: NBC's Risky Revelations Tries to Break through Taboo," *St. Louis Dispatch,* 24 April 2005. On the increasing number of references to religion in mainstream popular culture, see Donna Britt, "Pop Culture Slowly Moves into the Pew," *Washington Post,* 24 September 2004; Stephanie Kang, "Style and Substance: Pop Culture Gets Religion," *Wall Street Journal,* 5 May 2004; "Religion Surges into Pop Culture," *Chicago Tribune,* 19 April 2004; David Rooney, "The Gospel according to B'Way," *Variety* 25–27 March 2005, 36.

49   See, for example, Nicole JOA et al., "Favorite Joan and Adam Kiss?" Listserv message, 14 November 2004, http://p214.ezboard.com/fjoanandadamon-linefrm7.

50   Frances Early and Kathleen Kennedy, eds., *Athena's Daughters: Television's New Women Warriors* (Syracuse: Syracuse University Press, 2003); Sherrie A. Inness, ed., *Action Chicks: New Images of Tough Women in Popular Culture* (New York: Palgrave Macmillan, 2004).

51   McCormick, "The Father, the Son, and the Cafeteria Worker."

52   Fan demand led to the release of the entire (unaired) season of *Wonderfalls* on DVD.

53   Tona J. Hangen, *Redeeming the Dial: Radio, Religion, and Popular Culture in America* (Chapel Hill: University of North Carolina Press, 2002).

54   Lynn Schoefield Clark and Stewart M. Hoover, "At the Intersection of Media, Culture, and Religion: A Bibliographic Essay," in *Rethinking Media, Religion, and Culture,* ed. Stewart M. Hoover and Knut Lunby (Thousand Oaks, Calif.: Sage Publications, 1997); Razelle Frankl, *Televangelism: The Marketing of Popular Religion* (Carbondale: Southern Illinois University Press, 1987); Peter Horsfield, *Religious Television: The American Experience* (New York: Longman, 1984); Kenyan G. Tomaselli and Arnold Shepperson, " 'Speaking in Tongues, Writing in Vision': Orality and Literacy in Televangelistic Communications," in *Practicing Religion in the Age of the Media: Explorations in Media, Religion, and Culture,* ed. Stewart Hoover and Lynn Schofield Clark (New York: Columbia University Press, 2002); Quentin

Schultze, *Televangelism and American Culture: The Business of Popular Religion* (Grand Rapids: Baker Book House, 1991).

55   Bobby Alexander, *Televangelism Reconsidered: Ritual in the Search for Human Community* (Atlanta: Scholars Press, 1994); Heather Hendershot, *Shaking the World for Jesus: Media and Conservative Evangelical Culture* (Chicago: University of Chicago Press, 2004).

56   Robert Alley, "Television and Public Virtue," in *Channels of Belief: Religion and American Commercial Television*, ed. John P. Ferré (Ames: Iowa State University Press, 1990), 45–55; Michele Rosenthal, " 'Turn It Off!': TV Criticism in the *Christian Century* Magazine, 1946–1960," in Hoover, Schofield, and Clark, *Practicing Religion in the Age of the Media*. The conservative activist group Parents Television Council recently issued a report strongly criticizing TV networks for what they deemed negative treatments of Christianity on television. See "Mixed Messages/Faith in a Box/Conservative Advocacy Group Says Television Has No Respect for Religion," *Houston Chronicle*, 1 January 2005; and Joanne Ostrow, "TV Rant Preaches to the Mired," *Denver Post*, 19 December 2004.

57   William T. Fore, *Television and Religion: The Shaping of Faith, Values, and Culture* (Minneapolis: Augsburg Publishing House, 1987); Sam McFarland, "Keeping the Faith: The Roles of Selective Exposure and Avoidance in Maintaining Religious Beliefs," in *Religion and Mass Media: Audiences and Adaptations*, ed. Daniel A. Stout and Judith M. Buddenbaum (Thousand Oaks, Calif.: Sage Publishers, 1996); Carl Jeffrey Wright, *God's Vision or Television: How Television Influences What We Believe* (Chicago: Urban Ministries, 2004).

58   William D. Romanowski, "Evangelicals and Popular Music," in *Religion and Popular Culture in America*, ed. Bruce David Forbes and Jeffrey H. Mahan (Berkeley: University of California Press, 2000). For a concise summary of the these two different evangelical approaches to popular culture, see Quentin Schultze, "Touched by Angels and Demons: Religion's Love-Hate Relationship with Popular Culture," in *Religion and Popular Culture: Studies on the Interaction of Worldviews*, ed. Daniel A. Stout and Judith M. Buddenbaum (Ames: Iowa State University Press, 2001).

59   Jorge J. E. Gracia, *Mel Gibson's Passion and Philosophy: The Cross, the Questions, the Controversy* (La Salle, Ill.: Open Court, 2004); Thomas Lindlof, "The Passionate Audience: Community Inscriptions of The Last Temptation of Christ," in Stout and Buddenbaum, *Religion and Mass Media*; S. Brent Plate, ed., *Re-Viewing The Passion: Mel Gibson's Film and Its Critics* (New York: Palgrave Macmillan, 2004).

60   Tom Beaudoin, *Virtual Faith: The Irreverent Spiritual Quest of Generation X* (San Francisco: Jossey-Bass, 1998); Walter T. Davis Jr. et al., *Watching What We Watch: Prime-Time Television through the Lens of Faith* (Louisville, Ky.: Geneva Press, 2001); Craig Detweiler and Barry Taylor, *A Matrix of Meanings: Finding God in Pop Culture* (Grand Rapids: Baker Academic, 2003); John Wiley Nelson, *Your God Is Alive and Well and Appearing in Popular Culture* (Philadelphia: Westminster Press, 1976).

61   Roy M. Anker, *Catching Light: Looking for God in the Movies* (Grand Rapids: Wm. B. Eerdmans, 2005); Gareth Higgins, *How Movies Helped Save My Soul: Finding Spiritual Fingerprints in Culturally Significant Films* (Lake Mary, Iowa: Relevant Books, 2003); Clive Marsh and Gaye Ortiz, eds., *Explorations in Theology and Film: Movies and Meaning* (Malden, Mass.: Blackwell, 1997); Margaret Miles, *Seeing and Believing: Religion and Values in the Movies* (Boston: Beacon Press, 1996).

62   On *The Matrix*, see Stephen Faller, *Beyond the Matrix: Revolutions and Reve-lations* (Atlanta: Chalice Press, 2004), and Chris Seay and Greg Garrett, *The Gospel Reloaded: Exploring Spirituality and Faith in The Matrix* (Colorado Springs: Piñon Press, 2003). On *Star Trek*, see Michael Jindra, "It's about Faith in Our Future: Star Trek Fandom as Cultural Religion," in Forbes and Mahan, *Religion and Popular Culture in America*; and Jennifer Porter and Darcee L. McLaren, *Star Trek and Sacred Ground: Explorations of Star Trek, Religion, and American Culture* (Albany: State University of New York Press, 1999). On secular TV shows, see Horace Newcomb, "Religion on Televi-sion," in Ferré, *Channels of Belief*; Jay Newman, *Religion vs. Television: Com-petitors in Cultural Context* (Westport, Conn.: Praeger, 1996); Quentin Schultze, "Television Drama as a Sacred Text," in *Channels of Belief*; Elijah Seigler, "God in a Box: Religion in Contemporary Television Cop Shows," in *God in the Details: American Religion in Popular Culture*, ed. Eric Mazum and Kate McCarthy (New York: Routledge, 2001). For Christian interpreta-tions of other pop culture texts, see William Romanowski, *Eyes Wide Open: Looking for God in Popular Culture* (Grand Rapids: Brazos Press, 2001). For a discussion of religion and the Internet, see Jeff Zaleski, *The Soul of Cyber-space: How New Technology Is Changing Our Spiritual Lives* (New York: HarperEdge: 1997).

63   Douglas LeBlanc, "Hip Mission: A High School Girl Further Increases God's Prime-Time Exposure," *Christianity Today*, April 2004, 101–2.

64   James Martin, "God and the New Fall Shows," *America*, 13 October 2003, 22.

65   *Joan of Arcadia*, "The Fire and the Wood."

66   *Joan of Arcadia*, "The Devil Made Me Do It."

67   *Joan of Arcadia*, "Do the Math."

68   Franklin, "Down to Earth," 110.

69   *Joan of Arcadia*, "The Fire and the Wood."

70   See, for example, Franklin, "Down to Earth."

71   Ashley Merryman, "Challenge of *Joan of Arcadia* Is Our Own," *National Catholic Reporter*, February 2004, 15.

72   See, for example, Sally Steenland, *Growing Up in Prime Time: An Analysis of Adolescent Girls on Television* (Washington, D.C.: National Commission on Working Women, 1988).

Vocation as Proclamation of Love

1   Thérèse of Lisieux, *The Story of a Soul* (New York: Doubleday, 1989), 155.

2   In contemporary Christology the terms *descending Christology* and *ascending Christology* are used to refer to understandings of the nature and person of Christ that take as their starting point the divinity and humanity of Jesus, respectively. The present essay applies the terms *descending* and *ascending* to refer to the locus of departure for theological reflection on Christian anthro-pology, the divine activity on behalf of humankind, and the human response to God's saving action, respectively.

3   See Walter Kasper, *The God of Jesus Christ* (New York: Crossroads, 1984), 308–9.

4   Thomas Merton, *No Man Is an Island* (New York: Harcourt Brace, 1978), 3.

5   The Trinitarian theology articulated in this paragraph reflects the theologi-cal tradition of the church in the West, especially in terms of its reference to the procession of the Spirit from the Father and the Son.

6   John Paul II, "Letter to the Bishops of the Catholic Church on the Collaboration of Men and Women in the Church and in the World," *Origins* 34, no. 11 (2004): 171.

7   Karl Rahner, *Hearers of the Word* (New York: Sheed & Ward, 1969).

8   A helpful application of a phenomenological perspective in a Christian moral framework may be found in Russsell B. Connors Jr. and Patrick T. McCormick, *Character, Community, and Choices* (New York: Paulist Press, 1998), 27–33.

9   *Catechism of the Catholic Church*. 2nd ed. (Washington D.C.: United States Conference of Catholic Bishops, 1997), 1272–73.

10   Regis Duffy, "Baptism and Confirmation," in *Systematic Theology: Roman Catholic Perspectives*, vol. 2, ed. Francis Schussler Fiorenza and John P. Galvin (Minneapolis: Augsburg Fortress, 1991), 215.

11   *Catechism of the Catholic Church*, 258.

12   See Luigi Gambero, *Mary and the Fathers of the Church* (San Francisco: Ignatius Press, 1999), 124–25, 376.

13   J. M. R. Tillard, *Church of Churches: The Ecclesiology of Communion* (Collegeville: The Liturgical Press, 1992), 84–85.

Habits, Compartmentalization, and Vocation

1   Marc Parisi is now a campus minister at Calvert Hall High School in Towson, Maryland.

2   This theory is most explicitly laid out in Aquinas's *magnum opus*, the *Summa Theologica*. See especially the first half of part II, also called the *Prima Secundae* (or I–II). Aquinas relies on the thought of Aristotle for much of his work on virtue. See Aristotle's *Nicomachean Ethics*, 935–1112, in Richard McKeon, ed., *The Basic Works of Aristotle* (New York: Random House, 1941).

3   For a helpful and concise summary of human action and freedom, see the *Catechism of the Catholic Church*, 2nd ed. (United States: United States Conference of Catholic Bishops, 1997), 1730ff.

4   For a helpful discussion of intention, and Aquinas's thought on the whole, see Paul Wadell, *Primacy of Love: An Introduction to the Ethics of St. Thomas Aquinas* (New York: Paulist Press, 1992), 29–43.

5   See Wadell, *Primacy of Love*, 34. Wadell relies on John Finnis, *Fundamentals of Ethics* (Washington, D.C.: Georgetown University Press, 1983).

6   For Aquinas's discussion of habits, see his *Summa Theologica* I–II, 49–54. See also Wadell, *Primacy of Love*, 106–24.

7   The moral importance of how we "see" situations is a crucial contribution of virtue theory to ethical thought in the past few decades. Although virtue theory is several thousand years old, it has seen a great resurgence recently. One key book in instigating that resurgence—and a helpful discussion of the moral importance of how we "see"—is Iris Murdoch, *The Sovereignty of the Good* (London: Ark Paperbacks, 1970). For a more recent discussion of the moral importance of seeing, see Paul Wadell, *Becoming Friends: Worship, Justice, and the Practice of Christian Friendship* (Grand Rapids: Brazos Press, 2002).

8   See Aquinas, *Summa Theologica* II–II, 156. Aquinas is drawing here on Aristotle's *Nichomachean Ethics*, book 7.

Transforming the Artistic Vocation into a Calling

1   Regis J. Armstrong, J. A. Wayne Hellmann, and William J. Short, eds., *Francis of Assisi: Early Documents*, vol. 1 (New York: New City Press, 1999), 124.
2   Pseudo-Dionysius, *Letter Nine*, in *Pseudo-Dionysius: The Complete Works*, ed. John Farina (New York: Paulist Press, 1987), 283.
3   John Paul II, "Letter of His Holiness Pope John Paul II to Artists, 1999," sec. 3, and 11, http://www.vatican.va/holy_father/john_paul_ii/letters/documents/hf_jp-ii_let_23041999_artists_en.html.
4   John Paul II, "Letter to Artists, 1999" sec. 11.
5   Psuedo-Dionysius, *The Divine Names*, in *The Complete Works,* 74–75.
6   The three stages that I am proposing are similar but not identical to those proposed by Origen, which have had a subsequent influence on the development of Christian spirituality—the purgative, illuminative, and unitive stages of the spiritual journey. See Richard Byrne, "Journey Growth and Development in Spiritual Life," in *The New Dictionary of Catholic Spirituality*, ed. Michael Downey (Collegeville, Minn.: The Liturgical Press, 1993), 570.
7   Bonaventure, *The Life of Saint Francis*, in *Bonaventure: The Soul's Journey into God, The Tree of Life, The Life of Saint Francis*, ed. Richard Payne, trans. Ewert Cousins (New York: Paulist Press, 1978), 179, 228, 180.
8   David L. Schlindler further elaborates on this idea by saying: "Transcendence properly understood is not an experience of something alongside reality, something which fits in the empty spaces of which there are fewer and fewer in a consumer-technocratic culture. . . . The reason for this is that the transcendent God is immanent; as infinite, God is everywhere and reaches 'inside' everything." "Beauty, Transcendence, and the Face of the Other: Religion and Culture in America," *Communio: International Catholic Review* 26, no. 4 (1999): 917.
9   Pseudo-Dionysius, *The Celestial Hierarchy*, in *The Complete Works*, 146.
10   Pseudo-Dionysius, *The Celestial Hierarchy*, in *The Complete Works*, 146.
11   Alejandro Garcia-Rivera, *The Community of the Beautiful: A Theological Aesthetics* (Collegeville, Minn.: The Liturgical Press, 1999), 20.
12   John Paul II, "Letter to Artists, 1999," sec. 10.
13   John Paul II, "Letter to Artists, 1999," sec. 1.
14   John Paul II, "Letter to Artists, 1999," sec. 2.
15   Ewert Cousins, introduction to *Bonaventure*, 30 (quoting *The Soul's Journey into God*, II, 11).
16   *Bonaventure*, 67–68.
17   Teresa of Avila, *The Interior Castle*, in *The Collected Works of Teresa of Avila*, vol. 2, trans. by Kieran Kavanaugh and Otilio Rodriguez (Washington, D.C.: ICS Publications, 1980), 323.
18   John Paul II, "Letter to Artists, 1999," sec. 1.
19   *Bonaventure*, 229.
20   *Bonaventure*, 188.
21   Pseudo-Dionysius, *Letter Nine*, in *The Complete Works*, 283 (emphasis added).
22   John Paul II, "Letter to Artists, 1999," sec. 2.
23   John Paul II, "Letter to Artists, 1999," sec. 1.
24   *The Complete Letters of Vincent Van Gogh*, vol. 3 (Boston: Bulfinch Press, 2001), 180.
25   Michael Downey, ed., *The New Dictionary of Catholic Spirituality* (Collegeville, Minn.: The Liturgical Press: 1993), 209.

26   Simone Weil, *Selected Writings* (Maryknoll, N.Y.: Orbis Books, 1998), 92, 96, 91.
27   Armstrong, Hellman, and Short, *Francis of Assisi*, 1, 113.
28   *Bonaventure*, 255.
29   Garcia-Rivera, *Community of the Beautiful*, 8.
30   Otto Georg von Simson, *The Gothic Cathedral* (Princeton: Princeton University Press, 1988), 4.
31   Abbot Suger, *On the Abbey Church of St.-Denis and Its Art Treasures*, ed. and trans. by Erwin Panofsky (Princeton: Princeton University Press, 1979), 21 (emphasis added).
32   Pseudo-Dionysius, *The Mystical Theology*, in *The Complete Works*, 135.
33   John Paul II, "Letter to Artists, 1999," sec. 6.
34   Pseudo-Dionysius, *Mystical Theology*, 136–37.
35   Pseudo-Dionysius, *Mystical Theology*, 138.
36   Francoise Cachin, *Cézanne* (New York: Harry N. Abrams, 1996), 198.
37   *Bonaventure*, 263, 260, 180.
38   Armstrong, Hellmann, and Short, *Francis of Assisi,* 124.
39   Gregory of Nyssa, *The Life of Moses*, trans. Abraham J. Malherbe and Everett Ferguson (New York: Paulist Press, 1978), 113, 12, 30–31.
40   Pseudo-Dionysius, *The Divine Names*, in *The Complete Works*, 75.
41   Teresa of Avila, *Interior Castle,* 283–84, 276–77.
42   Gregory of Nyssa, *Life of Moses*, 114.
43   *Bonaventure*, 263, 228.
44   Garcia-Rivera, *Community of the Beautiful,* 88–89.
45   Pope John Paul II, "Letter to Artists, 1999," sec. 6 (quoting Macarius the Great).

Developing a Vocation of Work for Today

1   This is using the Standard Occupational Classification (SOC) and North American Industrial Classification System (NAICS). For details, see "Standard Occupational Classification (SOC) System," Bureau of Labor Statistics, http://www.bls.gov/soc; and "North American Industry Classification System (NAICS) at BLS," Bureau of Labor Statistics, http://www.bls.gov/bls/naics.htm.
2   Michael Horrigan, Bureau of Labor Statistics, "Introduction to the Projections," *Occupational Outlook Quarterly* (2003–4): 2.
3   Elaine Chao, "Message from the Secretary of Labor," *Report on the American Workforce* (United States Department of Labor, 2001).
4   Dorothy Sayers, "Why Work?" in *Creed or Chaos?* (New York: Harcourt, Brace, 1949), 46.
5   In her defense, she is aware of these problems. The first quote alludes to them (there must be a fit between worker and job, one's work must be something of value), but they were not the focus of the essay. Also, while her essay argues that people should serve the work rather than thinking about the community (because they lose track of doing a good job), she does not discuss whether this reasoning would imply that people should not be thinking about how their work serves God.
6   In work, we are to transform everything, both the external world (the objective, physical dimension) and ourselves (the subjective dimension). Work requires not just physical and intellectual exertion, but moral effort on the part of the person: discipline, perseverance, industriousness, etc.

These acts of will help the worker develop virtue, and the spiritual theology here assists in providing the motives for these acts. In the objective dimension, we subdue and master creation for our benefit. In the subjective sense, we subdue and master ourselves, and the growth in virtue this requires is often the most important and challenging elements of our vocation to work. However, in this essay I wanted to encourage people to think creatively about what they can do in their vocations to bring Christ to the world and thus have set aside the aspect of personal development in virtue through work. An excellent examination of the subjective dimension of work is provided in Samuel Gregg, *Challenging the Modern World: Karol Wojtyla/John Paul II and the Development of Catholic School Teaching* (Lanham, Md.: Lexington Books, 2003).

7   John Paul II, *Laborem Exercens* (Boston: Pauline Books & Media, 1981), sec. 24. All quotes from the church documents are given as written (emphases in original).

8   The headings for these three sections in *Laborem Exercens* are those used by the pope himself.

9   *Laborem Exercens*, sec. 25.

10   *Laborem Exercens,* quoting *Gaudium et Spes* (1965), sec. 34.

11   *Laborem Exercens,* quoting *Gaudium et Spes* (1965), sec. 34.

12   As *Laborem Exercens*, sec. 26, cites from *Gaudium et Spes* (sec. 35): "Just as human activity proceeds from man, so it is ordered toward man. For when a man works he not only alters things and society, he develops himself as well. He learns much, he cultivates his resources, he goes outside of himself and beyond himself. Rightly understood, this kind of growth is of greater value than any external riches which can be garnered. . . . Hence, the norm of human activity is this: that in accord with the divine plan and will, it should harmonize with the genuine good of the human race and allow people as individuals and as members of society to pursue their total vocation and fulfill it."

13   John Paul II, *Laborem Exercens*, sec. 25.

14   John Paul II, *Laborem Exercens*, sec. 25.

15   John Paul II, *Laborem Exercens*, sec. 36, quoting *Lumen Gentium*, sec. 36.

16   Although the pope did not do so in this section, two related points could also be made. First, though a carpenter would have been a respectable profession, it was hardly king or high priest. This incarnation in a particularly common profession surely proclaims that one is not one's work, that one's position before God is not determined by the position one holds in society. This idea is found in *Laborem Exercens,* sec. 6. Second, clearly carpentry was secondary to his later ministry of teaching, atonement, and resurrection. As I mentioned above, his model makes it clear how removed one's profession might be from the primary vocation to which God calls us.

17   John Paul II, *Laborem Exercens*, sec. 26.

18   Sayers, "Why Work?" 57.

19   Some translations of Luke 2:49 (e.g., NAB) use "house," while others use "business," but the vocational sense is clear.

20   John Paul II, *Laborem Exercens*, sec. 27.

21   Michael Novak, *Three in One: Essays in Democratic Capitalism, 1976–2000*, ed. Edward Younkins (Lanham, Md.: Rowman & Littlefield, 2001), 300.

22   Many of us will accomplish these obligations to serve others in ways unconnected to our work: singing in church, teaching catechism, coaching softball, volunteering at a homeless shelter, and so on. Those are all good, and

should be done. But the question here is how to use the skills from our work in service to others.

23   John Paul II, *Laborem Exercens*, sec. 25, quoting *Gaudium et Spes* (1965), sec. 34.

24   John Paul II, *Laborem Exercens*, sec. 24.

25   I focus on these as I believe transformation of our work is the hardest, and least socially accepted, part of our vocation in work, and thus most in need of illumination and encouragement. This isn't to imply that the only transformation must be a field-level transformation. For most of us, our daily work of transformation may only be to touch our coworkers. However, I take the harder cases to show how far some have gone with a proper spirit of vocation. If it can be done even in these hardest cases, surely it can for easier ones as well.

26   This is adapted from Jack Hayford and Gary Curtis, *Pathways to Pure Power: Learning the Depths of Love's Power, a Study of 1 Corinthians* (Nashville: Thomas Nelson, 1994), 47–48; Glenn Waddell and Judith Keegan, "Christian Conciliation: An Alternative to 'Ordinary' ADR," *Cumberland Law Review* 29 (1999): 583; and Christian Legal Service's Web site (now named Peacemaker Ministries): see http://www.hispeace.org.

27   This is adapted from Paul Vitz, "Psychology in Recovery," *First Things* 151 (March 2005): 17–22; and from Gregg Easterbrook, *The Progress Paradox: How Life Gets Better While People Feel Worse* (New York: Random House, 2003).

Our Common Calling to Holiness and Sanctity

1   For more about Dorothy Day see Paul Elie, *The Life You Save May Be Your Own: An American Pilgrimage* (New York: Farrar, Straus & Giroux, 2003).

2   Peter quotes Leviticus 11:44-45.

3   See also Exodus 3:4, 19:6; and 2 Timothy 1:9-10.

4   See also Romans 1:7; 1 Corinthians 1:2; and Matthew 5:48.

5   Thomas Hopko, *Finding One's Calling in Life* (Crestwood, N.Y.: St. Vladimir's Seminary Press, 2005), 4.

6   See David Farmer, *The Oxford Dictionary of Saints* (New York: Oxford University Press, 1992).

7   I am indebted to the work of my colleague Michael Plekon, whose writings have shaped my own thinking on the subject of holiness and sanctity; see especially *Living Icons: Persons of Faith in the Eastern Church* (Notre Dame, Ind.: University of Notre Dame, 2002); *Tradition Alive* (Lanham, Md.: Rowman & Littlefield, 2003); and cotranslated with Alexis Vinogradov, *In the World, of the Church: A Paul Evdokimov Reader* (Crestwood, N.Y.: SVS Press, 2001).

8   Sophie Koulumzine, *Many Worlds: A Russian Life* (Crestwood, N.Y.: St. Vladimir's Seminary Press, 1980).

9   Koulumzine, *Many Worlds,* 70.

10   John Meyendorff, "A Life Worth Living," in *Liturgy and Tradition*, ed. Thomas Fisch (New York: SVS Press, 1990), 147.

11   Meyendorff, "A Life Worth Living," 154.

12   This phrase is included in the anaphora (offertory) prayer of the Divine Liturgy of Saint John Chrysostom.

13   Alexander Schmemann, *Liturgy and Life: Christian Development through Liturgical Experience* (Syosset, N.Y.: Department of Religious Education-Orthodox Church in America, 1974), 5.

14   Alexander Schmemann, *The Journals of Father Alexander Schmemann*, trans. Juliana Schmemann (New York: SVS Press, 2000), 25.

15   Plekon, *Living Icons*, 190.

16   Chrysostom writes: "The altar is made of Christ's members, and the body of the Lord becomes your altar. Venerate it, you sacrifice the victim of the flesh of the Lord. The altar is more awesome than the one we use here, not just more than the one used in ancient times (in the Old Testament). No, do not object. The altar is awesome because of the sacrifice laid upon it, that, the one made of alms, is even more so, not just because of alms, but because it is the very sacrifice which makes others awesome. Again, this altar, only stone, becomes holy because Christ's body touches it, but that it is holy because it is itself Christ's body. So that altar is more awesome, sisters and brothers, than the one you are standing beside." *Flesh of the Church, Flesh of Christ: At the Source of the Ecclesiology of Communion*, ed. J. M. R. Tillard (Collegeville, Minn.: The Liturgical Press, 2001), 84.

17   See Wendy Mayer and Pauline Allen, *John Chrysostom* (New York: Routledge, 2000), and *St. John Chrysostom: On Wealth and Poverty*, ed. Catherine Roth (Crestwood, N.Y.: St. Vladimir's Seminary Press, 1984).

18   Alexander Schmemann, *Celebration of Faith*, vol. 2, trans. John Jillions (New York: SVS Press, 1997), 160–61.

19   Despite their both living in Paris, it is unclear whether Alexander Schmemann and Mother Maria ever crossed paths. It is interesting to note, however, that both were influenced by the same two men, Father Bulgakov and Metropolitan Evlogy (both to be discussed in more detail later in this chapter). Father Bulgakov was Mother Maria's spiritual adviser and Schmemann's academic mentor at the St. Sergius Theological Institute. Metropolitan Evlogy tonsured Mother Maria and was influential in Schmemann's early theological career.

20   Richard Pevear and Larissa Volokhonsky, *Mother Maria Skobtsova: Essential Writings* (Maryknoll, N.Y.: Orbis Books, 2003), 14.

21   Pevear and Volokhonsky, *Mother Maria Skobtsova*, 15.

22   Pevear and Volokhonsky, *Mother Maria Skobtsova*, 19.

23   Both Father Bulgakov and Metropolitan Evlogy were prominent figures in the Russian religious renaissance in Paris during this period.

24   Sergei Hackel, *Pearl of Great Price* (New York: SVS Press, 1981), 21.

25   Hackel, *Pearl of Great Price*, 36.

26   Mother Maria also established houses of hospitality at 43 rue Francois Gerard, 74 rue de Felix Faure, and a large country house at Noisy-le-Grand. Father Kyprian Kern was chaplain for Mother Maria's first house, at 77 rue de Lourmel, during the early 1940s. Interestingly, Schmemann was assigned to work with Father Kern after his ordination in 1946.

27   Pevear and Volokhonsky, *Mother Maria Skobtsova*, 30.

28   Hackel, *Pearl of Great Price*, 23.

29   Plekon, *Living Icons*, 270. Gauloises was a type of French cigarette.

30   Pevear and Volokhonsky, *Mother Maria Skobtsova*, 54.

31   Pevear and Volokhonsky, *Mother Maria Skobtsova*, 176.

32   Pevear and Volokhonsky, *Mother Maria Skobtsova*, 33.

33   Hackel, *Pearl of Great Price*, 130.

34   Pevear and Volokhonsky, *Mother Maria Skobtsova*, 42.

35   Plekon and Vinogradov, *In the World, of the Church*, 149.

The Ethics of Vocation and Military Service

1   "Commentary: Religious Views on War and U.S. Response," *Religion & Ethics Newsweekly*, 21 September 2001, episode no. 503, http://www.pbs. org/wnet/religionandethics/week503/perspectives.html.

2   Stanley Hauerwas, "No, This War Would Not Be Moral." *Time*, vol. 161, no. 9. 3 March 2003.

3   Chris Hedges, *War Is a Force That Gives Us Meaning* (New York: Anchor Books, 2003).

4   "Chris Hedges: The Costs of War," interview with Bob Abernathy on *Religion & Ethics Newsweekly*, 31 January 2003, episode no. 622, http://www. pbs.org/wnet/religionandethics/week622/cover.html.

5   Lloyd Steffen, "On a Mission: The Uses of American Power," *The Christian Century*, 122, no. 7 (2005): 33–38.

6   Elisabeth Sifton, *The Serenity Prayer: Faith and Politics in Times of Peace and War* (New York: W. W. Norton, 2005).

7   Robin W. Lovin, "On Prayer and Politics," essay for *Religion & Ethics Newsweekly*, 9 January 2004, episode no. 719, http://www.pbs.org/wnet/ religionandethics/week719/essay.html.

8   Reinhold Niebuhr, *Moral Man and Immoral Society* (New York: Scribner, 1995), xi, xii, 3, 18–19.

9   Miroslav Volf, *Exclusion and Embrace: A Theological Exploration of Identity, Otherness, and Reconciliation* (Nashville: Abingdon, 1996), 2–3.

10   Volf, *Exclusion and Embrace*, 1.

The Call of the Other

1   Alfred North Whitehead, *The Aims of Education* (New York: Macmillan, 1929), preface and 13.

2   Paul Ricoeur, *Oneself as Another*, trans. Kathleen Blamey (Chicago: University of Chicago Press, 1992).

3   Charles Taylor, *The Ethics of Authenticity* (Cambridge: Harvard University Press, 1991), *Sources of the Self* (Cambridge: Harvard University Press, 1989).

4   Alain Renaut, *The Era of the Individual: A Contribution to a History of Subjectivity*, trans. by M. B. DeBevoise and Franklin Philip (Princeton: Princeton University Press, 1997), 31.

5   Robert N. Bellah, *Habits of the Heart: Individualism and Commitment in American Life* (New York: Harper & Row, 1986), 142ff.

6   Bellah, *Habits of the Heart*, vii.

7   Renaut, *The Era of the Individual*, 52.

8   Taylor, *Ethics of Authenticity*, 4.

9   Alexis de Tocqueville, *Democracy in America*, ed., trans., and with an introduction by Harvey C. Mansfield and Delba Winthrop (New York: Penguin Books, 2003), 587.

10   de Tocqueville, *Democracy in America*, 588.

11   Taylor, *Ethics of Authenticity*, 9.

12   As cited in Charles Guignon, *On Being Authentic* (New York: Routledge, 2004), 34.

13   C. B. Macpherson, *The Political Theory of Possessive Individualism* (Oxford: Oxford University Press, 1962).

14   Macpherson, *Political Theory*, 48.

15   One common definition of commodity is a thing that by its properties sat-
        isfies human wants of some sort or another." *Rethinking Commodification:
        Cases and Readings in Law and Culture*, ed. Martha M. Ertman and Joan C.
        Williams (New York: New York University Press, 2005), 2.

16   Macpherson, *Possessive Individualism*, 48.

17   Ertman and Williams, *Rethinking Commodification*, 362ff.

18   Ertman and Williams, *Rethinking Commodification*, 257.

19   Joseph E. Davis, "The Commodification of Self," *Hedgehog Review* 5, no. 2
        (2003): 41–49.

20   Erich Fromm, *The Essential Fromm: Life between Having and Being* (New
        York: Continuum,1999), 72.

21   John Berger, *Ways of Seeing* (London: British Broadcasting and Penguin
        Books, 1973), 143.

22   Emmanuel Mounier, *The Character of Man*, trans. Cynthia Roland (New
        York: Harper & Row, 1965), 203.

23   Guignon, *On Being Authentic*, preface and xii.

24   Taylor, *Ethics of Authenticity*, 14.

25   Ricoeur, *Oneself as Another,* 3, 317, 187.

26   Ricoeur, *Oneself as Another,* 18.

27   Emmanuel Levinas, *Humanism of the Other*, trans. Nidra Poller (Chicago:
        University of Illinois Press, 2003), 67.

28   Richard A. Cohen, introduction to *Humanism of the Other*, xxxvii.

29   Jacques Derrida, "Eating Well," in *Who Comes after the Subject?*, ed. Eduardo
        Cadava (New York: Routledge, 1991), 100–101.

30   Emmanuel Levinas, *Entre Nous,* trans. Michael B. Smith and Barbara Har-
        shav (New York: Columbia University Press, 1998), xii–xiii.

31   Emmanuel Levinas, *Otherwise than Being*, trans. Alphonso Lingis (Pitts-
        burgh: Duquesne University Press, 1998), 117.

32   Ricoeur, *Oneself as Another*, 313–14.

33   Levinas, *Humanism of the Other*, 33.

34   Levinas, *Otherwise than Being*, 116.

35   Aristotle, *The Metaphysics*, book 2, 995A.

36   Ludwig Wittgenstein, *Tractatus Logico-Philosophicus*, 2nd ed. (New York:
        Routledge, 2001), 88.

37   Emmanuel Levinas, *Totality and Infinity*, trans. Alphonso Lingis (Pittsburgh:
        Duquesne Unversity Press, 1969), 279.

38   Michael Oakeshott, *The Voice of Liberal Learning: Michael Oakeshott on Edu-
        cation*, ed. Timothy Fuller (New Haven: Yale University Press, 1990), 41.

39   Ricoeur, *Oneself as Another, ,* 172, 330.

The Role of the University between Popular and Ecclesial Culture

Portions of this essay first appeared in "Behind the Scenes of Hollywood,"
Crisis Magazine, 14 June 2005; and "Some Great Calling," *The Baylor Line*,
15 March 2005. They are used with permission.

1   W. E. B. Du Bois, "St. Francis of Assisi," in *W.E.B. Du Bois: A Reader*, ed.
        Andrew Paschal, with an introduction by Arna Bontemps (New York:
        Macmillan, 1971), 290, 292.

2   Du Bois, "St. Francis of Assisi," 295.

3   Du Bois, "St. Francis of Assisi," 295, 291, 296.

4   Tom Wolfe, *I Am Charlotte Simmons* (New York: Farrar, Straus & Giroux, 2004), 86.

5   David Brooks, *On Paradise Drive* (New York: Simon & Schuster, 2004), 162.

6   Brooks, *On Paradise Drive*, 159, 180.

7   Mark Edmundson, "On the Uses of Liberal Education: As Lite Entertainment for Bored College Students," *Harper's*, September 1997, 40.

8   Edmundson, "On the Uses of Liberal Education," 43.

9   Mark Edmundson, *Nightmare on Main Street: Angels, Sadomasochism, and the Culture of Gothic* (Cambridge: Harvard University Press, 1997).

10   Goo Goo Dolls, "Iris" (Warner Brothers, 1998).

11   Andrew Delbanco, "Colleges: An Endangered Species?" *New York Review of Books*, 52, no. 4 (2005): 20, 19, 20.

12   Brooks, *On Paradise Drive*, 161.

13   David Thomson, *The Whole Equation: A History of Hollywood* (New York: Knopf, 2004), 220.

14   Thomson, *Whole Equation*, 49, 157, 98.

15   Thomson, *Whole Equation*, 218.

16   Thomson, *Whole Equation*, 221, 74, 157.

17   Thomson, *Whole Equation*.

18   Walker Percy, *The Moviegoer* (New York: Knopf, 1961), 13.

19   Søren Kierkegaard, from *The Sickness unto Death*, in Percy, *The Moviegoer*, 7.

20   Thomson, *Whole Equation*, 359, 295, 296.

21   Du Bois, "St. Francis of Assisi," 291.

22   Augustine, *Confessions*, book 6, chap. 6.

23   Blaise Pascal, *Pensées*, trans. A. J. Krailsheimer (New York: Penguin Books, 1995), 8.

24   Bernard Williams, *Truth and Truthfulness: An Essay in Genealogy* (Princeton: Princeton University Press, 2004), 94, 126.

25   John Paul II, *Fides et Ratio* (Boston: Pauline Books & Media, 1998).

26   Stanley Fish, "One University under God," *Chronicle of Higher Education* 51, no. 18 (2005): C1.

27   John Henry Newman, "Knowledge Viewed in Relation to Professional Skill," in his *The Idea of a University* (Notre Dame, Ind.: University of Notre Dame Press, 1982), 114–15.

28   Josef Pieper, *The Philosophical Act* (South Bend, Ind.: St. Augustine Press, 1998), 107.

29   Iris Murdoch, *Existentialists and Mystics* (New York: Penguin Books, 1997), 215, 369.

30   Pascal, *Pensées* , 8.

31   Augustine, *Confessions and Enchiridion*, ed. Albert Cook Outler (Philadelphia: Westminster Press, 1955), 194 (book 9, chap. 10).

Calling Students to Transformation

1   Robert Leamnson, *Thinking about Teaching and Learning: Developing Habits of Learning with First-Year College and University Students* (Sterling, Va.: Stylus Publishing, 1999), 1.

2   Mariano Azuela, *Los de Abajo*, ed. John E. Englekirk and Lawrence B. Kiddle (Prospect Heights, Ill.: Waveland Press, 1992), 36–37, 104; translations from this text are mine.

3   Gloria Fiero, *The Humanistic Tradition*, vol. 2, 4th ed. (New York: McGraw-Hill, 2002), 942.

4   Jorge Luis Borges, "The Library of Babel," trans. Anthony Kerrigan, in *Ficciones*, ed. Anthony Kerrigan (New York: Grove Press, 1962), 79, 80, 83, 80, 85–86.

5   Several critics and scholars have made the connection between Borges and the information age. See Dominic Gates "The Library of Babel: The Dream of Cyberspace as a Universal Library" (web.archive.org/web/2003060 5103629/www.pretext.com/oct97/features/story1.htm); William Hoffman, "The Library of Infinity Is Opening Near You" (http://mbbnet.umn.edu/ doric/ library.html); Garrett Rowland, "A Subaltern Horror" (www.themodernword.com/borges/borges_papers_rowlan.html); Douglas Walk, "Webmaster Borges" (www.salon.com/books/feature/1999/12/06/borges/index.html).

6   Harold Bloom, *Where Shall Wisdom Be Found?* (New York: Riverhead Books, 2004), 3, 2.

7   The twenty-one colleges and universities I surveyed were both secular and church-affiliated. Bridgewater College's mission statement included the following sentence: "On the premise that a recognition of one's capabilities is the beginning of *wisdom*, Bridgewater offers a liberal arts education designed to help the student gain as complete a self-understanding as knowledge makes possible." The statement was found in the 2003–2004 catalog (emphasis added). Interestingly, the wisdom that is referenced here is tied to self-knowledge and discerning one's calling.

8   Harry R. Lewis, "Has Harvard Lost Its Way?" *Chronicle of Higher Education: The Chronicle Review*, 24 March 2006, B6, B8.

9   Azuela, *Los de Abajo*, 114–15.

10   Borges, "Library of Babel," 80.

11   Donald DeMarco, *The Many Faces of Virtue* (Steubenville, Ohio: Emmaus Road Publishing, 2000), 54 (italics in the original).

12   Gregory the Great, *Life and Miracles of St. Benedict*, trans. Odo J. Zimmerman, O.S.B., and Benedict R. Avery, O.S.B. (Collegeville, Minn.: The Liturgical Press, 1949), 1–2.

13   Biagio D'Antonio de Firenze's *Allegory of the Liberal Arts* can be found in the Musée Condé of Chantilly. It is reproduced on the cover of Wilburn Stancil's *A Student's Guide to the Liberal Arts* (Kansas City, Mo.: Rockhurst University Press, 2003).

14   Marvin Perry, J. Wayne Baker, and Pamela Pfeiffer Hollinger, eds., *The Humanities in the Western Tradition: Ideas and Aesthetics,* vol. 2 (Boston: Houghton Mifflin, 2003), 127.

15   Msgr. Ronald Bashara, "The Heart of the Syriac Fathers," *Maronite Voice*, February 2004, 7.

16   DeMarco, *Many Faces,* 54.

17   Miguel de Unamuno, *San Manuel Bueno, Mártir* (St. Manuel the Good, Martyr; Madrid: Ediciones Cátedra, 1994), 133; translations from this text are mine.

18   Jorge Luis Borges, "Tlön, Uqbar, Orbis Tertius," trans. Alastair Reid, in *Ficciones*, ed. Anthony Kerrigan (New York: Grove Press, 1963), 34.

Formation of Catholic School Teachers

1   Helen Alvare's talk was delivered in the fall of 2003 at the University of St. Thomas (St. Paul, Minn.) and was sponsored by the Center for Catholic Studies. Selections of her talk are available in *Perspectives*, a magazine published by the Center for Catholic Studies (December 2003).

2   I am grateful for the various insights and suggestions made by Michael Naughton, Christopher Ruddy, Michael Miller, Anna Bonta Moreland, Don Briel, and Josh Grinolds.

3   I am using the term *values added* to refer to a certain approach to the formation of Christian professionals whereby there is a primary emphasis on mastering the skills, methods, and competencies of a certain field (often as defined by certain accrediting agencies in the field) and then, secondarily, adding Christian formation elements (theology courses and/or prayer/worship experiences) so as to give professional endeavors a Christian shape and direction.

4   This "values-added" approach is not exclusive to Catholic school teacher formation or to the area of education. Integrating Christian faith, particularly its intellectual dimensions, with professional competencies is a challenge in many fields.

5   In a National Catholic Educational Association (NCEA) monograph professional preparation is defined as "a process through which a person goes to achieve state certification by demonstrating competence in subject matter knowledge, methods of teaching, evaluation and understanding of human growth and development so that information, skills and attitudes can be related effectively to students" and teacher formation is that which "endeavors to foster knowledge and understanding of . . . basic teachings of Catholic education, revelation, scripture, tradition and documents of the Church." NCEA, *The Pre-Service Formation of Teachers for Catholic Schools: In Search of Patterns for the Future* (Washington, D.C.: NCEA, 1982), vii.

6   John L. Watzke, "Alternative Teacher Education and Professional Preparedness: A Study of Parochial and Public School Contexts," *Catholic Education: A Journal of Inquiry and Practice,* 8, no. 4 (2005): 464.

7   Since their peak enrollment in 1965 (5,253,791 students in 12,893 schools), Catholic schools have significantly decreased in number and have experienced an immense loss of students and staffing. However, national enrollments and staffing since 1994 have been relatively steady, with only slight decreases. In the 2004–2005 academic year, there were 7,799 Catholic schools serving more than 2,420,590 students. See Dale McDonald, P.B.V.M., *United States Catholic Elementary and Secondary Schools 2004–2005* (Washington, D.C.: National Catholic Education Association, 2005), 3.

8   Maurice Timothy Reidy, "Needed: The Vision Thing," *Commonweal,* 9 April 2004, 15–18.

9   John C. Cavadini, "Ignorant Catholics: The Alarming Void in Religious Education," *Commonweal,* 9 April 2004, 12–14; Peter Steinfels, *A People Adrift* (New York: Simon & Schuster, 2003), chap. 6.

10   Watzke notes, "Over consecutive decades, this percentage [of religious and clergy] markedly decreased without a planned or sustainable system for preparing lay educators for Catholic education" ("Alternative Teacher Education," 464–65). He also notes that many factors have contributed to the movement of Catholic higher education toward a more secular approach: "financial concerns; teacher candidate preference; state laws; lack of proximity, affiliation, or experience with Catholic schools" (463).

11   Mario O. D'Souza, C.S.B., "Jacques Maritain's Seven Misconceptions of Education: Implications for the Preparation of Catholic School Teachers," *Catholic Education: A Journal of Inquiry and Practice* 5 (2002): 435.

12   Franz DeHovre, *Philosophy in Education*, trans. E. B. Jordan (New York: Benziger Bros., 1930); John D. Redden and Francis A. Ryan, *A Catholic Philos-*

ophy of Education (Milwaukee: Bruce Publishing, 1942); William J. McGucken, S.J., "The Philosophy of Catholic Education," chap. 6 of *Philosophies of Education*, pt. 1, *Yearbook of the National Society for the Study of Education*, no. 41 (Chicago: University of Chicago Press, 1942); Jacques Maritain, *Education at the Crossroads* (New Haven: Yale University Press, 1960); Jacques Maritain, "Thomist Views of Education," in *Modern Philosophies and Education*, ed. Nelson B. Henry (Chicago: University of Chicago Press, 1955).

13   Maritain writes, "To have made education more experiential, closer to concrete life and permeated with social concerns from the very start is an achievement of which modern education is justly proud." *Education at the Crossroads*, 16.

14   Robert Henle, "A Roman Catholic View of Education," in *Philosophies of Education*, ed. Philip Phenix (New York: Wiley, 1965).

15   John L. Elias, "Whatever Happened to Catholic Philosophy of Education?" *Religious Education* 94, no. 1 (1999): 104.

16   Elias, "Whatever Happened," 93, 103. Elias explains: "Catholic philosophy of education was such a respected educational theory that its major theorists were invited to write a chapter on Catholic philosophy of education for the yearbooks of the National Society for the Study of Education, which were devoted to philosophy of education" (93). He also writes: "Few scholars identify themselves as Catholic philosophers of education as was done only twenty years ago. A number of Catholic scholars write on education but usually identify themselves as religious educators. In their writings they usually restrict themselves to issues relating to religious education and do not attempt to present a philosophy for all of Catholic education. The work of these authors, though possessing philosophical components, does not amount to a developed philosophy of Catholic education. Little explicit use is made of Thomistic principles, nor are the school, college, or university major foci of their work" (103).

17   Elias, "Whatever Happened," 104–5.

18   Elias notes that "in 1970 the *Catholic Educational Review*, a scholarly journal on Catholic education, ceased to exist when Catholic University declined to renew its subsidy" (104). Elias also notes that the decline in Catholic school enrollments in the 1970s and beyond that coincided with an increase in the number of students attending religious education classes may be an additional factor in the decline in a Catholic philosophy of education and a shift to theorizing about the task of religious education (104).

19   Catholic universities have typically offered a specific type of liberal arts education that includes philosophy and theology courses, which theoretically could connect with the development of a Catholic philosophy of education. However, without any deliberate attempt on the part of faculty and the curriculum to integrate Catholic philosophy or theology with the education profession, it is unlikely that students will make the connections between two increasingly specialized and compartmentalized areas.

20   John L. Watzke, "Teachers for Whom? A Study of Teacher Education Practices in Catholic Higher Education," *Catholic Education: A Journal of Inquiry and Practice* 6 (2002): 145. Watzke's study lays out some of the complexities behind why Catholic higher education has focused teacher preparation on public school teaching.

21   Watzke, "Teachers for Whom?" 146. One respondent in Watzke's study explained why preservice teaching experience favors public schools over

Catholic schools: "Parochial schools will hire someone who has taught in a public school, but our experience has found that many public schools will not hire someone who student taught in a parochial school" (147).

22 Watzke, "Teachers for Whom?" 482.

23 Michael Pressley, ed., *Teaching Service and Alternative Teaching Education: Notre Dame's Alliance for Catholic Education* (Notre Dame, Ind.: University of Notre Dame Press, 2002), 138–39.

24 I designed this course in summer 2000 with Dr. Margaret Reif from the University of St. Thomas School of Education. Other "Faith and the Professions" classes examine medicine, management, law, social work, and psychology.

25 This integration is spoken of regularly as one of the distinctive marks of Catholic schools. "The special character of the Catholic school and the underlying reason for its existence, the reason why Catholic parents prefer it, is precisely the quality of the religious instruction into the overall education of the students." John Paul II, cited in *The Religious Dimension of Education in a Catholic School, Congregation for Catholic Education* (Boston: Pauline Books & Media, 1988), sec. 66.

26 Certainly, various academic disciplines, such as theology, philosophy, history, and education, have their distinct methodologies and specialties, but at a Catholic university they are not incommensurable ways of knowing. Rather, each avenue of knowledge is grounded in the source of all created reality and reaches its end in Jesus Christ. It is in and through these various intellectual pursuits that Christianity finds its full expression. Furthermore, students participating in a distinctly Catholic understanding of knowledge experience an education that integrates various intellectual pursuits while showing the relationship between the spiritual, the intellectual, and the moral.

27 According to Archbishop Harry J. Flynn, "uniqueness includes provisions that students—full-time employees in the archdiocese's 223 parishes and 110 schools—pay no tuition and the university receives no income from student-credit production in the courses. . . . Since the program began, 400 archdiocesan employees have earned graduate degrees in educational leadership, curriculum and instruction, and religious education. Eighty-six percent of the graduates are still working in the archdiocese." *The Catholic Spirit*, St. Paul-Minneapolis Archdiocesan paper, 1 September 2005, 2A.

28 Mario D'Souza argues that philosophy is equally important to Catholic teacher preparation because "Catholic education . . . is more than religious education" ("Jacqus Maritain's Seven Misconceptions," 450).

29 This parallel track pattern is similar to the more general pattern of university education: first provide a liberal arts foundation, then give students their professional education. Often conceived of as a foundational approach to education, in reality it should be called an "alongside" approach where integration is left up to the students, resulting in a lack of integration. This lack of integration translates into a segmented curriculum that has lost a vision for how to organize, interconnect, and make sense of this array of material.

30 James T. Byrnes makes a similar observation: "Post-modernism has begun to be the philosophical base for many Catholic educators, which, although in actual educational practice may not be problematic, becomes problematic when faced with presenting the Christian metanarrative with Jesus as the Way, the Truth, and the Life. Thus, a certain schizophrenia is detectable

in many areas of Catholic education and among Catholic educators: on the one hand, significant agreement with the educational practices being proposed today and, on the other, disagreement with the rejection of the Gospel of Jesus. It is for this reason that Catholic educators must once again take up the task of renewing the rich heritage that is theirs in regard to a philosophy of education." *John Paul II and Educating for Life* (Washington, D.C.: Peter Lang, 2002), 3.

31 Vatican Congregation for Catholic Education, *Religious Dimension of Education*, sec. 14.

32 William F. Losito, "Reclaiming Inquiry in the Catholic Philosophy of Education," in *Catholic School Leadership*, ed. Thomas C. Hunt, Thomas E. Oldenski, S.M., and Theodore J. Wallace (New York: Falmer Press, 2000), 59.

33 Louis Drupe writes: "Yet all too often religion itself is presented as adding one more value to all others, thus relativizing what ought to be an absolute ground of values. In functional terms this means that we treat religion as if it were one among many things that we ought to cultivate and learn about. But the 'object' of religion does not tolerate this kind of compartmentalization: it either includes all aspects of life or none at all. If God were only the particular subject of an academic discipline called 'religious studies' or 'theology,' He would not be God. . . . [T]he transcendent presence in the educational process touches on all disciplines and above all, becomes the integrating factor of all moral education." "The Joys and Responsibilities of Being a Catholic Teacher," in *Faith and the Intellectual Life*, ed. James L. Heft, S.M. (Notre Dame, Ind.: University of Notre Dame Press, 1996), 66–67.

34 Evidence for the lack of current material on a Catholic philosophy of education is discussed by Ellis A. Joseph in "The Philosophy of Catholic Education" in *Handbook of Research on Catholic Education*, ed. Thomas Hunt, Ellis A. Joseph, and Ronald J. Nuzzi (Westport, Conn.: Greenwood Press, 2001). Joseph reports that a total of 184 authors contributed selections to a 1996 encyclopedia on the philosophy of education: "Not one contributor addressed either the Catholic philosophy of education or philosophy as it relates to Catholic schooling. Eleven of the contributors resided in Catholic institutions of higher learning. None discussed philosophy as it relates to Catholic education" (J. Chambliss, *Philosophy of Education: An Encyclopedia* [New York: Garland Publishing, 1996], 32).

35 Several scholars have observed that little if any progress has been made in identifying a distinctly Catholic philosophy of education since Maritain published *Education at the Crossroads* in 1943. See David Carr et al., "Return to the Crossroads: Maritain Fifty Years On," *British Journal of Educational Studies* 43 (1995): 162–78.

36 Losito, "Reclaiming Inquiry," 59–60.

37 Maritain, *Education at the Crossroads*, 1.

38 Maritain, *Education at the Crossroads*, 1.

39 Maritain, *Education at the Crossroads*, 5.

40 Maritain, *Education at the Crossroads*, 9–10.

41 Maritain, *Education at the Crossroads*, 8, 7.

42 Maritain, *Education at the Crossroads*, 11–12.

43 Maritain, *Education at the Crossroads*, 2.

44 Maritain, *Education at the Crossroads*, 1. It should be noted that Maritain's view of the human person as dynamic, not static, opens the way for discussion with contemporary studies in the sociology of knowledge whereby the influence of culture on understanding is taken seriously. John L. Elias sug-

gests that the development of a Catholic educational theory today needs to combine the insights of neo-Thomist philosophy (as seen in the works of Bernard Lonergan, S.J.) and the insights of contemporary social theory and analysis (as seen in the works of Paolo Freire). Acknowledging their different strengths, Elias writes, "Both thinkers attend to the issue that human persons are formed in a social situation. . . . [T]he social thought of these two thinkers, especially Freire's, provides a powerful basis for an educational theory that sees the goals of education in terms of human, social and cultural liberation." Elias, "Whatever Happened?" 106–7.

45   Maritain, *Education at the Crossroads,* 34.

46   Maritain strongly distinguishes the task of intellectual formation from "intellectualism" that reduces education to a bourgeois mastery of "dialectical or rhetorical skill" (*Education at the Crossroads*, 18).

47   Nurturing the intellect is inseparable from contributing to human beatitude. Yet, Maritain explains that the most important things in human life cannot be taught: "[N]othing in human life is of greater importance than intuition and love, and neither intuition nor love are a matter of training or learning. Yet education must be primarily concerned with them" ("Education for the Good Life," *Commonweal*, 3 May 1946, 68). In essence "intuition and love" play a critical role in Catholic education, yet there is something elusive about them because they depend more on grace than nature.

48   Maritain, *Education at the Crossroads*, 4.

50   Maritain, *Education at the Crossroads*, 15.

51   Sacred Congregation for Catholic Education, *The Catholic School*, 1977, sec. 56.

52   Second Vatican Council, *Gravissimum Educationis* (1965), in *Vatican II: The Conciliar and Post Conciliar Documents*, ed. Austin Flannery, O.P., new rev. ed. (New York: Costello, 1992), 725.

53   Second Vatican Council, *Gravissimum Educationis,* 733.

54   Anemona Hartocollis, "Who Needs Education Schools?" *The New York Times,* 31 July 2005.

55   Hartocollis, "Who Needs?"

56   Maritain, *Education at the Crossroads*, 8.

57   Hartocollis, "Who Needs?"

58   Maritain, *Education at the Crossroads*, 14.

59   National Council of Catholic Bishops (USA), *In Support of Catholic Elementary and Secondary Schools* (NCCB, 1990); *Principles for Education Reform in the United States* (Washington, D.C.: NCCB, 1995).

60   Wilton Gregory, Address, meeting of the National Catholic Educational Association, St. Louis, 29 March 2005.

The Art of Teaching and the Christian Vocation

Portions of this essay first appeared in "Liberal Learning and the Light of Faith: An Initiation into Wholeness," *The Cresset: A Review of Literature, the Arts, and Public Affairs* (Trinity 2004); and "Integrating Heart, Mind, and Soul: The Vocation of the Christian Teacher," in *Gladly Learn, Gladly Teach: Living Out One's Calling in the Twenty-First Century Academy*, ed. Mohn Marson Donaway (Macon, Ga.: Mercer University Press, 2005). They are used with permission.

1   For two such examples, see Alan Wolfe, "The Opening of the Evangelical Mind," *Atlantic Monthly* (October 2000); and James Burtchaell, *The Dying of*

the Light: The Disengagement of Colleges and Universities from Their Christian Churches (Grand Rapids: Wm. B. Eerdmans, 1998).

2   T. S. Eliot, "Journey of the Magi," in Collected Poems, 1909–1962 (New York: Harcourt, Brace & World, 1963), 99.

3   The Rites of the Catholic Church: Volume One, 3rd ed. (Collegeville, Minn.: The Liturgical Press, 1990), 160–61.

4   John Henry Newman, "The Three Offices of Christ," from The Works of Cardinal Newman: Sermons on Subjects of the Day (Westminster, Md.: Christian Classics, 1968), 52.

5   Rodney L. Petersen, "Church and University: The Threefold Ministry and the Offices of Christ," in The Contentious Triangle: Church, State, and University, ed. Rodney L. Petersen and Calvin Augustine Pater (Kirksville, Mo.: Thomas Jefferson University Press, 1999), 364. I am indebted to Petersen's article for alerting me to the treatment of this topic in John Henry Newman's and Yves Congar's works.

6   I am appealing to a particularly Catholic understanding of lay participation in the triplex munus Christi, one that assumes a distinction between the ministerial priesthood and the spiritual priesthood of all believers; according to this model, the ordained (bishops, priests, and deacons) participate in Christ's threefold work in a distinctive way, including sacramental provision, magisterial teaching, and church governance. The role of the laity will be discussed in the body of the text. As Rodney Petersen has shown, Protestant theology in its multiple expressions challenged Catholicism's hierarchical model of ministry and elaborated a different understanding of the munus Christi reflective of its various ecclesiologies (see Petersen, "Church and University").

7   Second Vatican Council, Lumen Gentium, in Vatican II: The Conciliar and Post Conciliar Documents, ed. Austin Flannery, O.P., new rev. ed. (New York: Costello, 1992), sec. 34.

8   Lumen Gentium, sec. 36.

9   Lumen Gentium, sec. 35.

10   John Henry Newman, "The Christian Ministry," in Parochial and Plain Sermons (London: Longmans, Green, 1918), 303.

11   Lumen Gentium, sec. 35.

12   Simone Weil, "Reflections on the Right Use of School Studies with a View to the Love of God," in The Simone Weil Reader, ed. George A. Panichas (New York: David McKay, 1977), 50.

13   John Paul II, Homily, Camden Yards, Baltimore, 8 October 1995.

14   John Henry Newman, "The Three Offices of Christ," 60–61.

15   Lumen Gentium, sec. 36.

16   Patrick Samway, Signposts in a Strange Land (New York: Picador, 2000).

17   E. O. Wilson, Consilience (New York: Knopf, 1998), 266, quoted in Wendell Berry, Life Is a Miracle: An Essay against Modern Superstition (Washington, D.C.: Counterpoint, 2000), 25.

18   Wilson, Consilience, 115, quoted in Berry, Life Is a Miracle, 30.

19   Berry, Life Is a Miracle, 31.

20   Wendell Berry, "The Loss of the University," in Home Economics (New York: North Point Press, 1987), 76–78.

21   E. F. Schumacher, A Guide for the Perplexed (New York: Harper Perennial, 1978), 43.

22   Berry, "Loss of the University," 82 (emphasis added).

23   James Taylor, Poetic Knowledge: The Recovery of Education (New York: State University of New York Press, 1998), 25.

24   Plato, *The Republic*, 403c, in Taylor, *Poetic Knowledge*, 17.

25   John Paul II, *Gospel of Life* (Boston: Pauline Books & Media, 1995), 12 (sec. 2).

26   Maritain, *Education at the Crossroads*, 7–8.

27   John Henry Newman, *Idea of a University*, 50.

28   *Lumen Gentium*, sec. 31.

29   John Paul II, *Christifidelis laici* (Boston: Pauline Books & Media, 2000), 62.

30   Martin Svaglic, introduction to Newman, *The Idea of a University*, xxii.

31   For instance, whereas Aristotle argues that happiness requires certain exter-
      nal goods, like freedom and health, Ciszek, writing as a former prisoner
      who was subjected to constant deprivation, provocatively asserts: "This
      simple truth, that the sole purpose of man's life on earth is to do the will of
      God, contains in it riches and resources enough for a lifetime. . . . In this
      subtle insight of the soul touched by God's divine power lies the root of true
      interior joy. And as long as this vision persists, as long as the soul does not
      lose sight of this great truth, the inner joy and peace that follow upon it per-
      sist through even the saddest and gravest moments of human trial and suf-
      fering. Pain and suffering do not thereby cease to exist; the ache and
      anguish of body and soul do not vanish from man's consciousness. But even
      they become a means of nourishing this joy, of fostering peace and con-
      formity to God's will, for they are seen as a continuation of Christ's passion."
      Walther Ciszek and Daniel Flaherty, *He Leadeth Me* (San Francisco: Ignatius
      Press, 1995), 117–18.

32   Yves M. J. Congar, O.P., *Lay People in the Church: A Study for a Theology of
      the Laity,* trans. Donald Attwater (Westminster, Md.: Newman Press, 1957),
      290. Congar goes on to note that some theologians specifically associate the
      prophetic mission of the baptized with their proclamation of the death of
      the Lord in the Eucharist ("For as often as you eat this bread and drink the
      cup, you proclaim the Lord's death until he comes" [1 Cor 11:26]).

Bibliography

Alexander, Bobby. *Televangelism Reconsidered: Ritual in the Search for Human Community.* Atlanta: Scholars Press, 1994.

Alley, Robert. "Television and Public Virtue." In Ferré, *Channels of Belief*, 45–55.

Anderson, C. Thomas. *Becoming a Millionaire God's Way.* Mesa, Ariz.: Winword Publishing, 2005.

Anker, Roy M. *Catching Light: Looking for God in the Movies.* Grand Rapids: Wm. B. Eerdmans, 2005.

Aquinas, Thomas. *Summa Theologica.* Translated by the English Dominicans. New York: Benziger Bros., 1948.

Aristotle. *Nicomachean Ethics.* In *The Basic Works of Aristotle,* edited by Richard McKeon. New York: Random House, 1941.

Armstrong, Regis J., J. A. Wayne Hellmann, and William J. Short, eds. *Francis of Assisi: Early Documents,* vol. 1. New York: New City Press, 1999.

Armstrong, Tracey. *Becoming a Pioneer of Success: God's Plan to Help You Win in Life and Business.* Shippensburg, Pa.: Destiny Image, 2004.

Augustine. *The Confessions.* Translated by John Ryan. New York: Image Books, 1960.

———. *Confessions and Enchiridion.* Edited by Albert Cook Outler. Philadelphia: Westminster Press, 1955.

Azuela, Mariano. *Los de Abajo.* Edited by John E. Englekirk and Lawrence B. Kiddle. Prospect Heights, Ill.: Waveland Press, 1992.

Bashara, Msgr. Ronald. "The Heart of the Syriac Fathers." *Maronite Voice,* February 2004: 7.

Beaudoin, Tom. *Virtual Faith: The Irreverent Spiritual Quest of Generation X.* San Francisco: Jossey-Bass, 1998.

Beenethum, Michael D. *Listen! God Is Calling! Luther Speaks of Vocation, Faith, and Work.* Minneapolis: Augsburg Fortress, 2003.

Bellah, Robert N. *Habits of the Heart: Individualism and Commitment in American Life.* New York: Harper & Row, 1986.

Berger, John. *Ways of Seeing.* London: British Broadcasting and Penguin Books, 1973.

Berry, Wendell. *Life Is a Miracle: An Essay against Modern Superstition.* Washington, D.C.: Counterpoint, 2000.

————. "The Loss of the University." In *Home Economics.* New York: North Point Press, 1987, 76–97.

Blaetz, Robin. *Visions of the Maid: Joan of Arc in American Film and Culture.* Charlottesville: University Press of Virginia, 2002.

Bloom, Harold. *Where Shall Wisdom Be Found?* New York: Riverhead Books, 2004.

Bonaventure. *Bonaventure: The Soul's Journey into God, The Tree of Life, The Life of Saint Francis.* Edited by Richard Payne. Translated by Ewert Cousins. New York: Paulist Press, 1978.

Bonhoeffer, Dietrich. *The Cost of Discipleship.* Translated by R. H. Fuller. New York: Touchstone, 1995.

Borges, Jorge Luis. *Ficciones.* Edited by Anthony Kerrigan. New York: Grove Press, 1962.

Brooks, David. *On Paradise Drive.* New York: Simon & Schuster, 2004.

Buechner, Frederick. *Wishful Thinking: A Seeker's ABC.* San Francisco: HarperSan Francisco, 1993.

Burtchaell, James. *The Dying of the Light: The Disengagement of Colleges and Universities from Their Christian Churches.* Grand Rapids: Wm. B. Eerdmans, 1998.

Byrne, Richard. "Journey Growth and Development in Spiritual Life." In *The New Dictionary of Catholic Spirituality,* edited by Michael Downey. Collegeville, Minn.: The Liturgical Press, 1993, 565–77.

Byrnes, James T. *John Paul II and Educating for Life.* Washington, D.C.: Peter Lang, 2002.

Cachin, Francoise. *Cézanne.* New York: Harry N. Abrams, 1996.

Caldwell, Kirbyjon, and Mark Seal. *The Gospel of Good Success: A Road Map to Spiritual, Emotional, and Financial Wholeness.* Wichita, Kans.: Fireside, 2000.

Carr, David, John Haldane, Terence McLaughlin, and Richard Pring. "Return to the Crossroads: Maritain Fifty Years On." *British Journal of Educational Studies* 43 (1995): 162–78.

Carter, Andria Y. "Get Right, Get Rich: Books Preaching the Theology of Prosperity Grow in Popularity," *Black Issues Book Review* 1 (2005): 70–74.

Catechism of the Catholic Church, 2nd ed. Washington, D.C.: United States Conference of Catholic Bishops, 1997.

Cavadini, John C. "Ignorant Catholics: The Alarming Void in Religious Education." *Commonweal,* 9 April 2004.

Chao, Elaine. "Message from the Secretary of Labor." *Report on the American Workforce.* United States Department of Labor, 2001.

Ciszek, Walter, and Daniel Flaherty. *He Leadeth Me.* San Francisco: Ignatius Press, 1995.

Cohen, Richard A. Introduction to *Humanism of the Other,* by Emannuel Levinas. Chicago: University of Illinois Press, 2003.

Cone, James. *God of the Oppressed.* 2nd ed. Maryknoll, N.Y.: Orbis Books, 1997.

Congar, Yves M. J., O.P. *Lay People in the Church: A Study for a Theology of the Laity.* Translated by Donald Attwater. Westminster, Md.: Newman Press, 1957.

Connors, Russsell B., Jr., and Patrick T. McCormick. *Character, Community, and Choices*. New York: Paulist Press, 1998.

Cousins, Ewert. Introduction to *Bonaventure: The Soul's Journey into God, The Tree of Life, The Life of Saint Francis*. New York: Paulist Press, 1978.

Davis, Joseph E. "The Commodification of Self." *Hedgehog Review* 5, no. 2 (2003): 41–49.

Davis, Walter T., Jr., Teresa Blyth, Gary Dreibelbis, Mark Scalese, S. J., Elizabeth Winans, and Donald J. Ashburn. *Watching What We Watch: Prime-Time Television through the Lens of Faith*. Louisville, Ky.: Geneva Press, 2001.

DeHovre, Franz. *Philosophy in Education*. Translated by E. B. Jordan. New York: Benziger Bros., 1930.

Delbanco, Andrew. "Colleges: An Endangered Species?" *New York Review of Books* 52, no. 4 (2005): 18–20.

DeMarco, Donald. *The Many Faces of Virtue*. Steubenville, Ohio: Emmaus Road, 2000.

Derrida, Jacques. "Eating Well." In *Who Comes after the Subject?* edited by Eduardo Cadava. New York: Routledge, 1991, 96–119.

Detweiler, Craig, and Barry Taylor. *A Matrix of Meanings: Finding God in Pop Culture*. Grand Rapids: Baker Academic, 2003.

Downey, Michael, ed. *The New Dictionary of Catholic Spirituality*. Collegeville, Minn.: The Liturgical Press: 1993.

Drupe, Louis. "The Joys and Responsibilities of Being a Catholic Teacher." In *Faith and the Intellectual Life*, edited by James L. Heft, S.M. Notre Dame, Ind.: University of Notre Dame Press, 1996, 61–70.

D'Souza, Mario O., C.S.B. "Jacques Maritain's Seven Misconceptions of Education: Implications for the Preparation of Catholic School Teachers." *Catholic Education: A Journal of Inquiry and Practice* 5 (2002): 435–53.

Du Bois, W. E. B. "St. Francis of Assisi." In *W.E.B. Du Bois: A Reader*, edited by Andrew Paschal with an introduction by Arna Bontemps. New York: Macmillan, 1971, 290–302.

Duffy, Regis. "Baptism and Confirmation." In *Systematic Theology: Roman Catholic Perspectives*, vol. 2, edited by Francis Schussler Fiorenza and John P. Galvin. Minneapolis: Augsburg Fortress, 1991, 211–30.

Early, Frances, and Kathleen Kennedy, eds. *Athena's Daughters: Television's New Women Warriors*. Syracuse: Syracuse University Press, 2003.

Easterbrook, Gregg. *The Progress Paradox: How Life Gets Better While People Feel Worse*. New York: Random House, 2003.

Edmundson, Mark. *Nightmare on Main Street: Angels, Sadomasochism, and the Culture of Gothic*. Cambridge: Harvard University Press, 1997.

———. "On the Uses of Liberal Education: As Lite Entertainment for Bored College Students." *Harper's* (September 1997): 39–50.

Elias, John L. "Whatever Happened to Catholic Philosophy of Education?" *Religious Education* 94, no. 1 (1999): 92–110.

Elie, Paul. *The Life You Save May Be Your Own: An American Pilgrimage*. New York: Farrar, Straus & Giroux, 2003.

Eliot, T. S. "Journey of the Magi." In *Collected Poems, 1909–1962*. New York: Harcourt, Brace & World, 1963.

Ertman, Martha M., and Joan C. Williams, eds. *Rethinking Commodification: Cases and Readings in Law and Culture*. New York: New York University Press, 2005.

Faller, Stephen. *Beyond the Matrix: Revolutions and Revelations*. Atlanta: Chalice Press, 2004.

Farmer, David. *The Oxford Dictionary of Saints*. New York: Oxford University Press, 1992.

Ferré, John P., ed. *Channels of Belief: Religion and American Commercial Television.* Ames: Iowa State University Press, 1990.

Fiero, Gloria. *The Humanistic Tradition*, vol. 2, 4th ed. New York: McGraw-Hill, 2002.

Finnis, John. *Fundamentals of Ethics.* Washington, D.C.: Georgetown University Press, 1983.

Foley, John Patrick. "Why Not More Programs like The Waltons?" In *Religion and Prime Time Television*, edited by Michael Suman. Westport, Conn.: Praeger, 1997, 7–8.

Forbes, Bruce David, and Jeffrey H. Mahan, eds. *Religion and Popular Culture in America.* Berkeley: University of California Press, 2000.

Fore, William T. *Television and Religion: The Shaping of Faith, Values, and Culture.* Minneapolis: Augsburg Publishing House, 1987.

Frankl, Razelle. *Televangelism: The Marketing of Popular Religion.* Carbondale: Southern Illinois University Press, 1987.

Fromm, Erich. *The Essential Fromm: Life between Having and Being.* New York: Continuum, 1999.

Gambero, Luigi. *Mary and the Fathers of the Church.* San Francisco: Ignatius Press, 1999.

Garcia-Rivera, Alejandro. *The Community of the Beautiful: A Theological Aesthetics.* Collegeville, Minn.: The Liturgical Press, 1999.

Gracia, Jorge J. E. *Mel Gibson's Passion and Philosophy: The Cross, the Questions, the Controversy.* La Salle, Ill.: Open Court, 2004.

Gregory of Nyssa. *The Life of Moses.* Translated by Abraham J. Malherbe and Everett Ferguson. New York: Paulist Press, 1978.

Gregory the Great. *Life and Miracles of St. Benedict.* Translated by Odo J. Zimmerman, O.S.B., and Benedict R. Avery, O.S.B. Collegeville, Minn.: The Liturgical Press, 1949.

Gregory, Wilton. Address, meeting of the National Catholic Educational Association, St. Louis, 29 March 2005.

Grisez, Germain, and Russell Shaw. *Personal Vocation: God Calls Everyone by Name.* Huntington, Ind.: Our Sunday Visitor, 2003.

Guignon, Charles. *On Being Authentic.* New York: Routledge, 2004.

Guinness, Os. *The Call: Finding and Fulfilling the Central Purpose of Your Life.* Nashville: Word, 1998.

Gutierrez, Gustavo. *A Theology of Liberation: History, Politics, and Salvation.* Maryknoll, N.Y.: Orbis Books, 1988.

Hackel, Sergei. *Pearl of Great Price.* New York: SVS Press, 1981.

Hangen, Tona J. *Redeeming the Dial: Radio, Religion, and Popular Culture in America.* Chapel Hill: University of North Carolina Press, 2002.

Hayford, Jack, and Gary Curtis. *Pathways to Pure Power: Learning the Depths of Love's Power, a Study of 1 Corinthians.* Nashville: Thomas Nelson, 1994.

Hedges, Chris. *War Is a Force That Gives Us Meaning.* New York: Anchor Books, 2003.

Heibert, Theodore. "Theophany in the Old Testament." In *The Anchor Bible Dictionary*, edited by David Noel Freedman. New York: Doubleday, 1992.

Hendershot, Heather. *Shaking the World for Jesus: Media and Conservative Evangelical Culture.* Chicago: University of Chicago Press, 2004.

Henle, Robert. "A Roman Catholic View of Education." In *Philosophies of Education*, edited by Philip Phenix. New York: Wiley, 1961, 75–83.

Higgins, Gareth. *How Movies Helped Save My Soul: Finding Spiritual Fingerprints in Culturally Significant Films.* Lake Mary, Fla.: Relevant Books, 2003.

Hoover, Stewart, and Lynn Schofield Clark, eds. *Practicing Religion in the Age of the Media: Explorations in Media, Religion, and Culture.* New York: Columbia University Press, 2002.

Hopko, Thomas. *Finding One's Calling in Life*. Crestwood, N.Y.: St. Vladimir's Seminary Press, 2005.

Horrigan, Michael. Bureau of Labor Statistics. "Introduction to the Projections." *Occupational Outlook Quarterly* (Winter 2003–4): 2–5.

Horsfield, Peter. *Religious Television: The American Experience*. New York: Longman, 1984.

Hudnut, Robert. *Call Waiting: How to Hear God Speak*. Downers Grove, Ill.: InterVarsity, 1999.

Ignatius of Antioch. *Early Christian Fathers*. Edited and translated by Cyril C. Richardson. New York: Touchstone, 1995.

Inness, Sherrie A., ed. *Action Chicks: New Images of Tough Women in Popular Culture*. New York: Palgrave Macmillan, 2004.

Jindra, Michael. "It's about Faith in Our Future: Star Trek Fandom as Cultural Religion." In Forbes and Mahan, *Religion and Popular Culture in America*, 165–79.

John Paul II. Encyclical Letter. *Centesimus Annus*. Boston: Pauline Books & Media, 1991.

———. Encyclical Letter. *Christifidelis laici*. Boston: Pauline Books & Media, 2000.

———. Encyclical Letter. *Fides et Ratio*. Boston: Pauline Books & Media, 1998.

———. Encyclical Letter. *Gospel of Life*. Boston: Pauline Books & Media, 1995.

———. Encyclical Letter. *Laborem Exercens*. Boston: Pauline Books & Media, 1981.

———. Homily, Camden Yards, Baltimore, 8 October 1995.

———. "Letter of His Holiness Pope John Paul II to Artists, 1999." Vatican. http://www.vatican.va/holy_father/john_paul_ii/letters/documents/hf_jp-ii_let _23041999_artists_en.html.

———. "Letter to the Bishops of the Catholic Church on the Collaboration of Men and Women in the Church and in the World." *Origins* 34, no. 11 (2004): 169–76.

Joseph, Ellis A. "The Philosophy of Catholic Education." In *Handbook of Research on Catholic Education*, edited by Thomas Hunt, Ellis A. Joseph, and Ronald J. Nuzzi. Westport, Conn.: Greenwood Press, 2001, 27–64.

Karaban, Roslyn. *Responding to God's Call: A Survival Guide*. San Jose, Calif.: Resource Publications, 1998.

Kasper, Walter. *The God of Jesus Christ*. New York: Crossroads, 1984.

Kierkegaard, Søren. *Fear and Trembling*. Translated and edited by Howard Hong and Edna Hong. Princeton: Princeton University Press, 1983.

Koulumzine, Sophie. *Many Worlds: A Russian Life*. Crestwood, N.Y.: St. Vladimir's Seminary Press, 1980.

Leamnson, Robert. *Thinking about Teaching and Learning: Developing Habits of Learning with First-Year College and University Students*. Sterling, Va.: Stylus, 1999.

Leider, R. J., and D. A. Shapiro. *Whistle While You Work: Heeding Your Life's Calling*. San Francisco: Berrett-Koehler, 2001.

Levinas, Emmanuel. *Entre Nous*. Translated by Michael B. Smith and Barbara Harshav. New York: Columbia University Press, 1998.

———. *Humanism of the Other*. Translated by Nidra Poller. Chicago: University of Illinois Press, 2003.

———. *Otherwise than Being*. Translated by Alphonso Lingis. Pittsburgh: Duquesne University Press, 1998.

———. *Totality and Infinity*. Translated by Alphonso Lingis. Pittsburgh: Duquesne University Press, 1969.

Levoy, Gregg. *Callings: Finding and Following an Authentic Life*. New York: Three Rivers Press, 1998.

Lindlof, Thomas. "The Passionate Audience: Community Inscriptions of The Last Temptation of Christ." In Stout and Buddenbaum, *Religion and Mass Media*,

148–68.

Little, Edward. *Ears to Hear: Recognizing and Responding to God's Call.* Harrisburg: Morehouse, 2003.

Losito, William F. "Reclaiming Inquiry in the Catholic Philosophy of Education." In *Catholic School Leadership*, edited by Thomas C. Hunt, Thomas E. Oldenski, S.M., and Theodore J. Wallace. New York: Falmer Press, 2000, 59–68.

Luther, Martin. "The Gospel for the Early Christmas Service." In *Luther's Works*, translated by John G. Kunstmann, vol. 52. Philadelphia: Fortress, 1974, 36–38.

———. "To the Christian Nobility of the German Nation." In *Three Treatises*, translated by C. M. Jacobs. Philadelphia: Muhlenberg, 1943, 1960, 13–16.

Macpherson, C. B. *The Political Theory of Possessive Individualism.* Oxford: Oxford University Press, 1962.

Maritain, Jacques. *Education at the Crossroads.* New Haven: Yale University Press, 1960.

———. "Education for the Good Life." *Commonweal*, 3 May 1946, 68–70.

———. "Thomist Views of Education." In *Modern Philosophies and Education*, edited by Nelson B. Henry. Chicago: University of Chicago Press, 1955, 57–90.

Marsh, Clive, and Gaye Ortiz, eds. *Explorations in Theology and Film: Movies and Meaning.* Malden, Mass.: Blackwell, 1997.

Mayer, Wendy, and Pauline Allen. *John Chrysostom.* New York: Routledge, 2000.

McFarland, Sam. "Keeping the Faith: The Roles of Selective Exposure and Avoidance in Maintaining Religious Beliefs." In Stout and Buddenbaum, *Religion and Mass Media*, 173–82.

McGucken, William J., S.J. "The Philosophy of Catholic Education." In *Philosophies of Education.* Pt. 1. *Yearbook of the National Society for the Study of Education*, no. 41. Chicago: University of Chicago Press, 1942, 251–88.

Merton, Thomas. *No Man Is an Island.* New York: Harcourt Brace, 1978.

Meyendorff, John. "A Life Worth Living." In *Liturgy and Tradition*, edited by Thomas Fisch. New York: SVS Press, 1990, 145–54.

Miles, Margaret. *Seeing and Believing: Religion and Values in the Movies.* Boston: Beacon Press, 1996.

Morsch, Gary, and Eddy Hall. *When There's No Burning Bush: Following Your Passions to Discovering God's Call.* Grand Rapids: Baker Books, 2004.

Mounier, Emmanuel. *The Character of Man.* Translated by Cynthia Roland. New York: Harper & Row, 1965.

Murdoch, Iris. *Existentialists and Mystics.* New York: Penguin Books, 1997.

———. *The Sovereignty of the Good.* London: Ark Paperbacks, 1970.

National Catholic Educational Association. *The Pre-Service Formation of Teachers for Catholic Schools: In Search of Patterns for the Future.* Washington, D.C.: NCEA, 1982.

National Council of Catholic Bishops (USA). *Principles for Education Reform in the United States.* Washington, D.C.: NCCB, 1995.

———. *In Support of Catholic Elementary and Secondary Schools.* Washington, D.C.: NCCB, 1990.

Nelson, John Wiley. *Your God Is Alive and Well and Appearing in Popular Culture.* Philadelphia: Westminster Press, 1976.

The New American Bible with Revised New Testament. National Conference of Catholic Bishops and United States Catholic Conference. Iowa Falls, Iowa: World Bible, 1986.

Newcomb, Horace. "Religion on Television." In Ferré, *Channels of Belief*, 29–44.

Newman, Jay. *Religion vs. Television: Competitors in Cultural Context.* Westport, Conn.: Praeger, 1996.

Newman, John Henry. "The Christian Ministry." In *Parochial and Plain Sermons.* London: Longmans, Green, 1918, 418–30.

———. "Divine Calls." In *Parochial and Plain Sermons*. New York: Ignatius Press, 1997, 1578–86.

———. *The Idea of a University*. Notre Dame, Ind.: University of Notre Dame Press, 1982.

———. "The Three Offices of Christ." In *The Works of Cardinal Newman: Sermons on Subjects of the Day*. Westminster, Md.: Christian Classics, 1968, 52–62.

Niebuhr, Reinhold. *Moral Man and Immoral Society*. New York: Scribner, 1995.

Niehaus, Jeffrey J. *God at Sinai: Covenant and Theophany in the Bible and Ancient Near East*. Grand Rapids: Zondervan, 1995.

Novak, Michael. *Business as a Calling: Work and the Examined Life*. New York: Free Press, 1996.

———. *Three in One: Essays in Democratic Capitalism, 1976–2000*. Edited by Edward Younkins. Lanham, Md.: Rowman & Littlefield, 2001.

Oakeshott, Michael. *The Voice of Liberal Learning: Michael Oakeshott on Education*. Edited by Timothy Fuller. New Haven: Yale University Press, 1989.

Palmer, Parker J. *Let Your Life Speak: Listening for the Voice of Vocation*. San Francisco: Jossey-Bass, 1999.

Parks, Sharon Daloz. *Big Questions, Worthy Dreams: Mentoring Young Adults in Their Search for Meaning, Purpose, and Faith*. San Francisco: Jossey-Bass, 2000.

Pascal, Blaise. *Pensées*. Translated by A. J. Krailsheimer. New York: Penguin Books, 1995.

Percy, Walker. *The Moviegoer*. New York: Knopf, 1961.

Perry, Marvin, J. Wayne Baker, and Pamela Pfeiffer Hollinger, eds. *The Humanities in the Western Tradition: Ideas and Aesthetics*, vol. 2. Boston: Houghton Mifflin, 2003.

Petersen, Rodney L. "Church and University: The Threefold Ministry and the Offices of Christ." In *The Contentious Triangle: Church, State, and University*, edited by Rodney L. Petersen and Calvin Augustine Pater. Kirksville, Mo.: Thomas Jefferson University Press, 1999, 359–81.

Petrella, Ivan. *The Future of Liberation Theology: An Argument and Manifesto*. Aldershot, N.H.: Ashgate, 2004.

Pevear, Richard, and Larissa Volokhonsky. *Mother Maria Skobtsova: Essential Writings*. Maryknoll, N.Y.: Orbis Books, 2003.

Pieper, Josef. *The Philosophical Act*. South Bend, Ind.: St. Augustine Press, 1998.

Pinsky, Mark. *The Gospel according to The Simpsons: The Spiritual Life of the World's Most Animated Family*. Louisville, Ky.: Westminster John Knox, 2001.

Placher, William C., ed. *Callings: Twenty Centuries of Christian Wisdom on Vocation*. Grand Rapids: Wm. B. Eerdmans, 2005.

Plate, S. Brent, ed. *Re-Viewing The Passion: Mel Gibson's Film and Its Critics*. New York: Palgrave Macmillan, 2004.

Plekon, Michael. *Living Icons: Persons of Faith in the Eastern Church*. South Bend, Ind.: University of Notre Dame, 2002.

———. *Tradition Alive*. Lanham, Md.: Rowman & Littlefield, 2003.

Plekon, Michael, and Alexis Vinogradov, trans. *In the World, of the Church: A Paul Evdokimov Reader*. Crestwood, N.Y.: SVS Press, 2001.

Porter, Jennifer, and Darcee L. McLaren. *Star Trek and Sacred Ground: Explorations of Star Trek, Religion, and American Culture*. Albany: State University of New York Press, 1999.

Pressley, Michael, ed. *Teaching Service and Alternative Teaching Education: Notre Dame's Alliance for Catholic Education*. Notre Dame, Ind.: University of Notre Dame Press, 2002.

Pseudo-Dionysius. *Pseudo-Dionysius: The Complete Works*. Edited by John Farina. New

York: Paulist Press, 1987.

Rahner, Karl. *Hearers of the Word.* New York: Sheed & Ward, 1969.

Redden, John D., and Francis A. Ryan, eds. *A Catholic Philosophy of Education.* Milwaukee: Bruce Publishing, 1942.

Renaut, Alain. *The Era of the Individual: A Contribution to a History of Subjectivity.* Translated by M. B. DeBevoise and Franklin Philip. Princeton: Princeton University Press, 1997.

Ricoeur, Paul. *Oneself as Another.* Translated by Kathleen Blamey. Chicago: University of Chicago Press, 1992.

The Rites of the Catholic Church: Volume One. 3rd ed. Collegeville, Minn.: The Liturgical Press, 1990.

Robinson, Bernard. "Moses at the Burning Bush." *Journal for the Study of the Old Testament* 75 (1997): 107–22.

Romanowski, William D. "Evangelicals and Popular Music." In Forbes and Mahan, *Religion and Popular Culture in America*, 105–24.

———. *Eyes Wide Open: Looking for God in Popular Culture.* Grand Rapids: Brazos Press, 2001.

Rosenthal, Michele. "'Turn It Off!': TV Criticism in the *Christian Century* Magazine, 1946–1960." In Hoover and Schofield Clark, *Practicing Religion in the Age of the Media*, 138–62.

Roth, Catherine, ed. *St. John Chrysostom: On Wealth and Poverty.* Crestwood, New York: St. Vladimir's Seminary Press, 1984.

Sacred Congregation for Catholic Education. The Catholic School, 1977.

Samway, Patrick. *Signposts in a Strange Land.* New York: Picador, 2000.

Sayers, Dorothy. "Why Work?" In *Creed or Chaos?* New York: Harcourt, Brace, 1949, 46–52.

Schlindler, David L. "Beauty, Transcendence, and the Face of the Other: Religion and Culture in America." *Communio: International Catholic Review* 26, no. 4 (1999): 916–21.

Schmemann, Alexander. *Celebration of Faith*, vol. 2. Translated by John Jillions. New York: SVS Press, 1997.

———. *The Journals of Father Alexander Schmemann.* Translated by Juliana Schmemann. New York: SVS Press, 2000.

———. *Liturgy and Life: Christian Development through Liturgical Experience.* Syosset, N.Y.: Department of Religious Education-Orthodox Church in America, 1974.

Schofield Clark, Lynn, and Stewart M. Hoover. "At the Intersection of Media, Culture, and Religion: A Bibliographic Essay." In *Rethinking Media, Religion, and Culture*, edited by Stewart M. Hoover and Knut Lunby. Thousand Oaks, Calif.: Sage Publications, 1997.

Schultze, Quentin. *Televangelism and American Culture: The Business of Popular Religion.* Grand Rapids: Baker Book House, 1991.

———. "Television Drama as a Sacred Text." In Ferré, *Channels of Belief*, 3–27.

———. "Touched by Angels and Demons: Religion's Love-Hate Relationship with Popular Culture." In *Religion and Popular Culture: Studies on the Interaction of Worldviews*, edited by Daniel Stout and Judith Buddenbaum. Ames: Iowa State University Press, 2001, 39–48.

Schumacher, E. F. *A Guide for the Perplexed.* New York: Harper Perennial, 1978.

Seay, Chris, and Greg Garrett. *The Gospel Reloaded: Exploring Spirituality and Faith in The Matrix.* Colorado Springs: Piñon Press, 2003.

Seigler, Elijah. "God in a Box: Religion in Contemporary Television Cop Shows." In *God in the Details: American Religion in Popular Culture*, edited by Eric Mazum and Kate McCarthy. New York: Routledge, 2001, 199–216.

Sherman, Doug, and William Hendricks. *Your Work Matters to God*. Colorado Springs: Navpress, 1987.

Sifton, Elisabeth. *The Serenity Prayer: Faith and Politics in Times of Peace and War*. New York: W. W. Norton, 2005.

Simson, Otto von. *The Gothic Cathedral*. Princeton: Princeton University Press, 1988.

Sinetar, Marsha. *Ordinary People as Monks and Mystics: Lifestyles for Self-Discovery*. New York: Paulist Press, 1986.

Skill, Thomas, James Robinson, John Lyon, and David Larson. "The Portrayal of Religion and Spirituality on Fictional Network Television." *Review of Religious Research* 35 (1994): 251–67.

Smith, Gordon. *Courage and Calling: Embracing Your God-Given Potential*. Westmont, Ill.: InterVarsity, 1999.

Sobrino, Jon, Paul Burns, and Francis McDonah. *Jesus the Liberator: A Historical-Theological Reading of Jesus of Nazareth*. Maryknoll, N.Y.: Orbis Books, 1994.

Steenland, Sally. *Growing Up in Prime Time: An Analysis of Adolescent Girls on Television*. Washington, D.C.: National Commission on Working Women, 1988.

Steffen, Lloyd. "On a Mission: The Uses of American Power." *The Christian Century* 122, no. 7 (2005): 33–38.

Steinfels, Peter. *A People Adrift*. New York: Simon & Schuster, 2003.

Stout, Daniel A., and Judith M. Buddenbaum, eds. *Religion and Mass Media: Audiences and Adaptations*. Thousand Oaks, Calif.: Sage Publications, 1996.

———. *Religion and Popular Culture: Studies on the Interaction of Worldviews*. Ames: Iowa State University Press, 2001.

Suger, Abbot. *On the Abbey Church of St.-Denis and Its Art Treasures*. Edited and translated by Erwin Panofsky. Princeton: Princeton University Press, 1979.

Svaglic, Martin. Introduction to *The Idea of a University*, by John Henry Newman. Notre Dame, Ind.: University of Notre Dame Press, 1982.

Taylor, Charles. *The Ethics of Authenticity*. Cambridge: Harvard University Press, 1991.

———. *Sources of the Self*. Cambridge: Harvard University Press, 1989.

Taylor, James. *Poetic Knowledge: The Recovery of Education*. New York: State University of New York Press, 1998.

Teresa of Avila. *The Interior Castle*. In *The Collected Works of Teresa of Avila*, vol. 2. Translated by Kieran Kavanaugh and Otilio Rodriguez. Washington, D.C.: ICS Publications, 1980, 31–196.

Thérèse of Lisieux. *The Story of a Soul*. New York: Doubleday, 1989.

Thomson, David. *The Whole Equation: A History of Hollywood*. New York: Knopf, 2004.

Tillard, J. M. R. *Church of Churches: The Ecclesiology of Communion*. Collegeville, Minn.: The Liturgical Press, 1992.

———. *Flesh of the Church, Flesh of Christ: At the Source of the Ecclesiology of Communion*. Collegeville, Minn.: The Liturgical Press, 2001.

Tocqueville, Alexis de. *Democracy in America*. Edited, translated, and with an introduction by Harvey C. Mansfield and Delba Winthrop. New York: Penguin Books, 2003.

Tomaselli, Kenyan G., and Arnold Shepperson. "'Speaking in Tongues, Writing in Vision': Orality and Literacy in Televangelistic Communications." In Hoover and Schofield Clark, *Practicing Religion in the Age of the Media*, 345–60.

Unamuno, Miguel de. *San Manuel Bueno, Mártir*. Madrid: Ediciones Cátedra, 1994.

———. *The Religious Dimension of Education in a Catholic School*. Boston: Pauline Books & Media, 1988.

van Gogh, Vincent. *The Complete Letters of Vincent Van Gogh*, vol. 3. Boston: Bulfinch Press, 2001), 180.

Vatican Council II: The Conciliar and Post Conciliar Documents. Edited by Austin Flannery, O.P., new rev. ed. Northport, N.Y.: Costello, 1992.

Vitz, Paul. "Psychology in Recovery." *First Things* (March 2005): 17–22.

Volf, Miroslav. *Exclusion and Embrace: A Theological Exploration of Identity, Otherness, and Reconciliation.* Nashville: Abingdon, 1996.

———. *Work in the Spirit: Towards a Theology of Work.* Oxford: Oxford University Press, 1991.

Waddell, Glenn, and Judith Keegan. "Christian Conciliation: An Alternative to 'Ordinary' ADR." *Cumberland Law Review* 29 (1999): 583.

Wadell, Paul. *Becoming Friends: Worship, Justice, and the Practice of Christian Friendship.* Grand Rapids: Brazos Press, 2002.

———. *Primacy of Love: An Introduction to the Ethics of St. Thomas Aquinas.* New York: Paulist Press, 1992.

Warren, Rick. *The Purpose-Driven Life: What on Earth Am I Here For?* Grand Rapids: Zondervan, 2002.

Watzke, John L. "Alternative Teacher Education and Professional Preparedness: A Study of Parochial and Public School Contexts." *Catholic Education: A Journal of Inquiry and Practice* 8, no. 4 (2005): 463–92.

———. "Teachers for Whom? A Study of Teacher Education Practices in Catholic Higher Education." *Catholic Education: A Journal of Inquiry and Practice* 6 (2002): 138–67.

Weil, Simone. "Reflections on the Right Use of School Studies with a View to the Love of God." In *The Simone Weil Reader,* edited by George A. Panichas. New York: David McKay, 1977. 44–52.

———. *Selected Writings.* New York: Orbis Books, 1998.

Whitehead, Alfred North. *The Aims of Education.* New York: Free Press, 1967.

Wilkinson, Bruce. *The Prayer of Jabez.* Sisters, Ore.: Multnomah, 2000.

Williams, Bernard. *Truth and Truthfulness: An Essay in Genealogy.* Princeton: Princeton University Press, 2004.

Wilson, E. O. *Consilience.* New York: Knopf, 1998.

Wittgenstein, Ludwig. *Tractatus Logico-Philosophicus,* 2nd ed. New York: Routledge, 2001.

Wolfe, Tom. *I Am Charlotte Simmons.* New York: Farrar, Straus & Giroux, 2004.

Wright, Carl Jeffrey. *God's Vision or Television: How Television Influences What We Believe.* Chicago: Urban Ministries, 2004.

Zaleski, Jeff. *The Soul of Cyberspace: How New Technology Is Changing Our Spiritual Lives.* New York: HarperEdge: 1997.

About the Contributors

THOMAS HIBBS is the Distinguished Professor of Ethics and Culture and dean of the Honors College at Baylor University. After receiving his Ph.D. in philosophy from the University of Notre Dame, Hibbs taught at St. Thomas Aquinas College in Santa Paula, California and Boston College, where he was full professor and department chair in philosophy. He has written several scholarly books on Aquinas, including *Virtue's Splendor: Wisdom, Prudence, and the Human Good* and *Dialectic and Narrative in Aquinas: An Interpretation of the Summa Contra Gentiles*. Hibbs regularly writes for the *Weekly Standard*, *National Review*, and the *Chronicle of Higher Education*, and lectures and writes on popular culture. He is the author of the book *Shows about Nothing*.

JEANNE HEFFERNAN is an assistant professor in the Department of Humanities and Augustinian Traditions and an affiliate professor at the School of Law at Villanova University. After earning her B.A. from Georgetown University, Heffernan earned an M.A. and Ph.D. in government from the University of Notre Dame, where she served as the assistant director of the Erasmus Institute. Before teaching at Villanova, Heffernan taught at Pepperdine University and was a visiting research fellow at the Ethics and Public Policy Center in

Washington, D.C. An author of numerous articles and book chapters, Heffernan's research interests include the connection between religion and social society, democratic theory, and Christian political thought.

CHARLENE KALINOSKI is a professor of Spanish at Roanoke College in Virginia. A Fulbright Scholar, Charlene earned her M.A. and Ph.D. from the University of Pennsylvania. Kalinoski lectures on many topics concerning modern languages and has cowritten several successful grants for and articles about international travel and scholarship.

JOHN LARRIVEE completed his B.A. and M.A. at Harvard University and his Ph.D. in economics at the University of Wisconsin. John serves as an assistant professor of economics at Mount St. Mary's University in Emmitsburg, Maryland. His research and publication interests focus on rural poverty/development, family and welfare policy, and religion.

THOMAS P. LOONEY is a member of the Congregation of Holy Cross and is the chairperson of the theology department at King's College in Wilkes-Barre, Pennsylvania. He received his M.Div. from the University of St. Michael's College in Toronto and his Ph.D. from the Catholic University of America. Widely published, Father Looney is also a member of the board of trustees for Stonehill College, North Easton, Massachusetts.

WILLIAM C. MATTISON III is an assistant professor of theology at Mount St. Mary's University in Emmitsburg, Maryland. He received his B.A. from Georgetown University and his Ph.D. from the University of Notre Dame, where he examined the role of the passions in the virtuous Christian life. Mattison is the editor of *New Wine, New Wineskins: A New Generation Reflects on Key Issues in Catholic Moral Theology*.

MICHAEL MILLER received his B.A. from the University of Notre Dame and his M.A. and Ph.D. from Boston College. Miller has a special interest in the thought of Thomas Aquinas and teaches philosophy at Mount St. Mary's University in Emmitsburg, Maryland.

WILLIAM C. MILLS earned his M.A. in theology and his M.Div. from St. Vladimir's Orthodox Theological Seminary, and his Ph.D. in pastoral theology from the Union Institute and University in Cincinnati, Ohio. The author of *Pascha to Pentecost: Reflections on the Gospel of John* and *Prepare O Bethlehem: Reflections on the Scripture Readings for the Christmas-Epiphany Season*, Mills also serves as rector of the Nativity of the Holy Virgin Orthodox Church in Charlotte, North Carolina, and as an adjunct professor in the Department of Religion and Philosophy at Queens University.

GAEL MOONEY is a professional artist living in New York City. After receiving her J.D. from Northeastern University School of Law and an LL.M. from Georgetown University, Mooney earned an M.F.A. from New York Academy of Art. She has taught drawing, painting, and art history at Queens College, CUNY, in the Department of Continuing Education, and art and theology at Dominican University in River Frost, Illinois. Mooney has studied theology at Fordham and the University of Notre Dame.

STEPHEN BUTLER MURRAY is the college chaplain at Skidmore College in Saratoga Springs, New York, where he also serves as the director of the Intercultural Center and a lecturer in religion. Murray followed his M.Div. from Yale University Divinity School with a M.Phil and Ph.D. in systematic theology from Union Theological Seminary in New York. He is also employed as a lecturer in theology and homiletics at Auburn Theological Seminary and serves as pastor of Charlton Freehold Presbyterian Church in Charlton, New York. Murray is coeditor of *Crossing by Faith: Sermons on the Transition from Youth to Adulthood, in Honor of Harry Baker Adams.*

JESSAMYN NEUHAUS is an assistant professor of history at the State University of New York in Plattsburgh. Widely published, Neuhaus received her M.A. and a Ph.D. from Claremont Graduate University, where she specialized in twentieth-century United States history, and the history of sexuality and cultural studies.

STANLEY NEVINS serves as chair for the Department of Philosophy at St. Joseph's College in New York. He received his M.A. and Ph.D. in philosophy from Fordham University. Published in both philosophy and psychology journals, Nevins also was honored with Professor of the Year at St. Joseph's.

MARC PARISI graduated from Mount St. Mary's University (2005) with a major in theology and a minor in sociology. He received his Professional Certificate in Youth Ministry from the Archdiocese of Baltimore and is employed as a campus minister at Calvert College in Towson, Maryland. While a student at the Mount, Marc directed three after-school theater programs for 4th and 5th grade students while serving as the formation director for the college campus ministry program.

DEBORAH WALLACE RUDDY received her B.A. in government and theology from Georgetown University and her M.A. and Ph.D. in systematic theology from Boston College. Ruddy's research interests include Catholic social thought and Catholic education. She serves as an assistant professor of Catholic studies at the University of St. Thomas in St. Paul, Minnesota, and is the director of the Catholic Social Teaching and Catholic Education Program.

Index